CW00474201

SHOPIFY, DROPSHIPPING AND BLOGGING

THE ULTIMATE GUIDE FOR BEGINNERS FOR
GROWING YOUR E-COMMERCE FROM YOUR
HOME BASE, BUILDING YOUR WEB STORE
STEP BY STEP, AND INCREASING YOUR
PASSIVE INCOME WITH YOUR BLOG.

PAUL J. ABRAMAH

Table Of Contents

Shopify Introduction

When it comes to starting a successful online business the online sales and marketing platform that you use can be either the flagship of your entire launch or the anchor around your new online store's neck. The right choice for many individuals and the one you are likely going to be the most satisfied with in the long run is Shopify.com. For nearly 2 decades Shopify has been providing ecommerce solutions for small business who want to take their business online.

When it comes to creating an online home for your store, there are many web building platforms and online payment solutions to choose from, Shopify takes all the hassle out of mixing and matching and puts all the tools for getting your online business up and running successfully in one place.

Shopify is more than a simple marketplace where goods are exchanged, it is also what is known as a payment gateway which means it handles the transaction verification process required to ensure that those who pay for your goods via debit or credit card actually have the funds to complete the purchase. It also means they are responsible for the security concerns related to these transactions which can be both complicated and expensive for merchants to pursue themselves.

When it comes to deciding how you want to use Shopify, the first thing you will need to determine is if you want to create your own site and then link it Shopify or if you are more interested in getting started as quickly, easily and cheaply as possible by using the store that Shopify will provide at all levels of service. While the option to create your own site will certainly cost more, it will give you complete control over the customer experience which is an important consideration if the niche you are considering working with is extremely competitive.

Starting your own online store is a major decision whether you are interested in building an active or a passive income stream and purchasing this book is a great step in the right direction. It is also the easiest step as setting up your own successful online store will require plenty of hard work and determination but that's not to say it won't be fun!

It is more than doable and the following chapters will discuss just how you can go about making your dream of an online store a reality. Inside you will learn all about the specifics of the Shopify platform and what makes it the best choice when it comes to starting your online store. You will also find tips related to choosing the products to sell that are right for you, getting your site up and running and marketing it properly. Finally, it ends with a look to the future and how you will know when to expand your product line.

Capitolo 1 What is Shopify and How Does it Work?

N o doubt you have already heard of Shopify. It is something of a household name now. Unless you have already delved deeply into it then the chances are you won't know what it can do for you and how it works so that's what I'm going to start by telling you before we look at the main advantages and disadvantages of using it.

So, what is it?

Shopify is a way of setting up a store online, providing you with an easy platform to sell just about anything that you want. It is incredibly popular with entrepreneurs and businesses who want an easy way to create an e-commerce shop that can operate alone or as part of an existing company.

One thing that sets Shopify aside from the competition is the fact that it is incredibly versatile. You don't need to have any experience in writing code. If all you want is a simple store to get up and running pretty much straight away, Shopify has a range of templates that you can choose from. These provide the skeleton of the store and can be customized so you can put your own unique stamp on your store. However, Shopify is not limited to small businesses or internet entrepreneurs; it is scalable, customizable and even multi-lingual, making it the perfect platform for any business even the biggest of brands like Red Bull, KKW Beauty, WaterAid and Budweiser – all using Shopify as their online store platform.

How does it Work?

Shopify is dead simple to use, one of the biggest reasons why it is so popular. It is a web-based software so there is no need to install it first. The platform is fully hosted by Shopify and this brings several advantages, including full customer support. There isn't any need to go through complex installations, worry about upgrades that might mess things up and you don't need to worry about any web servers – it's all done for you. And Shopify is compatible with all the major operating systems.

Setting up a store is simple, as you will see later. All you need to do is sign up for your free 14-day trial on Shopify and give it a go. Once the free trial period is up you need to decide whether to continue or not and which plan to choose. We'll be looking at those plans later on, but there are several to choose from, each with its own unique features and price. Then, you just need to decide on what to sell and add your payment details to pay for your subscription.

That's all there is to it. You can register a domain name so your Shopify store has the name you want it to have and if you already have a website or a domain name, simply integrate it all with Shopify - I'll show you how later.

Shopify Advantages

Shopify has several decent advantages and one of the biggest is that it offers more than 100 different themes for you to choose from for your storefront. This allows you to choose a professional look that also looks good on a mobile device. For those that have used WordPress, the approach to Shopify themes is quite similar – a store holds the themes and you can browse to choose what you want. Some are free, some require payment and you can also choose from themes set up for specific industries. These themes have been professionally designed and Shopify ensures that they consistent and compatible with its own software before they allow them into the store.

Another great advantage is the flexibility that Shopify offers, allowing to use the Shopify app store to add different functionalities. There are over 12oo apps to choose from and we'll be looking at some of them in a later. Again, some of them are free while some are paid and you can pick and choose the ones that help make your store easier to use and to automate certain aspects of it. There are social media apps, customer service, inventory management, accounting, even shipping apps, all available to add to your store to help run your new business. All of this makes Shopify more than a simple store; it is a complete business solution, providing assistance for the backend as well as the frontend. And if you worried about installing the apps, don't be because Shopify will do the work for you.

If there is one thing designed to send people into a panic, it's a glitch that causes their website to go down with no warning and leaving them with no idea how to get it all back again. Shopify is robust but, to deal with any issues that arise and any problems you may have their next advantage is that they operate a 24/7 customer support service. They offer several different phone numbers for different areas; they have email support and online chat so your problems can be solved straight away. Time is money as any business owner knows and the minimum amount of fuss and maximum speed to get an issue resolved is crucial.

The Shopify software is in the cloud so you have a great deal more flexibility because any web browser can be used to run it. You can work wherever you want, whenever you want, as long as you have a connection to the internet.

Security is not an issue either; Shopify does it all for you, ensuring all transactions are completely secure so you can concentrate on selling your goods.

Lastly, there is a Shopify POS (point of sale) app for both Android and iOS that helps take care of in-person transactions. Using it means you can sell anywhere – at a market, a fair, in a popup window, anywhere you want. Plus, it offers the versatility of accepting multiple methods of payment. The best of it is, the app fully syncs with your account so your orders can be monitored as can stock levels in real time, across all your points of sale – online, physical store, and so on.

Shopify Disadvantages

While Shopify has plenty of advantages, it also has a few disadvantages. Don't be too surprised; nothing is perfect and nothing can possibly suit everyone so make sure you are aware of the downsides before you start.

Unless you make use of the Shopify payments system, you will need to pay a fee on each sale and that can be anywhere from 0.5% to 2%, depending on which plan you are signed up to. If you opt for the basic plan, the transaction fee is 2% of each sale; the Shopify Plan is 1% and the Advanced Plan is 0.5%. How much of a disadvantage this proves to be is down to your perspective. In terms of money, it is equal to between $0.50 and $2 for every $100 sale – that isn't too bad and that money is used to pay for the payment management technology that Shopify uses. In simple terms, all you are doing is paying them to handle your transactions. Plus, Shopify doesn't hide their fees; they are completely upfront and you will always know what the charges are going to be.

Not all the apps are free to use. While they can offer huge amounts of functionality, some of them do have a monthly cost attached to them and this can soon bump up your monthly expenditure. Take MailChimp, for example, a popular mail app that helps you to run a mail campaign. If you have less than 2000 email subscribers then Mailchimp is free, but any more and the costs are anywhere between
$10 and $200 per month. Another one, FreshBooks, is a great accounting app but it will set you back almost $32 a month.

As far as apps go, if you have a small business most of them are free. But, grow your business larger and you may have to start paying out for those apps. For someone like you who is going to be starting a brand-new business, for now, you won't need to worry about that. And, if your business does grow, your revenue should grow with it and those all-important apps won't seem quite so expensive. You could try doing the accounting and marketing yourself to start with, but you will find that your attention will be on that and not on selling. You could also hire an external person to do for you, but that will definitely cost you more than the app would. Perhaps, in the long run, the best option is to bit the bullet and buy the app, saving yourself the time that you could be using to focus on selling.

Many platforms make use of CSS or HTML coding, but Shopify doesn't. Instead, it uses something called Liquid so store customization means you need to know the language or you need to know someone who does. That can prove expensive so, to begin with, stick with the themes on offer and leave the customization for later down the line.

While Shopify is incredibly flexible, and it can be highly customized, some parts of it can't unless you opt for the very expensive Shopify Plus plan so be aware of that from the start.

So, as you can see, most of the disadvantages revolve around costs and expense but, if you want a successful business, those are inevitable – you can't have it all for nothing. If you had a physical store, for example, you would have overheads in rent and utilities, not to mention taxes, staff, inventory and so on. With Shopify, the monthly subscription you choose is akin to these costs but much cheaper.

Capitolo 2 Develop a brand

I n the world of online commerce, you are competing with millions of people for attention and sales. Both of these things are important the online world. Without attention, you're not going to be able to gain awareness of all of your products, and without sales, your business will end up in the red. So, what makes your product any better than a competitor's? In a sea of people vying for a customer's dollar, the only thing that truly sets people apart is their brand.

A brand is a kind of identification that tells other people what your product is about. Brands are visual, conceptual and emotional in nature. They are designed to help people quickly understand what the product represents. Don't get confused here; branding isn't about what a product does but rather about what a product is.

Think about one of the most successful brands in America, or probably even the world, Coca-Cola. Coca-Cola sells a soft drink, but when they market Coke, they focus on things like togetherness, family, fun times and friendship. The beverage might be a soda, but the brand represents good times. And the world responded to that branding very positively.

Your goal should be to develop a good brand for your online store and product, so that people are able to associate your product with good values that are attractive to them. While it might seem like talking about the virtue of your product is important, that's really just advertising. Branding is about far more than just talking about your products. Rather, branding talks about what your company is about. People love to buy products, but if you can get them interested in your brand, then you will have a customer for life.

So, how can you get a customer interested in your brand? Well, it starts with knowing the attributes of a good brand. Let's take a look at each component of a brand, so you can learn how to appeal to customers.

Mission:

The first thing to remember about your brand is that it represents the whole picture of what your company is about. People need to have a perfect understanding of what your mission is before they are willing to get behind it. Of course, you're probably in business in order to make money; that's a given. But no one is going to support you if you say your mission is to get as rich as possible.

A mission is something that speaks to people's hearts and minds. It captures the imagination and excites them. A mission isn't about you, but it is about how your company is going to have an effect on the world at large. Don't underestimate how powerful a message can be to consumers. In the noisy world of advertisements, your mission can help set you apart.

Do you see how that is something you can nod your head to? Their mission has nothing to do with Warby Parker and everything to do with the world around them. They talk about a good price, a rebelliousness against the system and a desire to lead businesses in being more socially conscious. This mission is big, and when a customer learns about this desire, the company is immediately set apart from the rest of the pack. There are many places to get eyeglasses online, but there is only one Warby Parker.

Visual Identity:

Your brand needs to have some kind of visual identity attached to it. This identity includes colors, shapes or a logo. Most companies stick with one or two primary colors to put on all of their products, allowing people to readily recognize that a product is associated with a specific company. In addition to specific colors, you will also need a logo. You should probably hire a graphic designer or a freelancer to design a nice logo for your company if you don't already have one.

Uniqueness:

You also need to focus on highlighting what makes your product and your company different from all of the other products that are out there on the market. Remember, there is a vast ocean of products in the world, and they are all vying for your customer's attention. So, in order to brand yourself effectively, you need to create a strong image of being unique. Even if you are selling something that everyone else is selling, try to highlight what makes it unique to you.

Uniqueness isn't necessarily about quality, but it's about how you present your product to others. Think about medicine, for example. Most medications use the same ingredients, but they use branding to create a picture of uniqueness. They target a specific type of pain, or they have great customer service. These things are meant to help customers distinguish pain medication to be separate from the generic stuff sold in stores.

Presentation, quality and experience are the three major areas where you can work to create a great brand. You can focus on either or all of these areas, showing potential customers what makes you unique. Remember, you must always be able to answer the question: "Why should I buy from you specifically?" Work on your brand until you can come up with a sufficient answer that will motivate people to click the buy button.

Capitolo 3 Product Sourcing

In the establishing of an online store, most people start out with so much zeal and zest. They can identify niche markets that they can take advantage of and seemingly have everything set up. Everything except identifying where to source for products. This has often proved to be a big challenge for people setting up businesses whether they would be exploring the option of getting their own product manufactured or getting suppliers of the products from whom they will make wholesale purchases from. Identifying these people has not been considered the easiest job one is able to do. Let us then consider the fundamentals when it comes to identifying a supplier that is reliable and credible for your business.

We shall be considering different suppliers and these would be the people from whom we shall receive our inventory from and this may range from manufacturers to wholesale traders and even distributors.

The first step to successfully identify an appropriate supplier would be deciding the type of supplier you would want for your type of business. These include:

- Manufacturer: he is responsible for the production of your idea

- Supplier: This can be either a manufacturer, a wholesale trader or even a distributor of already prevailing products that you are interested in.

- Drop shipper: this might be only to supply goods and meet the orders of brands that are already prevailing.

Domestic suppliers against Overseas suppliers

For anyone getting into e-commerce business, they need to reach the decision of what type of suppliers they would want. One can take the option of keeping their product locally produced or they can take the other option of having their products sourced overseas. This could mean any territory overseas but it often alludes to countries in Asia like China and India.

Often, outsourcing supplies from overseas usually has a less financial implication on the business on every unit of product produced, however, it does require a high capital requirement initially. These two options have both their pros and cons which we shall explore.

Domestic Sourcing

Pros

- High quality of manufacturing and better labor standards
- No language barrier
- Appeal as a made in America product
- Easy verification of the manufacturers
- Shipping time is significantly reduced
- Better intellectual property right protection
- Increased security in payments and recourse

Cons

- Increased cost of manufacturing
- Little product choice

Overseas Sourcing

Pros

- Significantly reduced cost of manufacturing
- A wide variety of manufacturers
- Services such as those of Alibaba have eased the navigation of suppliers

Cons

- A perception of lower quality from the client base

- Often mired with cases of low labor and manufacturing standards.

- Miniature protection on intellectual property

- Language barrier

- Increased difficulty in the verification of manufacturers

- Increased shipping duration

- Differences in culture as ingrained in the business practices

- Dealing with clearance at customs during importation

- Reduced security of payment and recourse

So now that you are more informed of your choices and some of the advantages and disadvantages of either option on the shipping, it would then be important to consider what your options are and where you can start making your inquiries for suppliers. In the wake of the information age and digital era, the internet would be the ideal place to start your search from. However, to help narrow the search, one can explore the following options first:

Directories

This can prove to be one of the ideal sources for suppliers. There are tons of free online directories that have explicitly profiled thousands of potential suppliers, wholesalers, and manufacturers. These are some options of the most popular ones:

Domestic Directories (Online)

- Kompass

- Makers Row

- ThomasNet

- MFG

Overseas directories (Online)

- AliExpress

- Bambify

- Alibaba

- IndiaMart

- Oberlo

Google

In today's world, it is only expected that we could only go onto google and search for anything and whatever it is we were looking for would appear high in the results. However, most suppliers have not updated their websites or optimized them enough with the advancement of Google's algorithms that these pages would probably not be found in the top search results as we are accustomed to. Because of this, one might be required to go through many of the results' pages to find the suppliers. Also, one should put the effort into searching using different terms that would help narrow the search and give better outcomes.

Local Library

Many libraries have subscribed to online directories of businesses and manufacturers that would otherwise be difficult to gain access to as an individual. These include those such as the Scotts Online Business directory. In this directory, you would find many profiles of potential suppliers located in North America. One can get into contact with these libraries to find out if they are in possession of these directories.

Referrals

With the invention of social media, one can ask a great list of friends and family to recommend reliable suppliers at the click of a button. It is very likely to find people who are already involved in the space and therefore have contacts and networks either directly to the suppliers or to people who do. Use the power of referrals and social media to make your search easier.

Other methods

One can also find suppliers by searching for their products using their NAICS codes. The NAICS is the North American Industry Classification System which has assigned every product in every industry a code. Some organizations that deal in manufacturing and supplies list their products using these codes which exponentially makes it easier to identify these goods.

Request for a quotation

The way you approach a supplier and consequently find out their rates might seem a trivial task, however, it is anything but. One should take time to organize their thoughts and inquiries to suppliers which would subsequently better the chances of you getting a response from them and furthermore, one with correct and updated information. Here is a list of things that you might need to consider in your inquiry:

- Do they have a minimum order quantity and if yes, what is it? This is to help you decide if their MOQ is affordable and manageable for you.

- What is the pricing on their sample? It is important to get samples first before putting in a full order, therefore, ask about how they charge for these samples. You may be fortunate enough to find suppliers who would send you these samples at no cost.

- What is the pricing on their production? This question is vital as it will determine the pricing on your goods. This would also make it known to you if you will be able to get discounts on production of large volume.

- What is their average turnaround time? This will enable you to know how to plan for your business and when you can meet the demands and orders from your business.

- What are their payment terms? Many suppliers tend to request for full payments on their orders. This will help you know how to plan for the capital requirements. Also, one inquires if they offer payment plans for future supply orders.

In case you're searching for a supplier interestingly, you're going to rapidly find out about 'Minimum Order Quantities' (MOQ's). It's normal for a supplier to necessitate commitment to buy a huge number of units for your first request contingent upon the item and producer.

MOQ's strain this position when you have constrained capital, or essentially need to take no chances by beginning little to test the waters before making bigger buys. The best part about this is that MOQ's are quite often open to negotiations.

Prior to these negotiations, the initial step is to comprehend why the provider has forced a minimum. Is it because there is a considerable measure of work forthright? Or, on the other hand, possibly this is because them wanting to work with bigger purchasers. Understanding the purposes for the minimums will enable you to better comprehend their position and enable you to negotiate and propose to best counter offer. With this information, one can request for lower order quantities and middle ground can be reached including paying a higher rate on every unit or paying a large deposit on big order but receiving the stock in bits.

Capitolo 4 Choosing A Product Category

B efore you set up a shop on Shopify, it may be important to consider the types of products you can sell. In e-commerce, there are three basic product categories you can choose from, and Shopify is an excellent platform for all of them.

Digital Products

As you might have guessed, a digital product is something that can be delivered electronically. The largest perk of this product category is that it completely eliminates shipping, dramatically decreasing the time and costs involved in running your e-commerce store. The downside is that digital products often have to be produced, either by the store owner or by contractors. You can sell software from third parties as well, but the market is pretty saturated with this type of thing.

There are a large number of digital products you can sell, and a large part of understanding this market is either improving upon other such digital product concepts or providing something completely new. Some examples of digital products include:

•   Sounds samples for musicians and artists to use in their music.

•   Software for PC, MAC, etc. This can be the software you have developed, or you can work with software developers and offer their products. Note that selling certain software without a license from the company can violate the terms of service of Shopify.

•   Web design themes (customizable!)

•   Book cover designs (customizable!)

•   Other design elements.

• Ebooks, music, and videos. Whether it is instructional ebooks and online courses for surfing or ebooks and movies about high- school-aged werewolves on the wrestling team, Shopify is an excellent solution for content creators in need of a sales platform.

• Nearly anything that can be delivered digitally!

Physical Products

Physical products are probably the most common types of products sold through e-commerce, and while the logistics are a lot more involved than digital products, this is likely going to be the path you go down. As long as the product is legal and doesn't violate Shopify's terms of services, it can be sold on Shopify.

The upside to physical products is that they are easier to sell. The downside is that you'll have to ship them, handle defective orders and returns, have a place to store them prior to sales, and worst of all, you have to purchase them before you can sell them, making the overhead higher than selling digital goods.

Common physical products include:

• Technology, such as computers, cameras, smartphones, video game consoles, and more.

• Media, such as video games, movies, music.

• Clothing items and accessories

• Beauty products, such as makeup and hair products

• Handmade goods, including customizable clothing and mugs, soaps, one-of-a-kind creations and basically anything you can produce

• Private-label products, which are mass-produced products with your own branding on them.

- Pretty much anything.

We'll go into more detail later about how to research what market you want to sell in, how to source products, and alternative methods of handling physical sales, such as drop shipping.

Subscription Products

Subscription products are a rising market as the likes of LootCrate and similar monthly subscription services have exploded in recent years. While there are subscription-specific platforms for selling these types of items, Shopify offers far more tools, customization, customer service, and reliability than these others. Also, there's no reason you can't use more than one platform.

You may have some experience with subscription boxes. There's almost one for everything these days. There are shaving kits that come monthly. There are candy boxes. There are gourmet meat boxes, clothes, video games, movies, collectibles… it is truly endless.

The huge advantage of subscription boxes is that you have an approximation of the amount of product you will require to fulfill your orders because people pay for the product before you even have to assemble the boxes. While you'll likely need to have some product on hand, you can maintain an inventory that makes sense for the number of subscribers you currently have.

One of the disadvantages is that you need to retain subscribers in order to make this business model work. This means a couple of things for you. First, you'll need to continue to source new products so customers aren't receiving the same things over and over. Second, you need to be able to create a perceived value that exceeds the price you charge. Part of the struggle with subscription boxes is that customers are often disappointed with the offerings for the price, even if they are more than fair considering all of the additional work that goes into putting them together.

With the growth of subscription boxes being offered, it is also worth noting that coming up with an original idea is going to make a huge difference in your success. If the same subscription box you want to curate already exists, the amount of competition can be difficult to overcome. That doesn't mean there isn't room for more strange candy boxes in the world, but it does mean you need to set yourself apart somehow.

As a seller of physical goods, it is obviously possible to sell a subscription box on top of your usual products, and this is a model that many subscription box companies have started to follow through with to hook in customers that may not want the experience of unboxing items they don't truly want but will purchase one or two of the items separately.

Choosing One

You probably have some idea which of these types of product categories you would like to work with. If you are unsure, it is wise to take the time to come up with a general idea for all three, handle some market research, and determine from there which are the most viable, which you are the most passionate about, and how easily the market is to break into.

Capitolo 5 Setting Up Your Shopify Store

S etting your store up is actually quite easy once you know which features you want to use so that's what we are going to do now – set up the store, add a product and come up with a URL that will allow your customers to recognize you online.

Choose Your Platform

First, you must work out which service and platform you want to use. Let's see what the services are first. Most of these are pretty much identical in features, but the more expensive plans have more advanced features. And don't forget that credit card fee per transaction on top of the monthly fee for the service.

For those just getting their foot in the door, the lowest service is probably the best as it gives you a chance to test the waters and learn how things work before you upgrade. Once you get a handle on the basics and the money starts rolling in, you can choose to upgrade. Keep in mind that the Basic Shopify plan does come with quite a bit though.

Your next decision is which platform you want to use and by this, I am talking about the website you want your Shopify Store to be connected to. You can, if you choose, connect your store to several platforms at once so let's see which ones are available:

Facebook:

Facebook has a built-in store option and when Shopify is connected, your page will allow customers to either visit your store or purchase from right there on your Facebook page. If you have a page that is often shared, this can be a great idea because you get access to a wider audience who can see your products instantly and decide whether they want to buy straight away and see what else you have for sale. This works for those who have a large following on the social media platform.

Pinterest Buttons:

Pinterest is still one of the biggest social media sites and quite easily outpaces Twitter in user participation and growth so it should not be pushed to the wayside. Shopify partners with Pinterest so you can link product pins to your Shopify account, allowing customers to buy instantly. Even better, the purchase takes place in the Pinterest app so your customers don't have to jump through a ton of hoops to get access to your products – this can increase your sales percentage quite significantly.

Shopify Store:

Shopify provides space in their store for you to set up an online shop. They have a drag-and-drop interface that helps you to create a great-looking storefront. The upside to this system is that is easy and eliminates the need to spend hours working on designing and building a website. Shopify provides strong support for their sales platform and they also offer app support for WordPress and other websites. Shopify has all the customization you want to get a great store up and running in just minutes.

Your Own Website:

WordPress and Squarespace are good options for websites, but they don't really work too well with Shopify. Shopify has put a lot of hard work in to come up with their own platform and, while you could use WordPress, it takes a lot of work and a knowledge of coding to integrate Shopify. You also won't be able to use the apps n the Shopify stores. We'll be starting by using the Shopify platform as it is much easier so let's get started.

1.   Go to http://www.shopify.com and sign up for your free trial account. Input your email address and then click on Get Started.

2.   Create a password and note it down so you can remember it.

3.   Input your store name. If you don't really have one yet just type in anything; you can change it again later.

4.   Click on Create Your Store

5.   Next, you need to decide if it's an online store you want or you want to sell in a pop-up store or a physical store. For now, choose an online store because that will provide you with a website to sell your goods from.

6.   Click on Next and then input your name and address. These details are used for setting up your Shopify account so they won't show up in your store. Your store details will be set up later.

7.   Click the button for "This Is My Retail Store Address" ONLY if you want to use the name and address you input as your store address; if not, leave the box unticked.

8.   Click on "Take Me To My Store." Nobody can see your store yet because it has been protected by a password and only those with the password can see it. You only remove that password when you are ready for your store to go live.

9.   Now your store admin area is created. At the top of the browser window you will see a URL. Bookmark the page or write the URL down. This is your admin area, where your entire store is controlled. Click on "View Your Website" at the top of the screen and you will see your store.

That's it and your store is created and you are ready to start adding products.

ADDING YOUR PRODUCTS

Right now, your store is looking a little bit empty so let's add a product and see what it looks like.

1.   Click on "Back to Dashboard" so you go back to the Admin area and then click on "Add Products."

2.   Pick a product that you have an image for already and type a descriptive title in into the text box for Title

3.   Under the description, a number of fields will appear; fill them in with the correct details – these can be changed later so input anything for now.

4.   Obviously, "Price" is what the product will be sold at and "Compare at Price" shows you what you sold the product for previously – this can be left blank if it doesn't apply to you.

5.   Either input an SKU – a stock keeping unit – or leave it empty so one can be assigned. If you have an ISBN, an ASIN, or a barcode, the details go in the Barcode field. This lets the search engines easily index products, adding them, in Google's case, to their price comparison feature.

6.   Lastly, decide if you are keeping an inventory and whether the "Out of Stock" option should be shown by Shopify so you don't sell any more than currently in stock. You can leave the box for "Multiple Options" blank for now.

7.   Now click "Choose Files" and add some images of the product.

8.   For the "Visibility" option choose visible so you can see your store with your newly added products. Once you have seen it, you can delete the product or make it invisible but, once again, because your website is password protected, nobody can see it or buy the product.

9.   Click on "Save Product" and choose to "View in Website" – button at the top of the page.

Doesn't that look good? Add a few more products and then we'll move on to setting up your domain and emails.

DOMAINS AND EMAILS

Before your store goes live there are a few other details you need to deal with and the first is your domain name. When you choose one of the three main plans you get given a domain name but it isn't very exciting and it will do nothing for your credibility online. All that domain name consists of is your name followed by.shopify.com. You need a domain that is going to scream your brand or your product from the rooftops and Shopify helps you to do this by letting you buy a domain name through a domain registrar. When you purchase through an external registrar, that name is yours for as long as you choose, even if you, one day, decide to move on from Shopify.

Use a reputable domain registrar, like GoDaddy. You will find that most offer much the same service but do your homework thoroughly and don't forget to read the small print!

Once you have chosen your domain registrar, type in the domain name you want and click on Search. You will see a list of the domain names that match or come somewhere near what you typed in. If the name has already been taken, you will need to think of another – tip: before you go looking for a registrar, spend some time thinking of several names that will suit your business. It's highly unlikely that you will get the one you really want!

Your name needs to be memorable, not too long and easy to spell. People don't like complicated website names and will tend to move on to an easier one! You should pay no more than about $15 a year for a domain name if it is not a premium com or co.uk name – these will set you back a little more.

Chose which name you want and click on the "Checkout button" and decide how long a term you want to pay for. Longer periods tend to work out cheaper per year and 2 years seems to be the best bet – it's long enough to give your business chance to shine but doesn't tie you in for too long.

Input your payment and address details but be aware; if people search Who's for your domain name this address will show up. If you don't want your address made public, you can pay for an extra privacy feature on most registrars.

Once you have successfully ordered and paid for your domain name, you get a confirmation email. Click on the link in the email and you will be redirected to your control panel. Now you are ready to add that name to your Shopify site.

Return to the Shopify dashboard and click the option for the "Domains" menu. Click "Add an Existing Domain." Type your new domain name in and click "Add Domain." On your screen you will see a DNS address – write this down, you will need it in a minute. Also, write down the URL from the address bar – yourdomainname.myshopify.com.

In the control panel for your domain name (whichever registrar you chose), click on the option for "Manage Domains." Choose your domain name from the dropdown list and then go to the top of the page. Click on DNS and scroll through the list, clicking on "Show Advanced DNS Options."

Click to "Add a New Record" and type in the DNS number you wrote down – it must be exact, something along the lines of 205.95.223.56 (not this number!). In the Host box, type in your domain name, omitting the www from it. TTL needs to be set to 300.

Repeat these steps with CNAME and input your domain information.

It will take a while for all this to start working but, when they do, you will be able to use your own domain name to access your Shopify store.

Back in the dashboard for your Shopify store, click on "Domains" and then on "Set as Primary." Click on "Save" and you are ready to move on to the next step.

Setting up your Email Account

Now that your domain is all set up it's time to look at emails. You need a minimum of one email account for the domain name and this can be used for all your Shopify store contact details. Later on, you can set up one for each department or person in your business if you want.

When you purchase your domain name, the registrar will likely provide you with one email address and a number of forwarders so what you could do is set up a primary email account and use other addresses to forward emails to that main account. If you need extra mailboxes, you can buy upgrades.

In your domain registrar control panel, click on "Email" and then on "Add New Address." Where it says Account Name, type in what you want the email address to be, sticking with a generic name for now like sales or mail. This becomes your primary address.

Next, click on "Add New Forwarder" and input the addresses you require, forwarding them to the primary email address you created first.

Once your email account has been set up, you can use any email client to access them, but the easiest way is to use the client supplied by your domain account. So, find your main email account and click "Login" beside it. Input your email and your password and then click on "Compose."

Input a message, with a subject line and an email address to send it to – use your own personal one for this test – and click on "Send." Check your personal email account to make sure the email came through. Reply to it and then go back to your domain email account to make sure the reply came through okay. If it did, all is working well.

Now we can move on to setting up the remainder of your Shopify store.

Capitolo 6 How to Drive Traffic to Your Shopify Site?

Launching your own store is a onetime process. It is an opportunity for you to draw as much traffic and attention as you can. There are certain things or steps which you can take to get more traffic drawn towards your store during its grand inauguration. This will further help you in becoming a seasoned marketer with huge sales.

In this article, you will get to know more about how to get traffic for your new store with the help of influencers and drawing attention. Here we provide six templates and some tactics which will help you for your store's campaign. You can just copy and paste these templates. By the end of this chapter, you will also gain some valuable information and things which will help you in maintaining the momentum of a well-established business.

Let's start with the six different templates used to gain traffic.

1.   Provide Free samples to Instagram Users

One of the most loved social media applications Instagram is certainly considered to be a very efficient marketing channel for ecommerce merchants. As per the findings of a recent study, Instagram is a fast growing social platform which enhances the customer to reach of a brand by 25% than any other social platform does. Our own analysis proves that it generates a much higher average order value when compared to Facebook, Google Plus, Pinterest, and Twitter. It helps in driving a lot of traffic to your store when you know how to draw the influencer's attention. For example, let's assume that you are willing to start an online skin care product company.

- From where should you start promoting your products and gain attention for your store?

You can start by searching for popular accounts on Instagram that will allow you to feature your products to their followers.

- How will you find such accounts?

You can search with the help of WEBSTA. It is a website which records all the popular hashtags and account users on Instagram. You can easily locate these popular users and hashtags by just typing 'skincare' in the search bar. This will redirect you to those users who have the term 'skincare' mentioned in their bio or username. With the help of this, you can get the link to that user's contact page, email, and phone number.

You can also use the mobile app of Instagram for targeting the influencers. You can go through the popular pages on Instagram which contains the latest trending pictures. Click on any such trending picture to get the username or link of the user's account. Look for contact details like email in the bio of the user.

These users often provide their email address for advertisement, product placement, and partnership opportunities. After this, you have people's reach which has to be strategic. Not all users have a huge amount of followers. Targeting the perfect user for getting the job done is the most important part.

- What is a reach out campaign?

Suppose that you have targeted a user who has mentioned his/her business address. The next thing for you is to send a sample along with a note which describes your product. If there is no business address provided then send a note, asking whether the user is interested in featuring certain skincare products or not.

2. Get connected to press and bloggers

You can easily reach out to people like bloggers and vloggers who have a certain amount of followers on various websites and social media platforms. The process of contacting them is quite similar as contacting Instagram influencers.

Google can be the source for searching a blogger.

Pick some relevant keywords like 'skincare tips,' 'skincare methods' and 'skin care' to search on YouTube. Go through the videos posted on YouTube and check whether they post regularly or not. You may have to watch multiple videos before contacting anyone who will actually feature your product. You will find many people who take this as their mode of earning.

Another good option for gathering huge traffic is the press.

You might not get an opportunity to have your product published by a big newspaper, but you will get a scope to introduce your product to the press or local news site. If you can come up with some unique ideas and brilliant descriptions about your product, then there stands a chance for you to get your product featured. Construct a short, but effective pitch for your product as reporters have to go through a lot of pitches. Short and unique pitches are always welcomed to take up as a success story.

Just like any Instagram personality can give your product optimum exposure, a popular blogger, vlogger or the press can do the same if they agree to feature your product. It will help in drawing traffic, maximizing sales and gaining attention. Just as you can send a sample and a note to an Instagram user, similarly you can get in touch with a blogger or press.

What should you write to a blogger, vlogger or press?

This template will help you to get things started and sorted. To be published as a success story you can pitch for it. Prepare a note which you will like to send to the appropriate person. There are many people with huge audiences, and they gain a lot of attention while you are waiting for your shot at getting the success story covered. There is no such rule that you have to opt for the most successful and biggest people. You can opt for people with less amount of audience as they are not always crowded by people similar to you, looking to get featured. For your information, the retro video game seller, Chris Dammacco targets vloggers will small audiences on YouTube.

One thing which matters the most is the loyalty of the audience which is much similar to the size of the audience.

3.   Reddit your store

Reddit is basically the hangout hub for the internet users. Along with the main page of Reddit, there are multiple numbers of niches known as the subreddits. It a cumulative source of the most popular contents trending on the internet. You can search for a subreddit by just typing /r/sci-fi, /r/swimming, /r/gaming, etc. to help you and your store, you should follow some threads.

The first thing which everyone should be surfing is /r/entrepreneur subreddit. It has several interesting tips, facts, and discussions based on entrepreneurship made by its 79,000 subscribers. You will also find some threads like /r/small business which will fetch general information on business tactics. Give a brief description on your store and products. Give a catchy headline like, "Health care starts with skin care. My store brings you the best of skin care products for all types of skin."

Keep it short, effective, snappy but not sale-y. To know whether you are following the guidelines of Reddit, you can go through the Reddiquette guide. Check the subreddit rules which can be found in the right sidebar of subreddit. There are certain subreddits which do not allow posting promotional posts. So, what's an ad for you is a big no-no for them? Even if you are posting about your site in a subreddit which doesn't entertain such posts, you will be facing certain consequences like getting banned from the subreddit. Kindly follow the rules before posting anything.

4.   Ask your friend and family to share:

Are you already in that age where all your friends are posting pictures of their children and is it annoying when all you can think about is work? Well, there are people who do get sick of baby photos, but you can surely give them relief by selling your online store! People don't launch a startup very often, so you have high chances to make your work get an added eye within your circle of people.

Have you heard of Upworthy? I am sure you have! Their articles are all over our Facebook feed. You'd be surprised to know that their initial traffic generation happened with the help of their friends and families. They had a goal to get around 1,000 Facebook likes, and by the end of their first day, it actually worked out! This was the part that gave them their initial traction and everything took off. Things started rolling in, and it became a popular name. Thus, ask your well-wishers to do you an initial aid without making them feel irritated.

When you are on Facebook, talk about your store through updates. Talk to your family, extended family, relatives, and friends. Have them reunited through mails and send them a note about your store. They will not only share your work but also refer other people when they know someone who could need you. Don't stress on selling your products, but sell your concepts and show them how unique you are. Ask them to make simple promotions through sharing and networking. These people will be able to share your work and give you success by reaching out to the mutual and also the non-mutual people on your list.

5.   Engaging on Twitter proactively:

You don't really need to start selling before you have started engaging people onto your Twitter account. There are several ways to get people in your store. For example, Blackbird Baking Company from Toronto is a bakery that sells fresh bread. They had over 500 followers before their store had opened! If you have a few hundred people before you launch, you will not solely await your big day!

Now suppose you have something similar to sell. Post about your work on Twitter and see how people are reacting to it. You will be redirected to people who are interested in having a new bakery, and you are likely to get some restaurateurs and self-declared bread enthusiasts in your region!

Followerwonk is one tool that can be used for finding some relevant users who could be interested in following your page. As soon as you log onto Twitter, you will get relevant keywords, and you can browse through bios and profiles. This process helps you follow a neat tweeting strategy. The Blackbird baking company has been flourishing over the months and is selling their goods to interested stores across Toronto. They have also been adding several pictures on Instagram and Facebook which not only shows their success but also customer's interests. You should also check them out to realize how mouthwatering and shareable food could be!

It is pretty easy to active people through tweets and publicizes within your local community. You will get topics that include about the life in Toronto, their food, people and of course their bread. They have also mentioned important details like opening and closing time, new sells, etc. so you should always keep your customers updated.

Thus, the central strategy is, search for keywords in Twitter and get it related to the business. Look for several chances to introduce your work to the interested customers and higher your sales pitch. You will soon realize how valuable your tweets are to the concerned group of people!

6.   Create a blog, feature people and audience and then publicize:

Finally, the last part of this suggestion is to reach out to prospective buyers by connecting people through big audience and blogging. Rather than sending samples of products, you are likely to get more traffic in better way – writing a blog post and send them through mail or Twitter. Don't wait for them to feature you, when you can feature them before! You are anyway looking for influencers in your concerned industry. Write about the top people that you find and turn it into an easy blog post by featuring popular Instagramers, vloggers, bloggers, etc.

Some common examples of headlines are:

- Top 10 hairstyle bloggers to follow

- Top 15 Twitter profiles to follow

- Top 20 Instagramers to discover new hairstyles

- Top 4 YouTube personalities for style tutorials

In your post, add some blurb discussing who they are as you list them one by one. Circulate the post through your Twitter account. It is important to add their handles, but don't be obvious that you require their attention. You should be thoughtful and innovative, which will draw in all their concerns!

Your store will launch once you don't have a lot of problems to reach out to people. Do whatever it takes to draw in traffic and then turn visitors into customers. Once this is done, move towards your online store and work on it.

It is important to remember than drawing traffic is a continuous process, and you must stick to it. Even if you think you have enough followers, it is actually never enough. Keep engaging people so that you can market yourself a little every moment. You will soon have a pool of followers, and that might make you feel that it is enough, but in reality, you can never have too many followers or too much traffic. This just keeps on expanding you and bettering your work. So, simply gear up for what you have ahead and embrace yourself for lots of appreciation and love!

Capitolo 7 Platforms for Building Your Store

Most people think that building an ecommerce store is a hard task that requires advanced skills in site building, coding, and web design. They are totally wrong. Anyone can build their own online store with plug-and-play platforms that are available online. Here, I will look at two popular platforms that you can use to build your online store. However, before I go into that, you need to know that your online store will always be a work-in-progress. If you decide to wait until you have a perfect website before you launch your store, you might never launch. Do what you can and keep improving as you move on.

While there are several platforms for building online stores, the two most popular platforms are Shopify and WooCommerce.

Shopify: This is simply the best platform when it comes to building a standalone online store. Shopify takes care of all the technical aspects of setting up your ecommerce website and running it, from handling the web-hosting bits to making your site secure and processing credit card payments. By taking care of the technical aspects of your dropshipping business, they allow you to concentrate on marketing and driving traffic to your website. On top of that, they have thousands of apps that you can use to extend the functionalities of your online store.

WooCommerce: This is another powerful toolkit that you can use to build your online store. WooCommerce is an open source platform, which allows you to make whatever modifications and customizations you want on your site. Unlike Shopify, it doesn't exercise any controls over your site's data, which is a big plus. However, WooCommerce is more suitable for small businesses. Managing a big store with

WooCommerce can be a bit challenging. Unlike Shopify, WooCommerce is free, though you will need to pay for licenses and buy third-party plugins in order to extend your store's functionality.

Promoting Your Dropshipping Business

Once your dropshipping store goes live and is ready to meet its first customers, now is the time to get it in front of as many prospective customers as you can and attract them so they can become paying customers. This is one of the most challenging parts of starting a dropshipping business. However, without promoting your business, your chances of success are next to zero. Luckily, if you commit yourself and do it right, you will enjoy massive results.

There are several channels you can use to promote your dropshipping business. While each business has a different channel that works best for it, I am going to look at five proven methods you can use to promote your online store. You don't have to use all of them. Focus on the methods that suit you best.

Social Media Marketing (SMM)

Social media marketing is the use of social media sites to create brand awareness, create customer relationships, gain traffic, and drive sales. These can be done on major social media platforms such as Facebook, Twitter, Instagram, Pinterest, Google+, LinkedIn, and YouTube, as well as on online forums and blogs. While many people see social media as nothing more than a social tool, it is something that you can leverage to drive sales for your dropshipping business. When creating a social media marketing campaign for your business, you should avoid trying to market your business on every social media platform. While it might seem like a good strategy to gain maximum reach, it will be overwhelming for you and you will end up achieving dismal results on each of these sites. What you should do is identify two to three social media platforms that will deliver maximum results and dedicate all your focus to them. All in all, social media is a great tool for marketing your dropshipping business. Avoid social media marketing at your own risk.

Facebook Ads

While this is an off-shoot of social media marketing, it deserves its own mention because of its effectiveness as an online marketing tool. Facebook is the largest and the most popular social marketing platform in the world. The platform has over 1.71 billion monthly active users, which makes it the ideal place to advertise your dropshipping business. However, the effectiveness of Facebook as a marketing tool goes beyond the numbers. Unlike most advertising platforms which serve ads on query-based data, Facebook serves its ads based on contextual data. With query-based data, the advertising platform shows adverts that are relevant to what users are searching for on the internet. A good example of a query-based advertising platform is Google AdWords.

In contrast, platforms that serve advertisements based on contextual data allow advertisers to choose the demographics of the people they want to see their advertisements based on context. This makes it easier for you to target a specific audience. Are your products geared toward 25-year-old men living in California who have an obsession with sport bikes? You can target this exact group with Facebook ads. Facebook advertisements allow you to choose you audience based on factors like age, geographical location, interests, behavior, job position, and so much more. This means that Facebook advertisements are more relevant and are more likely to drive conversions.

To make your Facebook advertising campaign more effective, you should first come up with a clear objective for the campaign. Is your aim to create awareness for your brand? Is it to drive people to your dropshipping store? Is it to increase your sales? Having a clear objective will help you craft an effective marketing campaign. On top of that, Facebook provides you with a variety of options that make it easier for you to achieve your marketing objectives.

The other things you should keep in mind in order to create a relevant Facebook advertisement is to ensure that you use persuasive, relevant, and actionable copy, use relevant and attention-grabbing images, and use a clear and concise Call to Action (CTA).

Search Engine Optimization (SEO)

Search Engine Optimization is the process of finetuning your site in order to capture traffic from search engines like Google. In other words, it is the process of ensuring that your dropshipping business can be found on search engines. SEO is a broad topic and consists of many elements. However, to make it simpler to understand, SEO can be broken down into the steps. The first one is defining the keywords that you want your site to rank for. This means that when people search for these keywords, they should be able to find your site on the first page of Google. You will have to do extensive keyword research to find appropriate keywords that you want to rank for. The second step is optimizing your site for the keywords you defined in step one. Step three is building backlinks to your dropshipping store. Having many backlinks on your dropshipping store gives Google's algorithms the perception that your site is an authoritative one, which in turn leads to a higher ranking on the search engine results pages.

By properly utilizing SEO tactics, your dropshipping store will rank higher on search engines, which means that you will have more people finding your store, visiting it, and buying your products. SEO allows you to direct traffic to your dropshipping store without having to pay for it.

While performing proper SEO to ensure your store ranks high on search results is not a necessarily easy task, it is still doable.

Defining the keywords, you want to rank for and optimizing your store for these keywords is the easy part. The hard part is trying to outrank your competitors for the same keywords, especially when your store is still relatively new and has yet to build some authority. This is where backlinks come in handy. Backlinks from high-quality sources will help raise your store's authority.

SEO is something you want to ensure you are doing right. According to data by Custora, organic search traffic drives about 26% of all orders on ecommerce stores. By improving your site's SEO, you can increase your sales by up to 26% percent. One thing you should keep in mind is that you won't see immediate results with SEO. Initially, you will hardly see any results, but in the long run, you will reap exponential rewards.

Email Marketing

Email is one of the most cost-effective tools you can use to market your dropshipping business and gain customer engagement. Email generates high-quality leads and high-quality conversions, which is why it has a return on investment (ROI) of 44%. If you do it right, you will see massive results. Email is so effective because people share their contact details voluntarily, which is a sure-fire sign that they are interested in your products. Email marketing also allows you to accumulate your prospect's personal data, which you can use in further interactions. By providing quality content through email, you can create more demand for your products.

To run an effective email marketing campaign, you should have an attractive lead magnet for your site. As a dropshipping business, your lead magnet can be a loyalty program that provides subscribers with exclusive discounts. You should have a well-designed email template and ensure that your regularly communicate with your subscribers. However, this does not mean constantly spamming them with sales emails. This will only lead to people opting out of your email list.

Instead, you should always strive to provide value through your email newsletters.

Video Marketing

The greatest thing about video marketing is that it makes it possible for you to create an instant connection with your audience. Posts with videos lead to more time spent on your site and increased engagement. Search engine algorithms also tend to give more importance to videos, which means that using videos will improve your ranking, increase your conversions, and have greater results on your brand awareness campaign.

The most effective way of using videos to promote your dropshipping business is to create video reviews of the products you sell in your store. These can range from amateur reviews by previous customers to professional and detailed reviews of a product's features, performance, and benefits. If you decide on using video marketing to promote your store, create a YouTube channel that matches your store design, provide information about your business on the channel, and make sure that your channel is also optimized for search engines.

Capitolo 8 Create Your Online Empire and Succeed in Ecommerce Business with Shopify

W ho wouldn't like to enjoy an online empire and do an impressive ecommerce business while sitting at home? To make your dream come true, let's first understand how to set up one's online store using Shopify.

Setting Up Your Online Store

Online store or online shopping is the latest buzz word you often get to hear. Here is an interesting offer from Shopify with a 14-day free trial that can be signed up from the main homepage. You can also click on the Free Trial button available on the menu bar. Provide your email, password and create a store name.

The URL of the page contains your store name; however, if you wish to change it later, the page allows you to change. It is always better to create a simple name which reads like you.myshopify.com because choosing multiple words will show the link like your-business-name.myshopify.com. In case, you don't want to be redirected to a URL from your domain like store.yourdomain.com to you.myshopify.com; then you must keep a store name/URL ready on hand. You will have to provide all your basic details such name, address, and phone number while creating your account on Shopify. After this process, you will be taken to the admin dashboard to start creating your online store. Check out the 7 steps guide to ease the process.

1. Add your products

Start adding products to your store by manual addition or a bulk upload from a CSV file or import from platforms like Magento and eBay. If you have digital products, then firstly you need to install an app for digital product delivery, add your products using this app. The Shopify's online manual. throws more light on the selling of digital products. If you have selling services that you are attempting to sell, then opt for an app like Product Options with which you can customize your service offerings. Shopify store allows you to have 100 variations for the products which typically have options as for size, color, and finish. This site gives you the feasibility to add a product with a set of options, and there is no limit as such if it is a physical product. For example, you have 3 options for your e-book, i.e., just the e-book, the second is e-book along with supporting material and a 3rd option which is inclusive of everything plus access to a private member forum. The Shopify Documentation clearly tells you how to set up products.

2.   Customize your design

The next step is to add custom design by choosing a theme. You can choose a theme from Shopify theme store which has various designs for free as well as paid. If you do not have any plan as such and simply chose some theme, you can always edit the theme by using the template editor or theme settings editor for modifying the coding. One common place where you would want to edit is the footer because that is the space you may choose for providing social links, payment methods, and various other details.

There will be some example themes that might be great to start out with. There are tons to choose from, but these ones are some of the best to look at off the bat.

3. Select Your Domain Name

The Shopify online manual encompasses all the information related to setting up of the custom domain name of your store. So, instead of being forced to choose a domain like you.myshopify.com, you can select from the options like store.yourdomain.com or yourdomain.com.

4. Set up Shipping and Tax Rates

You will be required to add taxes as well as additional shipping costs to your items and also notify Shopify about the same. Shopify would list the basic prices, but it depends on the product you sell, and you may need to customize more options.

4. Set up payments

This is the critical part of all the steps. Shopify Payments accept the credit cards if you are in USA, Canada or the UK, this facility would not require any third-party payment gateways or merchant account. Shopify incorporates other payment processing services that includes PayPal, Amazon Payments, and Google Wallet.

6. Settings

Your complete profile needs to be set up carefully, most of these details get filled while you do it step-by-step. However, it doesn't ask for the information required for adding your Google Analytics code, store description, and store title in the profile section as all this information is required to be filled in the general settings.

7. Open Your Store and Prove it to the world

Once all the details are entered, and you are ready with you online store, you can make it public. Till such time, it will be password protected, and you can also test the same to ensure if everything is functioning the way it is supposed to. Make sure that you check everything before the customer notices the loopholes.

Choosing Apps for Additional Functionality and Features

Shopify provides hundreds of free and premium apps which can be used to improvise your online store; they are categorized as:

- Accounting — Link your Shopify store to any of the popular accounting solutions such as QuickBooks, FreshBooks, and Xero.

- Customer Service — It always helps both the customer and the seller if you add contact forms, live chat, feedback, and other features for customer support.

- Inventory — Inventory management systems if integrated with your online store will help in the process simplification.

- Marketing — This category helps you include your email, search, and social media marketing into your online store.

- Reporting — You can check for additional analytics related to your online business with the usage of these apps. It will help you in measuring conversion rates, sales data as well as customer behavior.

- Sales — This category helps you in increasing the sales with the help of product reviews, customer loyalty programs, upsells, and recommendations given by others.

- Shipping — Create your product shipment process easier and simpler with apps that help in managing the order fulfillment process and link you with your preferred shipping service.

- Social Media — This is one category not to be missed on, keep yourself connected with the customers and engage them on social media platform using these apps.

- Tools — You will find tools that would help you in handling all the features required for running an online store successfully. The best part and the most convenient thing for the users is that it also offers setting up of bulk redirects, fighting fraud, language translators as well as RSS feeds.

Unsure of how and where to start your online store, then you may have to reconfigure your SEO settings for your product pages and in addition to that, add email marketing support so that the customers can be added to your email list. These email marketing services often guide you how to connect your Shopify store to their system.

Social Selling

This has become a totally new concept of selling and widely used these days. If you are one person who wants to sell products on your blog, then here it is. Shopify provides plugins and widgets for WordPress, Drupal and Joomla users by which you can show products in your posts, pages, and sidebar. If you are creating content based on customer's interest, this would increase traffic to your domain. Another interesting way to keep your customers in loop and engaged is to create a Facebook page and also post interesting stuff. Shopify offers various Facebook integrations that would allow you to turn your Facebook page into an e-commerce store.

What About Affiliates?

Shopify offers various apps that allow you to create your own affiliate program to keep track of referrals made by customers and supporters. You can do this if you would not mind sharing your profits with others, this will also create some publicity.

Where You Can Go to Learn More

If you are a person with zeal to learn about Ecommerce and succeed in marketing your online store, then there is no stopping. You can simply find reading material like, e-books, guides, tutorials and videos to help you learn more at Ecommerce University. You could also check Shopify Wiki where you can go through everything you are required to know about while using Shopify and the design/development of your store. Shopify also has a support section in which you can find over 200 troubleshooting articles. Just in case, if you happen to come across some new or weird issue, you even have forums to look for support. Forums often have thousands of topics related to e-commerce.

Where You Can Get Help

This is the last resort wherein if you fail to help yourself with the troubleshooting guides, you can always seek professional help from the Shopify Experts. This area provides help with the store setup, designers, developers, marketers and photographers who can indeed make your e-commerce store into a successful business.

Capitolo 9 Extensive Template Options

The company provides highly professional templates that you cannot find in other e-commerce platforms. You can find more than 100 themes, which are offered free or as paid. Paid options range from $80 and go up to $180.The design and themes featured in Shopify are stunning and elegant. The numerous free and premium templates feature themes created by big names in web design including Clearleft, Pixel Union and Happy Cog.

Setting up

Once you choose from the various themes present, the next step is to customize the feel and appearance of your site. You need to just open Shopify's template editor. The steps for editing are easy to follow, so you can make the necessary changes until you are satisfied with the look. Once you have perfected the appearance of the theme, you can upload it by visiting the Theme page. On the page, you will have to click on the upload theme option. Your theme will be added. It's as simple as that!

Website customization

At Shopify, each website template has its own individual settings. This helps you to effectively customize the design of your website. The templates have certain key concepts, which are easy to understand and help customize your site efficiently. The important concepts in the templates include

Products

These form the base unit and are the core of theme building. The feature has several subsections such as title, its description, image, price and the variants like weight, size, color, etc. These and the product variants can be created and constantly updated through the online admin and the dashboard.

The variants form a powerful feature in Shopify. You can use them to display products in numerous attractive and appealing way in your templates.

Collections

After products, you need to classify them into various collections. This is necessary to categorize all the products successfully. The collections can be further organized in different ways such as alphabetically, by price, date or bestselling feature, etc.

Product tags

Tags add more information to the product and help in better filtering of the collection.

Themes

Themes help to increase the appeal of the store. Shopify has over 55 themes, which are available in over 140 styles. So you can have plenty of options to choose from when you are searching for the right theme for your online store. As mobile accounts for over 50 percent of all traffic in e-commerce, it is absolutely important for your store to be mobile responsive. Most of the themes at Shopify are of this category.

The editor feature in theme settings allows you to preview a template as you make changes in the template. This way you can have total control over how your store will look.

Expert help

If you are in need of a completely customized template design, Shopify design experts recommend you on the ideal template set up. The service has expert developers, marketers, and designers to advice on setting up a successful business online.

Without the hassles of hosting and web design limitations, Shopify provides a customer-friendly admin that helps you include all you have dreamed of about your store in a template. The professional features of Shopify further help you complete the set up in a full-fledged way. And one important advantage that Shopify has with regard to its templates is, you will not find any logos or ads in the templates. You will have to look very hard to identify that the site is supported by Shopify.

Best enhancing features

Shopify is an all-inclusive e-commerce platform that provides a comprehensive feature-rich solution for your online store. Once you have chosen a template from the Theme store at Shopify and improve the design, you can customize and optimize your site effectively. The Liquid template language enables easy control of template optimization, even if you do not have sufficient knowledge about CSS and HTML coding.

When you have optimized the template with change colors, logo and other features, you can start creating the product catalog with tools like Brand Names, Attributes, Categories, and Pricing. Promotions are also easier with the promotion tool, which offers automated discounts on products at a particular period of sale. After the period of promotion, the products will revert to the original price present before the sale.

Here are landmark features of Shopify

Design features

In web design, the advantages with Shopify include

•   Professional and appealing e-commerce site, which is quick to set up and starts operating in minutes

•   Customizable and compliant with standards free templates provided with the account

- Total control over CSS and HTML of your website.

- Liquid template language encourages dynamic content layout in a flexible way

- The facility of linking media assets to the entire shop or to individual products

- Forums and communities of Shopify designers to help with strategies and tips.

Content management features

The dynamic CMS in Shopify can help create web pages, blog posts, contact us feature and other features directly from the dashboard administration. It features SEO marketing tools and tools or coupon codes, besides having a full-fledged integral mobile commerce feature.

Order and pricing

The purchase features are highly efficient. Shopify provides secure payments via credit cards and PayPal via 50 payment channels. Customers have plenty of options for payments including eChecks, credit cards, PayPal, Google Checkout and much more.

The smart information collection features enable detection of the country based on the IP address. This will result in automatic changes in the currency, tax rates, language customization in the checkout page including the checkout at the shopping cart page.

Shipping calculators are also provided with Shopify. You can set up return and refund policies with the various order processing tools enabling a streamlined checkout process.

Background features

The infrastructural features in Shopify are well designed to ensure optimal data security. The PCI compliant Level I certification makes sure that customer information is guarded safely. With its open-source foundation, Shopify continues to tweak its features and improve them. The software is compatible with several direct payment systems and operates from a state of the art data center. Other salient features that reinforce the infrastructure of the e-commerce platform include

• Ruby on Rails framework

• Open SBD firewall guarded Debian Linus Server hosting

• MySQL database support providing speed and reliability

Point-Of-Sale

The POS feature in Shopify allows both online and physical location sales. When compared to competitors this feature has several enhanced items such as card reader, cash drawer, receipt printer, and barcode scanner. All these are available for purchase as an entire package or individually, according to your requirements. With an iPad, it is possible to use Shopify effectively to

• Sell from a stall in the market

• Pop up store

• Store in events

• Permanent retail outlet

The stock and inventory are kept automatically synced with the various locations, enabling you to manage multiple stores from a single point.

Domains and Emails

Before your store goes live there are a few other details you need to deal with and the first is your domain name. When you choose one of the three main plans you get given a domain name but it isn't very exciting and it will do nothing for your credibility online. All that domain name consists of is your name followed by shopify.com. You need a domain that is going to scream your brand or your product from the rooftops and Shopify helps you to do this by letting you buy a domain name through a domain registrar. When you purchase through an external registrar, that name is yours for as long as you choose, even if you, one day, decide to move on from Shopify.

Use a reputable domain registrar, like GoDaddy. You will find that most offer much the same service but do your homework thoroughly and don't forget to read the small print!

Once you have chosen your domain registrar, type in the domain name you want and click on Search. You will see a list of the domain names that match or come somewhere near what you typed in. If the name has already been taken, you will need to think of another – tip: Before you go looking for a registrar, spend some time thinking of several names that will suit your business. It's highly unlikely that you will get the one you really want!

Your name needs to be memorable, not too long and easy to spell. People don't like complicated website names and will tend to move on to an easier one! You should pay no more than about $15 a year for a domain name if it is not a premium com or co.uk name – these will set you back a little more.

Chose which name you want and click on the "Checkout button" and decide how long a term you want to pay for. Longer periods tend to work out cheaper per year and 2 years seems to be the best bet – it's long enough to give your business chance to shine but doesn't tie you in for too long.

Input your payment and address details but be aware; if people search Whois for your domain name this address will show up. If you don't want your address made public, you can pay for an extra privacy feature on most registrars.

Once you have successfully ordered and paid for your domain name, you get a confirmation email. Click on the link in the email and you will be redirected to your control panel. Now you are ready to add that name to your Shopify site.

Return to the Shopify dashboard and click the option for the "Domains" menu. Click "Add an Existing Domain." Type your new domain name in and click "Add Domain." On your screen you will see a DNS address – write this down, you will need it in a minute. Also, write down the URL from the address bar – yourdomainname.myshopify.com.

In the control panel for your domain name (whichever registrar you chose), click on the option for "Manage Domains." Choose your domain name from the dropdown list and then go to the top of the page. Click on DNS and scroll through the list, click on "Show Advanced DNS Options."

Click to "Add a New Record" and type in the DNS number you wrote down – it must be exact, something along the lines of 205.95.223.56 (not this number!). In the Host box, type in your domain name, omitting the www from it. TTL needs to be set to 300.

Repeat these steps with CNAME and input your domain information.

It will take a while for all this to start working but, when they do, you will be able to use your own domain name to access your Shopify store.

Back in the dashboard for your Shopify store, click on "Domains" and then on "Set as Primary." Click on "Save" and you are ready to move on to the next step.

Setting up your Email Account

Now that your domain is all set up it's time to look at emails. You need a minimum of one email account for the domain name and this can be used for all your Shopify store contact details. Later on, you can set up one for each department or person in your business if you want. When you purchase your domain name, the registrar will likely provide you with one email address and a number of forwarders so what you could do is set up a primary email account and use other addresses to forward emails to that main account. If you need extra mailboxes, you can buy upgrades.

In your domain registrar control panel, click on "Email" and then on "Add New Address."

Where it says Account Name, type in what you want the email address to be, sticking with a generic name for now like sales or mail. This becomes your primary address.

Next, click on "Add New Forwarder" and input the addresses you require, forwarding them to the primary email address you created first.

Once your email account has been set up, you can use any email client to access them, but the easiest way is to use the client supplied by your domain account. So, find your main email account and click "Login" beside it. Input your email and your password and then click on "Compose."

Input a message, with a subject line and an email address to send it to – use your own personal one for this test – and click on "Send." Check your personal email account to make sure the email came through. Reply to it and then go back to your domain email account to make sure the reply came through okay. If it did, all is working well.

Now we can move on to setting up the remainder of your Shopify store.

Capitolo 10 Risks Involved and Major Pitfalls to be Avoided

It is thought that as many as fifty percent of start-ups will fail within the first year of business. There will be tough times; the same is true even for established businesses, but a good plan and a level approach can ensure you find a path through. In fact, your business should survive a tough time and emerge stronger and better than it was before!

It is essential to be aware of the risks involved in dropshipping before you start:

Reliance

Even if you follow the guidelines in this book and ensure you can source your products from several sources; you are still reliant on your supplier. They hold the stock and must send it to your customer within the timeframe agreed by you with your customer. Once you have passed the order onto your supplier it is out of your hands and there is very little you can do to control the process. The majority of the time everything happens smoothly and within the expected tie constraints. When it does go wrong you are stuck between an irate customer; who can seriously damage your reputation and a wholesaler that you need for the ongoing success of your business! It is not an easy position to be in!

Multiple Sources

It is essential to have a contract with several suppliers to ensure you are able to source a product when you need to. However, this does not mean listing products from different suppliers on your website. If you do list fifty items and there are ten items from each supplier, there is a very real risk that your customer will order items from different suppliers. This will push up the shipping costs for them and cost you the sale! Every supplier's products should be listed on a separate website. You may prefer to only establish one website at a time as there is a small cost to establishing a new site. If this is the case then you need to be aware of the stock levels and manually redirect and order, absorbing the additional carriage cost, in order to fulfil the order.

Alternatively you can add additional sites knowing that the links you create between your sites will help with the search engine rankings! Either decision is acceptable.

Tracking

Your reliance on a third party to ship your product creates a scenario where you will have difficulty, or may even find it impossible, to locate the product whilst it is in the delivery stages. This could be a serious issue as it will not make your business look very professional and your customer will not know what is happening with their product. In fact, your customer may even question the entire order if this is the case as tracking is now the norm in most transactions. This can be a particularly difficult issue at busy times of the year, such as Christmas, when more parcels go missing than normal.

There have been several steps forward in recent years regarding the electronic software packages which pass information between couriers and suppliers. It is advisable to check the situation regarding your own supplier before you sign up and dedicate your business to them!

Product Difference

Particularly when building your business you may be focused on adding products, building contacts and pushing your social media profile. You will not be focused on whether the product you have already added to your site has been changed, or even removed from sale! This can leave you appearing extremely red faced and can cause serious damage to your reputation when a customer receives a product that is not the same as described. The newer version may be a better version, but more expensive and cost you money in the process. It may simply not do the one thing that attracted your customer to buy it.

Missing such a vital piece of information is exceptionally easy to do and can have a serious effect on your business. When choosing your supplier it is imperative to choose one which provides product updates if items are changed or removed from stock. It will increase the likelihood of you spotting it and updating your site accordingly.

Failure to Plan

The more detailed and well thought out the plan the better you will be able to deal with any situation.

However, there are two issues associated with the planning stage which can place your new business at significant risk of failure.

• Failing to Plan means that you have no idea of what you will be likely to come up against, you will have no idea about the likely obstacles or even the best way to start in business. This does not mean you will fail completely; in fact it is possible to survive and even flourish. But, you will be surviving by luck and learning every lesson the hard way.

• Over planning can be just as bad for your business. There are two sides to this. The first is that you spend too long planning and never actually start trading because you are too busy trying to work out every possible thing that can go right or wrong. In fact, this is impossible and the reason that your business will not succeed; you have not even started! The alternative is to plan your approach and start the business. But, you become too adhered to the plan; you are only able to react according to what your plan says and you are unable to be flexible in your approach. This will mean you lose sales and opportunities as you are unable to risk taking them!

Alongside the risks there are some fairly major pitfalls which can derail your business just as you start to feel you are getting somewhere!

Many of these can be avoided if you are aware of them and prepared for them:

Competition

Dropshipping is an easy business to start in as there are very few start-up costs. Unfortunately, this means that many people attempt this kind of business and the competition for customers can be significant. In fact, the market becomes so saturated that it is barely possible to make a profit on the selling price. It is important to have a low price, if you do not you will not even be considered by the customer. However, this does not mean you need to have the lowest price.

The best way to avoid this is to ensure that you are recognized as offering more than just a product; you are offering excellent customer service and aftercare as well as knowledge of the product. You can also offer a better shipping package which will enable your customer to get their product faster or even a small free gift which will entice them to return to you.

Logistics

For you to make a living and a successful business out of dropshipping it is essential to have multiple websites, multiple suppliers and even multiple product ranges. However, all of this requires logistical support. You will need to ensure all orders are processed quickly by your systems so that the supplier can respond and dispatch the product as fast as possible.

The best way of doing this is to automate your systems as much as possible; if you do not then you will find it is very easy to miss an order when manually processing them or miss-key the information so that the customer gets the wrong product. The logistics involved in processing and tracking several orders from different locations and to different suppliers will become complicated and may take up a large part of your day. This will prevent you from undertaking tasks which can push your business forward and improve your profit and reputation.

Too Much Social Media

Just as you can spend too much time sorting the logistics of your orders you can also devote too much time to your social media profiles. This is incredibly easy to do as you are basically having conversations with people. Unfortunately this will quickly go past the point when it is beneficial to your business and merely be a means of procrastinating. If this is the case you are not devoting the time to your business that it needs and other; more important matters will not be dealt with.

To ensure you do not spend too much time on social media you should put a schedule in place; and stick to it!

Means to an End

Many people look at dropshipping as a business in its own right and do not have a plan to go beyond that. However, in reality, it is an excellent way to start in business with minimal funds and minimal risk. But, it should also be seen as a part of a long term plan which will involve dropshipping and physically holding your own stock.

Long term dropshipping will always leave you open to the whims of your suppliers and the fickleness of your market; with very little opportunity to respond if the market changes rapidly or your supplier ceases trading. To gain a satisfactory level of control and reduce the risk of your hard work being destroyed in a moment, you should plan for dropshipping to be a part of your wider business.

Product Descriptions

It is very tempting to copy the product description from the supplier's website or to enter a short description in order to add more products to your site. However, a full, copied description will not help your ratings in the search engines and may even lead your customers directly to your supplier; cutting you out of the game! A description which is too short will simply not provide enough information for your customer.

Put yourself into their shoes and work out what you would want to know if you were looking to buy one of your products. Then you can include this information in your product description, in your own words and maximize the effect of your description.

Working with a Dropshipper

Before you sign up with anyone to supply and deliver parcels on your behalf it is essential to check them out! You should confirm the length of time they have been in business and that they are a reputable supplier. Perhaps most importantly, you should check that they are the supplier and not a dropshipper themselves. The logistics would get even more complicated if you are ordering through a fellow dropshipper. Not only would you lose even more control over your product you would also find it difficult to compete on price!

Always take your time when considering a new supplier, ideally order a couple of test products from them to establish their speed and customer service level. This is an important part of the process and it is better to take a little longer to get it right than to rush it and give yourself a huge headache a few weeks down the road.

Stock Levels and Back Orders

Any supplier you integrate with must have an automated stock system which you can connect to. This will ensure that your site will always advertise the correct stock level and you will not be faced with having to tell your customer that the item they want is not currently in stock. Equally, you do not want to start agreeing to put customer orders on back order. Whilst this will keep the sale, assuming the customer is happy to wait, it will quickly become a logistical nightmare and one that you will have difficulty dealing with. The result can easily be a loss of faith by your customer as they wait for a back order which you have forgotten about and have no control over. This can seriously damage your reputation.

Capitolo 11 Shipping Methods

Throughout the book, so far, we went through a very large part that deals with setting up the commercial store online. We have learned all about setting up an e-commerce store and with that saw the things that we may require getting started. We have gone through the legalities involved. In our heads, we already analyzed the market and the products and settled on one that we were going to trade-in. Without shipping, without delivering the products to different clients, you have no business. Without being able to send your product from your storehouse to the clients, you cannot be involved in e-commerce. It would be more fitting to say that you are in the warehousing business.

Through this chapter, we will explore the different options we have when it comes to shipping our products to our customers and after looking at this we will be able to decide what option will be the best fit for our business and what will be the best fit for our customer base. Therefore, considering this, we need to decide what method we are going to use before making any order. We will need to go to the shipping settings on our store by clicking the shipping button on the admin screen to set up the different options. But before that, let us look at what they are.

The shipping methods and strategies you choose for your store will probably evolve with the evolving of your store and its growth. Among some of the choices, you will have to make, is what are the rates that you are going to charge for shipping. So below are some options that you can explore.

- Flat rate shipping

- Charge exact shipping costs

- Free shipping

Flat rate shipping

This involves charging a flat or standard charge for every package. This can also be varied to mean having a flat rate for a weight range, destinations of the goods or even the cart totals. When using this strategy, it is important to know the average cost of shipping to keep the price reasonable. This avoids undercharging that will eat into your profits and overcharging that will be exploiting your customer base. An example one can use for this type of rate is putting a $5 shipping fee for all the goods that are being shipped domestically.

Charge Exact Shipping costs

This method is just as is implied by its name; one charges exactly what it would cost for the shipping of the product from where the inventory is held to the doorstep of your client. For businesses in the United States and in Canada, Shopify goes a step further to help you out with this. One can take advantage of Shopify shipping and with this, they are able to display the shipping rates that are already calculated at checkout or your own customers. This is the best strategy, in my opinion for businesses that are still new and might be frugal with the funds that are available to them. This strategy has the customer cover their exact shipping costs and this reduces the financial constraints on the fledgling business.

Free Shipping

As suggested by the name already, this is a strategy for shipping where the business handles the cost of the shipping for the clients. Offering this option usually influences the cart conversions for your store in a positive manner. You might be thinking that this is impractical for new businesses that need to save up more and more of their limited funds to run the store but there are a few ways through which you can still offer free shipping to your customers in a way that is favorable to your new business. This can be by adding the shipping cost onto the sticker price of your product which would then insulate your business from taking an economic hit every time you ship a good for free. Another strategy one can employ is by giving free shipping on sales over a certain value of sales. This can be determined by either value-based or mass-based free shipping tolls.

Optimizing Shipping Rates

Being that you are now enabled to obtain rates that are already calculated for shipping from your store, it is important to ensure that these prices charged are accurate. This can be done in either one of two ways:

- Choosing to package

- Using product weights

Your store obtains rates on shipping depends on the weight of the cart and the size of the box the good will be shipped in. Adding the weights of all your products and the dimensions of the boxes that they will be shipped I would go a long way in improving the accuracy of this number. If this box is what is used for all your shipping, choose this box by setting it as the default making the calculation of the shipping rate faster.

Setting up shipping on your store

There are a few steps that can be used in setting this up from one's admin screen:

1.   Enter the shipping origin of your goods

2.   Add the shipping zones to it

3.   Add the different rates calculated for the different shipping zones

4.   If you are using Shopify to purchase your labeling, select the printer of the label and the packaging types that will be the store defaults.

Fulfill orders

The whole process that involved shipping your goods to the clients is known as the fulfillment of orders. These orders can be fulfilled manually by the owner of the store. A person can also involve carriers who will adjust the cost of shipping for the client and one can also use fulfillment services to ensure that their orders are shipped.

Customer Experience

After setting these settings up, a new store owner should test to see if the system and the application of the rates are precise by placing a test order to best get a feel of the customer's experience.

After a client has chosen a good, checked out, and entered their shipping address, the store consequently calculates the cost of the different shipping options that are applicable to them. The cheapest rate is what is usually set as the default and appears top of the list of the customer's options. In the cases of the customer retracting and changing their orders, their shipping rates are bound to change depending on the change in their order.

That is all there is to shipping and the different shipping options available to your customers in your store.

Capitolo 12 How to Operate Your Business?

If you are a novice in the dropshipping business, you could end up wasting a lot of time trying to figure out the ins and outs of running the business. To enable you to hit the ground running and to get ahead of the learning curve, let's discuss how you should operate your business once it's fully set up.

First, you have to understand that things are going to get mixed up at some point—that is the nature of the dropshipping business. The fact that most logistical functions are handled by third parties (manufacturers, wholesalers, and suppliers) means that there are lots of things that are out of your control, and so you should be mentally prepared to deal with mistakes and screw-ups.

Your suppliers will occasionally mess up your customers' orders, and sometimes, they may even run out of stock. When this happens, you may feel frustrated, and you may be tempted to give in or even to switch to a different business model. We can't lie to you and say that there won't be any challenges, but we can guarantee you that you will be able to handle most challenges if you are adequately prepared, and if you have taken the time to establish rules and protocols for all types of challenging scenarios.

One thing you need to remember is that the dropshipping model is already complicated by its very nature, so you should try as much as possible to keep things simple on your end. Try to find simple solutions to any problems that arise, rather than wasting time and resources trying to figure out the perfect solution for your problems. Things move fast in this business, and if you focus too much attention on singular events, you are going to get overwhelmed. Have a simple structure for your business, and make sure that all your operations move along smoothly.

Since mistakes are bound to happen, you shouldn't spin your wheels too much when they actually do occur. Even the best suppliers will occasionally mess up an order, and the customer will end up getting disappointed by the package he receives. Whatever the error, don't waste time passing around blame.

When addressing a customer's complaint, own up to the mistake and apologize, then take quick measures to make it up to him by seeing to it that your supplier fixes the issue. Think of every mistake as an opportunity to learn and grow.

Most professional suppliers will own up to mistakes that are genuinely theirs, so you don't have to be too confrontational when you report your customers' complaints to them. It's important to maintain a good rapport with your suppliers throughout because your success as a drop-shipper depends on it. However, if a supplier makes a habit out of messing up your orders, it may be wise to conclude your association with that supplier, because he may drag you down the path of failure.

Even though drop-shippers don't personally handle inventory, one of the biggest challenges that you will have to deal with as a drop-shipper will be the management and coordination of inventory, given the fact that you will most likely be working with multiple suppliers (we've already discussed why it's important to build redundancy into your supply system by having backup suppliers for each product in case there is a problem with your primary supplier). Managing and monitoring inventory is quite complicated, but as you gain more experience, you will become much better at it.

Even if you have a supplier and a backup supplier for a given product, you should keep a list of every other supplier who stocks the products that you are selling so that you can monitor things like price changes or the introduction of new models of the product to the market. If you don't keep tabs on all suppliers in the market, you could miss major market changes that could either render your prices unsustainable or make your products less viable. For instance, if you sell fashion accessories, your suppliers may be late to introduce new trendy items, and you would be stuck selling outdated items while your competitors cash in on the new trend.

If multiple suppliers are operating in the same niche, they may not all stock the same exact products, but chances are they all have the best-selling items in their catalogs. Always go with the supplier who offers you the best deal and don't be too hung up on loyalty—your primary aim is to increase your profit margin and make more money.

You should also exercise a lot of wisdom when selecting the products that you want to carry in your store. Try to select products that are readily available in multiple stores so that you can always have options when you have lots of order to fulfill. If you pick a product that is only available from one supplier, you run a much bigger risk of failing to fulfill an order if your supplier runs out of stock because there are no other sources of that product.

You should use generic product descriptions on your sales pages if you want to be able to fulfill orders using products from multiple suppliers. You may find that suppliers have products that perform the same exact function, but they have slight differences. For example, if you are selling accessories such as third-party chargers, they may be meant for use with the same exact phone, but they could differ slightly when it comes to aspects such as cord length, brand, color, or shape. When you list a product of this nature in your website, don't be too specific in your description because you want to have some wiggle room in case you have to fulfill customers' orders with items that have slight variations.

If the brand of a product is not well known, and it doesn't hold any value in the mind of the customer, don't constrain yourself by listing that name in your description. Instead, list the brand as "generic" because this will give you some flexibility if you found a cheaper version of the same product later on.

When you choose the products that you want to list, you should dig deep and find out if they are always available.

You may find a great product, list it, and start selling it, only to discover later that it is only available for a few weeks or months, or that the manufacturer discontinued its production. Most suppliers will keep availability records for their products, so you should inquire about that. Some products could only be available during specific seasons, while others could be in shorter supply than you expected.

Knowing about a product's availability could give you an insight on how to properly market it. If a product has limited availability and you still feel like you could make some profit out of it, you could market it as a 'limited edition' product. However, if you are not very experienced as a drop-shipper, we recommend sticking with products that have high availability rates.

Even if you plan properly, you may still find that all your suppliers are out of stock at the same time and that there is no way for you to fulfill a specific order. When that happens, you should try to find a similar but slightly superior product and use it to replace the one that is out of stock. If customers have already ordered the old product, offer to upgrade their orders to the new and better one, but don't charge them extra. Most customers will be happy to get a better product for the price of the product they ordered. Even if you don't make a profit out of that particular sale, you should remember that it's always better to make zero profit than to turn away a customer.

If you have multiple suppliers who have your listed product in stock at the same time, how do you choose the one with whom to place your orders?

Well, there are several criteria that you can use to make this decision. One option is to always go with your favorite supplier. This will be the one who has always been the most reliable, the one who offers the best customer service or the one with the most affordable prices. In that case, that would be your primary suppliers, and the others will be backups.

You can assign orders based on the availability of the product in each supplier's inventory. For each product that you are selling, find out which one of your suppliers has the highest amount of inventory, and then choose them as your primary supplier for that particular product. Figuring that out can be tedious if you are doing it manually, but there are services like eCommHub that can help you automate the process.

Another option is to assign orders to different suppliers based on their geographical locations. When the customer puts in an order, you will have to find out which one of your suppliers is closest to where that customer lives, and then assign the order to that supplier. There are two benefits of using this criterion—it can reduce the time taken to deliver the product to the customer, and it can also help you cut down on shipping costs.

You can also assign orders to suppliers based on the prices that they offer for each item on your store. Even if the prices from the suppliers vary by only a few cents per item, you should consider taking advantage of that because small price margins tend to add up especially if you are dealing with consumer products that sell in high volumes. When you are allocating orders to suppliers based on price, make sure that it's the total price of the sale that you are considering (that means listed price plus shipping price and any other charges that may apply).

Of all those methods, there is none that is inherently better than the rest, so select the one that you find suits you best or the one that is easiest for you to implement.

When operating a dropshipping business, you should be very much concerned with security and fraud issues because you will be handling a lot of credit card data from customers. Many merchants have found that storing their customers' credit card info simplifies things when customers want to make more purchases in the future. However, the problem with storing people's credit card information is that it's very risky, and you could end up being liable in case that information gets hacked.

For you to be allowed to store your customers' card information, you will have to comply with rules from regulatory institutions and you would have to foot the bill for expensive compliance audits. For this reason, it's much easier for you not to store customers' credit card information. Instead, if you want repeat customers, it's cheaper to invest more in marketing and scaling. If you run your dropshipping store on a platform instead of doing it on your own website, you may be allowed to store customer credit card data because most platforms are already compliant with industry regulations.

You should also be concerned about scammers posing as customers in an attempt to defraud you, or those who use stolen credit card information to make purchases from your store. There are ways to tell if an order that you have received is a fraudulent one. For example, if a customer seems to have different billing and shipping addresses, there is a high probability that he could be a scammer.

Roughly 95% of all fraudulent purchases are done by customers with different billing and shipping addresses, so make sure you take a closer look at such purchases. If it turns out that the names on the two addresses are also different, the possibility could even be much higher. However, there is always a chance that you are dealing with a gift purchase, so don't jump to conclusions.

You should also take a closer look at purchases that are made through email addresses that bear no resemblance to the customer's name (or to a real name for that matter). If the email address is formed from a random string of letters instead of sensible sounding names or words, it could be a fraudulent purchase made by a hasty scammer or even a robot.

You should also take a closer look at purchase orders that require expedited shipping. Fraudsters who charge their purchases on stolen cards may either want the purchase to be delivered fast before the real owner cancels the card or maybe they just don't care if they use the most expensive delivery method since it's not their money anyway.

To prevent fraud, you can use AVS (Address Verification System). This is a system that obligates customers to enter the address that you have on file along with the credit card number before their transaction can go through. This method has been known to significantly reduce cases of fraud in the e-commerce websites that implement it.

Capitolo 13 Marketing

O nce your Shopify page is up and running all that is left to do now is to market it like crazy to ensure that you grow your brand as quickly and steadily as possible.

Find your target audience

When you found the products you are now selling, you committed to a niche of the population that is interested in that product. The next step is to segment that niche down even further and determine just who you are likely going to sell the most products too. The easiest way to go about doing so is to first collect some information on customers who have purchased products from your store so far which means you will want to implement a survey on your confirmation page to try and gain as much information about your customers as possible.

Once you can start looking at the metrics of the people who are purchasing your products, you can start honing in on who purchases your products the most. Your goal should be to determine a general range of individuals most interested in your products and shift the majority of your marketing to targeting those groups.

Once you have a clear idea of who you want to target, with most of your marketing, you will want to determine how you are going to go about conveying to them what your unique selling point (USP) is. To do this you are going to want to start by making a list of all of the features that your products have and then cross off the ones that more than a single competitor can also offer. Don't forget to consider emotional needs that your product fills. Finally, you will want to clearly express the features and needs and spell them out on each product page.

Build your brand

Building your brand is an important part of ensuring your online store will see success in the long term. Building your brand is a culmination of many different elements including the colors of your store, the logo you choose to represent your store and the mission statement and ethics that your store represents.

When it comes to choosing the colors for your store, the first thing you should consider is a few core colors that complement one another as well as few more colors that are variations on the first. It is important to keep the color variation to a minimum as simple, clean looks are currently in fashion. Certain colors are also known to stimulate certain responses which make them natural choices when it comes to selling certain products.

Brown is known to reassure shoppers while also coming off as confident. Orange is an energetic color that radiates warmth, originality, passion and a fresh start, likewise, when it is paired with blue it will make the customer view the related content as new and exciting. Yellow is an attention grabbing color that is also playful as long as it is used in moderation; yellow that is too strong is known to decrease customer interest. Green is a positive color that conjures up harmony, safety, relaxation and positivity. Blue is peaceful, thoughtful and productive, but it should not be used if you are selling items related to food as it is known to decrease the appetite.

When it comes to designing a logo, it is important to consider what you ultimately go with long and hard as your logo is going to be seen more than any other aspect of your business. When it comes to finding the right logo for you, a good place to start is with common symbols as when done properly your logo will spring to mind whenever that symbol is used. When thinking about your logo it is important to consider how it looks when it is the size of a thumbnail as it is when it is filling your screen completely. You never know where your logo might end up and it is important to plan accordingly. Likewise, it is important to pick a logo that can default to colors that resemble the colors of your store but it should be just as recognizable when any other colors are inserted into the mix.

When choosing a logo, it is important to pick something that is timeless instead of cashing in on a current trend. While a trendy logo might get you some notice today, it is much more likely to be a hindrance in the long run. Create a logo that you are sure will be comfortable with for the foreseeable future.

When it comes to determining your mission statement and ethics there are several important things to try and cover. You will want to make it clear what the purpose of your company is in a way that can be inspirational to your customers. You will want to make it clear what values your company holds in the highest regard and how you plan to conduct business in a general sense. You should also make it clear how this goal directly benefits those who purchase your products.

Additionally, you will want to include any thoughts you have on the character of your business or any types of social or behavioral standards you are willing to promise to always try and uphold. It is important to create a mission statement that makes it clear what sets you apart from other similar stores, while at the same time not limiting your potential growth. While it is easy to start making promise to customers, it is important to keep yourself in check and only promise things that you know you can deliver on in both the short and the long term.

Consider Content Marketing

Especially when you are first starting your Shopify store, there are few ways of more effectively marketing your existence then doing everything in your power to be seen as an expert on the niche in question. This process can take a fair amount of work but the results will pay for themselves countless times over when done properly. To get started with content marketing you will want to take advantage of ability to build a blog on your Shopify page and then start filling it with content that your target audience will genuinely appreciate.

Create the type of content that your target audience considers both relevant and useful will serve several purposes. First, as the quality of your content becomes more widely known, it will drive traffic to your website that you can then potentially convert into sales. Indeed, every piece of content you create can be seen as a direct contribution to your marketing efforts. What's more, some of this content can be discussions of products that you are currently selling on your site as well as breakdowns of the specifics of each. These blog posts can then contain links to the sales page, closing the loop on customers who only look at the blog and never at the rest of the site.

In addition to directly driving customers, and sales depending, to your Shopify page, regularly generating content that your customers either find interesting or easy to relate to serves a larger purpose as well. This is to cement you as an expert in the niche in question which will then serve the added bonus of making any products you write about or recommend carry an added weight that being an expert conveys. When it comes to creating the type of well thought out and useful content that you will want to generate in order to create the image you are hoping to achieve the first thing you are going to want to do is some homework.

In this case it means really learning everything there is to know about a portion of the niche that your target audience is a part of. This means more than simply reading the related Wikipedia page, though that is a good place to start though only for the sources that are referenced at the bottom of the page. You are going to need to go deep if you are hoping for this type of marketing approach to be successful, as you are going to need to be able to generate new and relevant content on a regular basis if you hope to see any results on this front.

Once you are very familiar with your topic, the next step to being seen as an expert is to get your name out there in niche-specific circles. This means posting thoughtful comments to the subreddits related to your niche, popular social media destinations for your target audience and even on the blogs of other Shopify users who are dealing in the same niche. Your goal should be to make it so that your potential customers can't go anywhere in the digital world without seeing your name in relation to the products and your niche in question. Always include your logo in all of your comments as well as a link to your page when appropriate.

If you are looking for another easy way to make yourself appear as though you are an expert in the niche in question, one of the easiest ways is publishing as an eBook on the topic, and then displaying that book prominently on your Shopify page. As an added bonus, the book can be given away for free to stimulate email address collection for the email marketing tips described below. Publishing an eBook is as easy as going to UpWork.com or similar websites and looking for a ghostwriter whom you can often procure for around $1 per 100 words which means a hefty 12,000-word book like this one will run your around $120. From there around the same amount gets you a finished book that you can post to the Kindle Marketplace for free.

Consider Email Marketing

While public opinion has turned against email marketing in the last decade, the reality is that it is still the single most effective type of marketing that an online business can partake in. When done properly, email marketing is said to have a return on investment of nearly 4,000 percent.

When it comes to generating emails that your former customers are likely to open, you will again want to include the types of useful content that your target audience is sure to be interested in. You can even start blog posts on your blog and then finish them in your email marketing newsletter as a way of building a list of interested parties. When generating content, it is important to include enough sales material to ensure that you see a return on your investment, without making the entire newsletter nothing more than one long advertisement. When in doubt err on the side of too much useful content instead of not enough.

To create an effective email marketing strategy, the first thing you are going to want to do is determine just what your goals with email marketing are going to be. This will allow you to tailor your content in a way that generate the greatest amount of positive results in the shortest period of time. When it comes to generating goals, consider how much content you plan to create each week, how you will connect the email newsletter with sales, how you will attract new subscribers and how the email newsletter can tie into your broader marketing goals.

From there it is simply a matter of generating the right email newsletter list which can be easier said than done. The first thing you will need to do is create a new page on your site to link people to who are interested in signing up for your email newsletter. There should be a link to this page from your blog as well as on the order confirmation page that every customer sees after they have completed their order, these are the most valuable customers you have as they have already bought products from you once which makes them more likely to do so again in the future.

When it comes to attracting new email subscribers, the best way to do so is to promise access to something with a perceived value, say an eBook you had written, in exchange for signing up for your newsletter. It is important to not use underhanded tactics to get people to sign up for your newsletter or to gain their email address through other means and then send an unsolicited email. Either of these actions are only going to get your email marked as spam, they will never, ever get anyone to open them unsolicited.

Once you have a new subscriber, you will want to ensure they open the first email they receive from you by including the right subject line. The subject line is one of the only things that you can reliably assume your subscribers are going to see which makes it extremely important when it comes to influencing open rates. Surprisingly, studies show that the true determining factor as to whether an email will be opened is not the content of the subject line, but its length. This means that subject lines under 60 characters or over 70 character will likely see an average open rate, while those with a subject line of between 60 and 70 will see dramatically less. All told, less than 40 total characters tends to see the best results.

Additionally, you will want to time your weekly email newsletters to go out on Friday or Saturday night, after 9 pm. Studies show that the best time to capture subscribers' interest is to ensure they are likely to start interacting with your email first thing in the morning or on the weekends. In other words, the more time they have to interact with your content the better.

Cashing in on holidays

When it comes to preparing for holiday sales, discounts and deals are nice, but so is an optimized customer experience. This means it is important to check each of your product pages as well as your checkout services to ensure that everything is working as smoothly as possible on both your mobile site and your traditional site. Especially during the holiday rush, customers are in search of as many ways to make their lives easier as possible which means they are likely to bolt at the first sign of inconvenience.

Likewise, you are likely to see a much higher number of conversions if you offer a wider range of shipping options to facilitate those who are shopping at the last minute. Don't worry about the extravagant costs, people will pay them eventually. Additionally, you will see a higher number of conversions farther out from the actual holiday if you bite the bullet and eat the shipping costs for a specified period of time.

Ensure your customers are aware of the timeframe and watch your sales soar.

While you may be tempted to lower your prices to grab a few extra customers, the strategy of offering deep discounts occasionally is actually less productive than you might think. For starters, around the holidays anyone who is looking for a present related to your niche is likely going to purchase your products anyway, that's the benefit of working in a niche. Second, while it will likely create a spike in sales in the short term, in the long term you are likely to notice a slightly lower overall sales rate because you have trained some of your customers to hold off making a purchase in hopes that you will drop the price on the item they have their eye on.

Paying for Advertising

Depending on the type of niche store you are selling, there are numerous types of advertising you should try before you begin to explore the options relating to paying for advertising. After that it will help to have a good idea of just what you can expect when it comes to various types of paid advertising.

Banner ads: Banner ads are the most common type of internet advertisements and they can be seen on everything from webpages to next to these very words if you are using a free third party eBook reader. These ads are extremely prevalent online to the point that many users ignore them entirely. They are useful if targeted properly, however and can be purchased on either a pay per visitor model or a pay per 1,000 views model.

If you plan on using this type of advertising, you will want to have a very clear idea of just what your conversation rates from this advertising is.

Text advertising: This type of advertising is often found on Google search engine results and consists of just text and a link to your page. Depending on the niche in question this can be a valuable advertising tool if you can set your business apart from others in the same niche in just a few words.

Google AdWords: This type of advertising is often considered the most popular among those who own and operate an online store. Google offers text and display ads in relation to keywords or phrased that you specify. Additionally, the long that you pay for Google AdWords advertising, the higher your related quality score is going to be. Having a higher quality score makes it more likely that your advertising will appear when the targeted keywords are used.

Capitolo 14 Mistakes to Avoid When Starting the Business

Here are some common mistakes that many novice drop-shippers tend to make. We will discuss why people find themselves making these mistakes, and what you should do to avoid making them:

Starting Without Learning the Ins and Outs of Dropshipping

There has been much hype around the topic of dropshipping, and a lot of misinformation came along with it. Many self-proclaimed "dropshipping gurus" have been telling people how easy it is to start a dropshipping business, and this has led a lot of people to assume that you don't need to learn any technical aspects of the business to succeed. The truth is that the dropshipping game is evolving pretty fast, and there is stiff competition in every niche, so you should avoid jumping into the business without taking a little time to learn as much as you can about the trade.

Choosing Bad Suppliers

Many newbies fail to look into the history of suppliers to find out if they have a reputation for unreliability. They assume that in order to maximize their profits, they need to go with the supplier who offers the lowest prices, but the truth is that the quality of service and the reliability of a supplier is much more important for a drop-shipper than saving a few cents on each order. If a supplier messes up and makes a lot of excuses during your first few weeks of operation, you should drop him and find a more reliable one before your business gets stuck with a bunch of negative reviews.

Lacking Faith in the Dropshipping Model

For you to succeed as a drop-shipper, you have to stick to the model. Some first-timers make the mistake of doubting how the model works, so they try to blend dropshipping with other forms of retail e-commerce. This often happens when newbie drop-shippers worry about their suppliers running out of stock, so they go out and use their own money to buy some inventory. If you have chosen to be a drop- shipper, you should stick with it and concentrate on scaling your business, and you should avoid complicating things unnecessarily. Have faith that the system will work.

Expecting Money to Come Easily

Again, the notion that dropshipping brings in quick and easy money comes from the so-called experts who misinform people because of their own personal agendas. As a drop-shipper, don't assume that you will set up a store, launch it, then sit back and start watching the money flow in. Success in dropshipping requires hard work, proactivity, and a competitive attitude. Customers don't just come to your shop, you have to go out there on the internet, find them and bring them in through advertising and content marketing. Dropshipping is not a get rich quick scheme.

Failing to Retarget Your Site Visitors

Retargeting site visitors is probably the most effective marketing strategy out there in terms of the sales that it generates. If you don't take advantage of retargeting ads on Facebook or Google, that's akin to throwing money away. People visit a shopping site or a sales page because on some level, they really would like to buy that product, so if you keep reminding them about it, one day, as soon as they can get some money, they are highly likely to come back and make that purchase. If you have limited marketing funds, make retargeting ads a priority in your marketing strategy.

Using Low-Quality Product Images

First-time drop-shippers are encouraged to use free photos as a cost-cutting measure, but that doesn't mean that you should use low-resolution product photos. If your supplier provides low-quality photos, try to find better photos of the product elsewhere online, or you can order a sample of the product and take your own photos of it. Online shoppers don't get to see the products they are buying beforehand, so they rely on photos to make purchase decisions. To be fully convinced about the quality of a product, most of them would want to see lots of high-resolution photos from different angles so that they can zoom in and study the product in detail.

Misleading Your Customers About Your Shipping Time

Many new drop-shippers are afraid that the customer might go elsewhere if they think that the shipping time for a product is too long. Some drop-shippers are tempted to either conceal the real shipping time or to straight up lie about it. If you can't guarantee fast shipping for a certain product, you should be honest about it, and offer an explanation as to why it's taking longer than expected (perhaps you are shipping it from abroad). Misleading customers about your shipping time counts as terrible customer service, and if a customer has to wait longer for a package that he was promised, he is highly likely to take his business elsewhere.

Being Afraid to Reinvest Your Money in the Business

When dropshipping novices make a little money from their businesses at the beginning, some are usually afraid of putting the money back into the business for fear that they could end up losing it all. However, the right approach is to reinvest at least some of the money you make into the business through adverting or SEO. There are lots of ways to advertise one's dropshipping business—you could hire influencers, buy PPC ads, etc. Your business won't grow if you take every cent you make out of it. Use your proceeds to scale your business in order to make more profits.

Failing to Work with Instagram Influencers

Right now, Instagram is one of the hottest platforms if you are looking to advertise any kind of product. People follow influencers on Instagram to an almost religious extent, and you would be surprised at how many people will be willing to buy a product just because one influencer mentioned it. You can easily find an influencer within your niche who is willing to give your store or product a shout out for a bit of cash. The bigger you dream, the bigger you'll grow, so don't be afraid to spend a lump sum of cash for an endorsement from a few powerful influencers.

Using Complicated Shipping Fee Structures

First-time drop-shippers tend to publish complicated shipping fee structures on their websites or to display shipping fees under the price tag of every item in their shops. This can be confusing and off-putting for many customers. Customers don't need to see your cost breakdowns; they just want to know how much the whole thing is going to cost them. Instead of having separate shipping fees for all listed items, you should just set prices that account for shipping costs and then offer free shipping. This is a neat marketing trick that can make customers think that you are offering them a great deal.

Creating Unclear Policies

Many novice drop-shippers make the mistake of thinking that store policies are mere formalities, so they fail to make them as clear as necessary. You should avoid having unclear policies. If you don't know how to create such policies, you can borrow ideas from other similar businesses, or you can use online tools provided by industry players such as Shopify. For example, if you don't explicitly state in your policies that a customer has to include a tracking number when returning a package, and then the customer claims that he sends back the package without producing a tracking number to prove it, you won't have any recourse if the package "gets lost in the mail."

Mishandling Product Returns

Product returns are complicated and frustrating for drop-shippers because they require a lot of correspondence, and they cost money. However, they are also an opportunity for you to deliver good customer service, and they help you learn the weaknesses in your system so that you can fix them. Many first-time drop-shippers mishandle product returns by trying to shortchange the customer or by taking their frustrations out on the supplier. You have to remember that returns are part of the business and in the end, they are inevitable. You should prepare for them by outlining clear rules on how they ought to be handled and by sticking to those rules even if things get frustrating.

Relying Too Much on One Supplier

Many drop-shippers make the mistake of counting too much on a single supplier. This leaves them unprepared in case anything unexpected happens. You should always have several backup suppliers for every product in your store. If something happens, say your supplier runs out of stock or hikes up his prices, you can count on your backups to fill your orders. If you are in a situation where your business could live or die depending on the actions of a single supplier, then you are not managing your risks properly.

Failing to Test Several Products

You may have a niche in mind when you start your business, and you may select great products that bring in a decent profit, but that shouldn't be the end of it, you should keep testing new products to see if you can make money off of them. If you are inflexible about the products that you carry in your store, you could wake up one day to find that there is a universal shortage of your best-selling product, so it's good to have backup products. By testing several products, you can identify those that may come in handy when you want to scale your business.

Focusing on Price Competition

Many first-time drop-shippers make the mistake of thinking that they can beat out the competition by setting their prices lower than everyone else. While it's true that customers like bargains and low prices, there are other more sustainable ways to make your store stand out from the competition. If you start a price war, you will be digging your own grave. Whenever businesses start undercutting each other, it's the ones that have few resources that end up losing. You cannot undercut dominant online retailers because they are always willing to match the lowest price, so you have to differentiate yourself by offering great service with a personal touch.

Selling Products That Violate Trademark or Copyright Laws

Just because a supplier has a product available in his inventory doesn't mean that it is entirely legal. There are many cases where suppliers stock knockoff products that are often imported from Asia. You may also see clothes or accessories with nice logos from popular Western franchises and decide to sell them in your store. You should be extremely careful in these situations because some of those products may violate the legal rights of other businesses, and you could get sued by the companies that own the trademarks, copyrights, or other intellectual properties that were used to make those products.

Capitolo 15 Expanding Your Product Line

O nce you have finally gotten everything up and rolling there is nothing left to do but keep your nose to the grindstone and keeping marketing your store until you find success. Eventually you are going to feel the need to begin expanding the types of products that your store sells, and in doing so you will open yourself up too many new questions and concerns.

Adding products tactically

The life cycle of the products on your page can be seen as being in one of four primary cycles. The startup phase is when a product first comes on the market and you are building awareness of it. The second is growth when sales of that particular product are growing the most; this is followed by maturity when the product begins to regularly sell an expected amount of units. Finally, the maturity stage is then sometimes followed by the exit stage is when the interest for the product is in a decline. While not every product hits all the stages, when a product begins to decline in sales you need to know what to do.

When you are ready to start expanding your stock, what you need to do is look at the analytics and determine just which of your products are producing the most consistent conversions.

From there, it is simply a matter of analyzing the data and determining if adding another similar item would likely split the number of sales or if it is likely to double them. If this does not appear to be a step in the right direction, instead it might be better to determine why interest has dropped off on the product in question. Many of the common reasons for a product's decline have to do with a newer version being released or a change in the practices related to how that product is made or used. If this is the case, then something as simple as a few minutes' research can totally refresh your product line.

Find out what your customers want by including a survey regarding a product expansion in an email newsletter. There is nothing to be gained by beating around the bush in this instance and, because only your best customers are likely going to interact with your newsletter, you have a way to directly ask your target audience what they want to buy from you. Take the time to draft up a realistic grouping of new products and also leave room for a write in section, you may be surprised at the results you find.

Finding new products

When it comes to looking for new products to sell, the first thing you are going to want to do is take a look at your existing stock and see if there are any obvious holes in your product line. If nothing sticks out to you at this point, your next best bet is likely to be to get offline and out into the world of brick and mortar retail stores. Take the time to seek out local variations on the theme of your niche and you might be surprised at how easily a new product idea or service comes to mind.

Back online, another viable alternative that more and more online stores are embracing is the world of Kickstarter manufacturers. Finding niche relevant content in this area is as easy as going to Kickstarter.com and looking through successfully funded Kickstarter pages to find products that might speak to your niche. Getting in touch with these types of manufacturers can often lead to a mutually beneficial relationship wherein they get a way to sell their product once they have delivered on their initial backer promises and you get an exclusive item that there is a proven demand for.

With that being said, it is important to ensure that the demand in question hasn't burned out with the fulfillment of the Kickstarter campaign, do some research and search out any additional demand or the product, the faster the better as if you don't meet the demand someone else will. While forming a good relationship with a Kickstarter manufacturer can lead to great things, it is important to do your research and only deal with manufacturers who have already successfully shipped product.

The great thing about Kickstarter is that anyone with an idea can get it funded, but this means that oftentimes people need to adapt to new roles on the fly which can be more difficult than it might first appear. Ensuring that the company has shipped product first will go a long way towards weeding out many of the problems inherent in the early days of a manufacturing company. Regardless, it is important to never offer to pay for exclusivity and to always get everything in writing as you will not be able to safely assume the company is not going to fold until they have sent you a few shipments of products.

Capitolo 16 Shopify Tips and Tricks

Tips and tricks are always great for anything new that you are learning- it makes us do things better, more efficiently, in less time and achieve better results. Here are 8 tips to master your online business:

Going Premium with Themes

Themes are the backbone of your site and free themes only take you a certain distance in your business goals. Shopify is known for its amazing all-in-one themes that are contemporary, classy, and crisp, and using these make your store more upscale than the price tag of your theme. Speaking of the price tag, it is worth to invest in the theme of your choice just so that your store stands out from everyone else's.

Making your store beautiful will attract sales. Not only that, investing in premium themes enables your e-commerce site to be seamlessly functional but they also tell your brand story. The need to invest in the theme of your choice is crucial because it represents the look and feel of your products and your customers will have a more pleasurable experience browsing and buying products of your site.

Premium themes can make your store exclusive so this is a wise investment especially if you see your site growing.

Keep your eye on the ball

Your main goal is to create profits right? So that should be your focus. Do not get carried away by flashy graphics and so call 'must-haves' for your website or even long content that apparently 'speaks' to your audience. You do not want to lengthen the time it takes for your customers to decide to purchase your product. The idea is to get them to your site, browse for what they want, click on the product, read a short description and click on Add to Cart > Proceed to Checkout. Keep things moving forward and avoid anything that detracts from this mission.

Practice SEO

Part of your marketing should also be SEO. SEO is not dead so long as keywords are still used to search for anything and everything on the internet. You need to use SEO wisely not only on your website but also on your social media which is from content, titles, tags, image tags, descriptions- the whole nine yards. You will be found much easier through specific keywords.

Think like a customer

One of the reasons why you need to stick to a niche that you know and one that you are passionate about is so you understand customer pain points. What do you look for when you are on someone's website? What do you expect to find there? What kind of buying process makes you feel you purchase things fast? What makes you like the website you usually purchase from? Knowing the pain points yourself makes you understand what your customers want and how your product can help them accomplish their needs.

Product Reviews

The best way for any customer to know that the products that they are purchasing value for money are by reading reviews. Customers will click on products that have higher ratings and the likelihood of them purchasing it is if has good reviews and high ratings.DO not cheat on your reviews. If you have a product that always gets bad reviews- trash it. When you do, let your customers know that you are discontinuing it because this will help increase their confidence in your site. The fact that you have heard them and you are doing something about it increases brand trust.

Mix your marketing

There are many ways to reach your customers depending on who they are and what they do. For most e-commerce marketing methods, social media marketing and email marketing is the way to go. But you should not rely on it entirely. On and off, it is also good to meet with your customers and see who they are. Give product giveaways, hold online workshops or seminars, have an online meet-and-greet, feature your customers using your product or give them a shout out!

Make your logistics work well

Have strong and clear agreements on any potential logistical issues that you may encounter in your e-commerce business. Outline these in your contract and also have this on your website. Inform customers what to do if they have returned. Outline this with your supplier as well and establish standard operating procedures for returns, damaged items and so on. Outline what the shipping costs are as well between yourself and the supplier and what is the expected delivery date for your items between supplier and customer.

Establish your relationship with your supplier

Establishing and maintaining close relationships with your suppliers ensure that you can also extend the benefits to your customers. When your supplier trusts you, there will be many things that you can get done such as offer personalized packaging to your customers, ensuring speedy shipping, have lesser time in managing any issues you have to deal with if there are any delays. Collaboration is based on trust and the soonest you establish trust, the better.

Communicate your Product Strategy

Strong product descriptions ensure higher success rates of purchasing. This information is critical to your customer- they want to know what they are buying and the better you describe your product, the faster it would be for your customers to make a purchasing decision. Do not give long and vague descriptions and also do not put on duplicate content. Duplicate content will be penalized by search engines.

Using Apps that are Necessary

Apps bring in immense value to your site and that is what store owners on Shopify love about the platform. The value and power of your site rest not only in the design and content but also the add-ins you place to make the user experience powerful. These apps help you automate shipping information, scheduling, sending out emails, managing your inventory as well as your purchase orders. In short, it helps you save time as well as money.

That said, not all worth paying for or investing in it so you need to know which are worth to invest in and which apps are great as free versions. In order for you to do that, here are some tips:

-       Research the kinds of apps that store owners are talking about and then test them out yourself. If they work great for others, chances are they will work excellently well for you too.

-       Apps usually offer free trials before you sign up, so use the trial period to gauge if this app is what you need before you make a commitment.

-       Be careful where your money goes because monthly subscription fees for your app may cause a dent into your monthly budget but if it does give you more sales, then the app is worth it. It is good to stick with an app on a monthly basis for a few months to know whether it helps with your store before committing to a yearly plan.

Maximize your PPC ROI

The Pay-Per-Click PPC game is ensuring that you use the right keywords to attract the right audience using the content that you place in your pages, especially your landing pages. PPC is a must-have strategy when it comes to e-commerce.

Use PPC to publicize your new products as well as drive traffic to your deals and offers. Optimize your PPC by ensuring that you use the right keywords at the right products or pages.

Shopify also assists new store owners by giving them extra AdWords credit so use this wisely. Store owners get about $100 for AdWords whenever you spend $25 on Shopify so to ensure that you get the most of this, you also need to work on creating a viable content and marketing strategy.

PPC's success relies entirely on conversions and social media is one of the ways that you can grow your source of revenue. Think about using these channels to engage and direct your target market to your site.

Keeping your business Online

You can take the stress out of selling by running your business on the go, using Shopify's mobile app. Use the app and save yourself some time as push notifications to your mobile ensures that you can always keep tabs on your sales figures as and when you need to.

Online business is great with Shopify as you can run your business with the flexibility of time and space- literally anytime, anywhere.

You can also make your business work for you by taking it on the road, using the mobile app. Speak to suppliers, update your store, check on inventory and many more without having the need to be in your office space.

Capitolo 17 Build A Mailing List

Once you have finished setting up your store and getting your apps in place, it's time to start focusing on how to market your website and your product. Remember this simple rule: it doesn't matter how great your product is; if you don't market it, no one will find it.

This is a very simple rule that is worth guiding your entire marketing policy. Sometimes, we can get too caught up in how interesting and well-made our products are, to the point where we erroneously come to the conclusion that all we really need is a good product. However, there are extreme limits when it comes to things like word-of-mouth marketing. You need something stronger.

The mailing list is the single most powerful marketing tool that you should have in your arsenal. If you aren't working on building a mailing list, then you are going to be losing out on the ability to send specials, offers, and reminders to a potential customer base. Essentially, the mailing list comprises a list of people who have voluntarily handed their email addresses over to you. You are then free to email them as often as you like.

You need an email list because no other marketing system is as useful and direct as an email.

All other forms of advertising rely on people noticing your ads and clicking on them, but an email arrives directly in their inbox and begs to be opened. There is no hoping to catch attention because unless they delete it without looking at it, they will read it, even if it's just for a moment.

Starting an email list isn't too difficult. There are plenty of different and unique services that you can utilize when it comes to building your mailing list. The one we would recommend would be MailChimp because it's intuitive, easy to use and free until you reach over 2,000 subscribers. MailChimp also lets you send custom campaigns and track the number of people who have opened, read and clicked on links within your emails. This kind of data is valuable because it allows you to know just how many people are engaging with your promotions.

Setting up an email list is easy, but getting emails on that list is the hard part. There are a variety of different ways that you can generate emails, but you'll want to be careful. Focus on getting quality emails, also known as leads. A quality lead is someone who is in your target demographic and would be interested in buying your product. One quality lead is better than 10 emails because you want to find emails that have a big chance of buying products from you. This means that you should develop email list building patterns composed only of high-quality leads who will actually purchase things from you. If you have 1,000 poor quality leads, you can email them until you're blue in the face, but you'll get lucky if even one person buys. However, if you had 100 high-quality leads, they might purchase far more because they are part of your target demographic.

So, if you are wanting to gain emails, you're going to need what is commonly referred to as a lead generation system. This means that you have some kind of attraction program in place that will gather leads for you. People don't just give their emails away; rather, they are cautious with their information until they come across a deal that is beneficial to them. Then, they are willing to trade their email in exchange for some kind of item.

The item can be a free product, a discount code, an eBook or any other thing of value. It's got to be valuable enough to encourage a potential customer to sign up, but not too valuable that it would attract people outside of your target demographic. For example, if you sold knitting patterns, you could have a free eBook with knitting patterns, which in turn would attract people who were into knitting. But if you were to offer a free crocheted hat, many people who find the product value but have no interest in knitting patterns would sign up for it. This costs you a lot of your money and, worst of all, doesn't provide you with much value.

One of the most tried and true methods of lead generation is the free eBook giveaway. You simply offer the eBook on your website in exchange for an email address. This is one of the best ways to start a relationship with a potential customer because the eBook will give them an opportunity to sample some of your work. If you aren't much of a writer, you can always hire a freelancer or a ghostwriter to make something for you. The book doesn't have to be really long; it just has to add some kind of value to your potential client's life.

Promotions, contests, and giveaways are all great ways to generate leads as well, but you should always make sure that they are only appealing to your target demographic. Going outside of your demo is a costly endeavor and is ultimately a waste of time. Instead, keep your focus on finding quality leads by developing good giveaways or, as they are called, lead magnets.

You might be wondering how exactly people are going to find out about your giveaways. You can have the best lead magnet in the world, but if people aren't landing on your website, then how are they going to hear about it?

Capitolo 18 Simplicity at Its Best

Whether you have a B2B business realm or a B2C model, you need a platform that does more than the normal software functions such as transactions. A comprehensive model such as Shopify will make you competitive in the fast-paced and robust markets present now. It can provide the significant advantage you need over your competitors who do not have the support of similar technology.

Shopify supplies you with the tools you need to build your store online. Once you know the basic setup, which is easy to master, you can expect a seamless functioning of the store. And you have 24/7 phone or online support from the service. So, creating an e-commerce site for your business is just a breeze with Shopify. You will not need to know any technical codes or other background knowledge to set up your store online.

An overview of Shopify

Shopify is one of the best e-commerce shopping carts that is completely web-based. With Shopify, you will be able to sell your services or goods online in an effective manner. All the aspects of an online store set up such as building a website, choosing the right design, customizing the site to fit your brand and products, managing orders and customers, tweaking the various features, receiving reports on sales, etc., are streamlined and easier to deal with when you use Shopify.

Shopify is a feature enriched sales register appropriate for small and big online retailers. The best thing about the software is you need not spend towards maintaining servers of your own, as the software is taken care of by Shopify's servers. This effectively curbs all the efforts and costs involved in server maintenance.

Founded in the year 2006, Shopify has its headquarters in Ontario, Canada. It was originally developed by Daniel Welland, Scott Lake and Tobias Lutke for the snowboarding business they owned together. The idea for Shopify was born, when they required a shopping cart with better features than what was available at that time. They designed their own solution that met with all their requirements. The efficacy of the software made them decide on marketing it. Soon Shopify became a very popular and trusted service in the e-commerce shopping cart segment.

At present, Shopify serves over 243,000 merchants and the businesses using the service are continuously growing. Shopify has clients such as Amnesty International, Github, Foo Fighters, etc. The company has done transactions that amount to more than $14 billion.

While the original version was very popular, the subsequent version Shopify 2, launched in the year 2013, surpassed the reputation of the earlier version as a highly effective e-commerce platform. The newer version had strong merchant minded and cleaner backend features. The Live Theme Editor feature and the enhanced search and filter features added to the service further increased its effectiveness. Other highlights of Shopify 2 include improved analytics, better reporting tools and facility to issue part of the refunds, instead of doing the transaction via PayPal.

Convenience and simplicity

Although Shopify has numerous features in it, you need not be overwhelmed. The system is structured logically. The entire set up of your online store is easier without any complicated procedures. You will need just a few minutes to set up the basic store. Other than the designing aspect, which needs some attention because you need to balance the colors for the theme at the backend, Shopify is quite an easy to use service. Once the basic store is built, you can easily add on to it to create a fantabulous store.

Exclusive features

Some important features that make Shopify an excellent option are:

•   You can put your online store to a trial run before you launch it officially. This trial run is done in two ways. One is through a live editor feature and the other way is doing it online.

•   To own a domain name for your store, you can do it easily via the Shopify dashboard. This is quick and easy when compared to other services, which make it mandatory to purchase the domain via third party services.

Customer-facing or front end features

A convenient and easy to use interface is one of the significant features a shopping cart should have. A customer should be able to navigate through the site smoothly, select the items needed, buy them and complete the transaction successfully.

If on the other hand, the process is frustrating, it will be difficult for the customer to buy a product, even if it is a good one. Thus with a difficult navigation feature, you will be left with numerous abandoned carts. And to make matters worse, customers will definitely not return to the site, nor will they recommend the store to others.

When you consider Shopify, it excels in the convenience feature. It is very easy to build a store using Shopify. Managing is also a breeze. Both in terms of administration and customer-facing end, the software is easy to manage.

Customers who transact through a site backed by Shopify will feel assured about the business. They would consider the business to be a well-organized, professional and legitimate retail establishment. And one of the best and most admired parts of using Shopify software is, you will not find any of its brandings in your site, leaving a very consistent and great shopping experience.

Administration Panel or Back end management

For building your online store, you need just a few minutes. You can easily open and build the basic structure of your online store. From the beginning stage, you have the facility to preview your site, so you will know how it will look like before you launch it live. This can be done using the live editor backend feature or by a password online. The password is sent to you via email after you sign up for the free trial version.

To make the entire process easier, you are guided on the right way to use the present URL of your store. The domain set up mentioned earlier also helps a great deal. You can find this feature, when you click on the Store Settings and opt for a domain.

The admin homepage provides you with four important steps. These steps help you to create the necessary groundwork before you begin selling. These include

1.   Adding products

2.   Customization of brand

3.   Domain set up

4.   DECIDING ON SHIPPING AND TAXES INFORMATION

While these are the basic steps, there are other steps to consider too such as creating store policies, including a description of your shop and the details of the product, add on features such as Google Analytics, and others.

Features such as customer information, images, items, categories, and other related options are very direct and easy to understand. Partial returns and enhanced fraud detection features of the updated software version further make the software more effective.

Customer satisfaction

When it comes to shopping online, simplicity is vital. If a retail business has to invest more time in learning the basic set up and management of its store, it would start looking for an efficient and manageable shopping cart option. Shopify scores in this aspect, as it is easy to lay the groundwork with the software. The service is created in an efficient way, so you are able to tweak the features later on without having to do everything at the initial stage itself.

Outstanding user-friendly features

Other than the above-mentioned advantages of Shopify, here are a few more:

You can add products easily when compared to the competitors

It is easy to include links in the navigation menu for rearranging them

The article or blog section feature available with the standard Shopify format is a good one. You can add blog posts or pages easily.

Themes can be edited in a simple way.

What you need to have

As Shopify is an e-commerce software that is web-based, your requirements are very simple. You need to have a proper internet connection. For the software to function smoothly, an updated and current browser such as Safar, Firefox or Chrome is necessary.

While the operating system or hardware requirements are not much elaborate, if your system has updated technology, it would facilitate easier set up of your online store. In case, you are in need of hardware addition at your physical retail store, the service has retail packages for hardware, which it supports fully.

When you go through all the convenient and easy to use features you will understand that Shopify has made its platform as easy as possible without compromising on the innovative features, which are needed for customers to have a competitive edge.

Shopify Conclusion

Today multi-channel selling is popular, which entails making a sale across multiple platforms. Do not just wait for the customers to visit your website, rather attract them using platforms such as Facebook, Twitter, and Instagram. You should not be ignorant of such trends because they play an important role in connecting you with customers.

Also, you are encouraged to do a proper assessment when seeking to set up a successful Shopify store. This is where you identify a market niche. You need to identify the products that you will be dealing with, which are, those you know have a broad market and ensure customers will be willing and able to buy them online.

For instance, health and fitness products have gained significant popularity in the market. It is common to come across blogs encouraging people to be attentive with what they are eating and to exercise regularly. This increased awareness of health issues has created a market for health and fitness products. Also, there is a growing market for consumer electronics such as personal computers, laptops, smartphones, and TVs, among others. Furthermore, Millennials have created a broad market for beauty and fashion products. You should take advantage of these markets and target certain customers, provide suitable content, and give people offers that will attract them to your store.

You have been provided with an extensive discussion on how to find reliable suppliers. It has been noted that not all businesses you come across will be legitimate wholesalers, you must take your time in researching for suitable suppliers.

An aspect that you be aware of is ensuring you are selling your products at as low a price as possible. To ensure you are dealing with competitive prices and making profits at the same time, you will need to look for legitimate wholesalers or suppliers who will give you suitable market prices. From there you will be able to sell at a mark-up price.

Be cautious of the retailers who pretend to be wholesalers. They will be selling their products at a higher cost than wholesalers. When you engage with such suppliers, you will end up selling at higher prices than the competitors.

Another aspect you have to compare is local and international suppliers. For instance, cost, quality, and the customers' social class will determine whether to deal with a local or international supplier. You can also come across ideal suppliers through referral, Google search, attending trade shows, or contacting manufacturers.

As noted, you need a marketing plan to succeed in differentiating your brand. A marketing plan is important because it enables you to carry out calculated and assessed actions.

When you engage in marketing planning, you get the opportunity to think and become more conversant with aspects relating to the target customers. Look at the marketing plan as a strategic plan that informs you of customer needs and wants. Also, you get to learn how to attract them, reach them, and tell them what they want to hear. It will then be possible to engage them, follow up, and convert them into customers, which in turn will increase your sales.

Dropshipping Introduction

B efore you begin any business venture, it is always a good idea to know exactly what you are getting into. This way, you can make an informed choice with your time and money.
Furthermore, knowing what you are getting into means that you can have an easier time actually creating your business because you know exactly what it takes to create success with that business model, which means you are more likely to be successful overall.

Instead of jumping straight into talking about how you can find products and suppliers and how to build your dropshipping business, we are going to start with the very basics. Imagine that you have never heard of dropshipping before and that you are brand new to this concept, and that you are curious about how you can legitimately turn this into a business. This way, you are able to ensure that you have a strong understanding of exactly what it is that you are about to begin creating!

To make it simple: dropshipping is a form of retail fulfillment where you have a company that is not responsible for keeping the products that it sells in its own possession. Rather than you being responsible for sourcing, purchasing, storing, shipping, and otherwise managing the products involved in your business, someone else takes care of all of this. When you sell merchandise from your store, the company responsible for your products will receive notification of the sale and fulfill the shipping for that product. They will also manage any returns or other product-related functions that need to happen in order for your business to run. You will only be responsible for paying that company for the products that you sell to your customers.

The possession of inventory and the way that inventory is managed, is the primary difference between dropshipping and standard retail companies. If you were running a standard retail company online, you would be required to purchase, store, and manage your entire inventory. This part of running a retail business can be incredibly time- consuming, as well as expensive, which is why many people do not begin retail businesses. If you can cut this part out, however, you can make the business far more sustainable while still having the capacity to earn a fairly strong income from your business. This is where dropshipping comes in, and is why dropshipping can be such a powerful way to create an income with your business.

Dropshipping is an excellent business model for just about anyone to get started with. If you are brand new to online business, if you are an entrepreneur looking to spread out your income channels, if you are looking to get into entrepreneurship but have a low budget, or if you are testing out a niche, dropshipping is excellent for you to get started with. This business model does not require a large amount of capital to start with, and it can offer a high payoff fairly quickly. If you remain consistent in your efforts and follow a proven successful strategy from the start, you can use dropshipping to help you earn more money while also learning more about the market.

Capitolo 19 Pros & Cons of Dropshipping

Dropshipping is different from the other retail's models due to this major factor - the retail owner or merchant does not own inventory or stock. The merchant instead purchases this inventory as and when it is needed from their third-party supplier that focuses on manufacturing or wholesaling, in order to meet customer demands.

In other words, dropshipping works as below:

• The customer makes an order for a product seen on the merchant's online store.

• The merchant records the order purchase and automatically sends this to the dropship supplier, complete with order details and customer information.

• The dropship supplier packages the product and ships it according to the customer's given information.

This is an extremely effective and attractive business model as it eliminates the purpose of the merchant to have a physical business venue like an office space or even a warehouse. All they ever need is internet access, a website and a device connected to the internet to upload, update and store information on their products and services if any.

Pros of Dropshipping

There are plenty of benefits to this dropshipping business model. These are:

• It is extremely easy to set up. Unlike setting up a brick-and-mortar business space, this retail model only involves just three steps which is i) finding the supplier ii) setting up a good website and once that is done iii) selling your products and services

• This model is easy to understand and implement especially for a new coming into the e-commerce industry

• To set up your business with the dropship model, the cost involved is literally next to nothing. Unlike in traditional business models where the major costs go into the setting and running of the operations, in dropshipping this step is eliminated and all the cost you need to think of is the applications you need to run your website, domain registration, hosting as well as themes you use - which is not much.

• Dropshipping risks are significantly lower because there is little to no pressure about selling inventory.

• This type of business model can be run from anywhere meaning the business owner or merchant's location independent. There is no warehouse, no sales location, no offices, not much employees and no hassles.

• There is little to absolutely no commitment to a physical space requirement which means the business owner can run their business by the beach, in their home, while flying on the plane. All you need is an internet connection and your laptop, iPad, tablet or any device you can access the internet with.

• You can sell just about anything over the internet and there's a dropship supplier for almost anything out there. Either sell only one product, or a mix of products - it is entirely up to you. Just find your niche and the right dropship supplier you need.

• You will have more time and resources to look into scaling your business. With traditional business models, the more you profit, the more work you have to put in and the more you need to invest in the resource section.

•   Dropshipping also reduces losses on damaged goods. Shipment is directly from supplier to customer and because there are fewer shipment steps involved, the risk of the items being damaged is also reduced.

Cons of Dropshipping

Where there are pros, there are also cons even when it comes to dropshipping. Here are some of them:

•   You must bear complete liability if anything goes wrong, even if it is the supplier's fault. The customer purchases the product from your site- the merchant's website. In the event, something happens or if the supplier doesn't keep their end of the bargain or messes up, it is still the merchant's fault. Your customers will contact you because you are the face of the brand. Therefore, it is extremely important to hire the right dropship supplier.

•   You have lower control over the creative process. Your customers will have lesser satisfaction with your product because you will not be able to determine personalized packaging or the branding of the shipped products- this is dependent on the supplier.

•   You have less control over how your product is presented during the fulfillment and delivery process as this is the supplier's job to ship the products to the customers. However, having the right supplier and establishing a good relationship with them will give you better control as some suppliers will go the extra mile in ensuring your creative process is delivered through the product. However, this may cost more.

•   There may be more issues especially when it comes to shipping. Selling multiple products is a good idea as it can increase sales and make you profit; however, it can also pose a problem if the merchant has too many suppliers to deal with for each product they sell. Also, different suppliers will change different shipping costs as this would depend on where they are located and what kind of product you have.

•   The competition in dropshipping retail is extremely high due to the attractiveness and the popularity of this business model. Unless the merchant caters to an extremely specific niche, the competition is detrimental.

•   It is hard to keep track of the inventory from the supplier. Due to miscommunications due to cancellations and having backorders. However, with new software coming in and improved communication abilities, this matter can be solved. Of course, this software also comes with a price and may also increase your overhead costs.

How Viable and Profitable is Dropshipping?

Profit margins for dropshipping usually range from 15% to 45%. For consumer goods such as luxury items and durables, the profit margin can be up to 100%. When it comes to dropshipping, it entirely depends on the kind of niche you are in and then getting the right supplier. You do not want to enter a heavily saturated market.

One of the better ways to ensure higher margins is to source directly from the manufacturer and not the vendor/supplier. This cuts out the middleman. Once the business gains traction, it can become an effective money-making means that it only involves little input. To potential to earn up to one million dollars is real, although not for every dropshipping business.

Who is Dropshipping for?

If you are a first timer entering the online business, then dropshipping is a great business model, to begin with. It is low-risk and low-investment which is great for novices starting their own business. It does not involve much monetary gamble.

It is ideal for someone who is a current owner of a retail store and already has an inventory, but looking to reach newer, wider markets.

This business model, however, does not give you amazing results from the get-go. Dropshipping margins are relatively lower so this might not bode well for a startup brand because these businesses do not have ultimate control where customer satisfaction, related to brand experience and branding is concerned.

Here Are the Types of Entrepreneurs Dropshipping Will Benefit:

• The Validating Entrepreneur

Dropshipping is a great way to test new products or even new startup products before an entrepreneur can begin heavily ingesting into the inventory required to sell. This makes it the perfect business model for entrepreneurs that require high levels of product validation before they begin investing heavily.

• The Budget Entrepreneur

Dropship qualifies as the least expensive business model for online selling because you do not need to purchase inventory upfront. Due to this, the dropshipping method sells effectively for entrepreneurs that are on a budget or are looking to keep startup costs low.

• The First Time Entrepreneur

Selling online is not as easy as it seems to be so for the first-time online entrepreneur, the dropshipping method works well. Understanding how to market the product online and drive and convert traffic takes time to figure out as well as optimize. Dropshipping allows online entrepreneurs to learn the ropes of online commerce, conversion and driving traffic before they begin investing thousands in an inventory.

• The Multi-Variety Entrepreneur

Dropshipping is an ideal model to use for retailers who want to sell a variety of products simple for the reason that you do not need to purchase inventory upfront.

Who Isn't Dropshipping for?

- The Brand Centric Entrepreneur

Building a brand around a product is difficult but the rewards are long-term and worthwhile. However, it is exponentially difficult to build a brand using the dropshipping retail method because there are plenty of other elements connected to the entire customer experience that the brand-centric entrepreneur will not be part of.

For instance, there will be times when a customer has made a purchase for a product. You, the merchant finds it's sold out with the dropship supplier. This is not only inconvenient for you as the merchant but also frustrating to the customer. It is even more frustrating to coordinate between dropshipper and customer to determine a solution. Since you are not shipping the product on your own, you also do not have control of the packaging which is an extension of the brand experience.

While some merchants are okay with that, asking yourself if this bothers you will help determine if dropshipping is for you. You also will not be able to create a relationship with shipping companies because you do not do the shipping. When something goes wrong in the shipping process, coordinating with the shipping companies can prove to be difficult. You need to coordinate with the shipping account representative, who is already busy, and this might take a few days to sort out.

- The Margin Focused Entrepreneur

One of the biggest problems with dropshipping is its thin margin lines. Gross margins for traditional dropshipping products are around 10 to 20%. After you pay off your credit card transaction fees, e-commerce fees, and other online services, you are looking at only a small percent of your margin left. While there are online entrepreneurs who earn big, up to a million dollars of revenue each year, their profit margins are around 40k to 50k once all these fees are deducted.

- The Non-Creative Marketer

With more manufacturers, chances are they're also dropshippers of their own products and they also have the same exact goals in sales which are about 30% coming from direct-to-consumer sales and this is usually from their own e-commerce site. This would mean that to sell their product, you are competing directly with your own supplier. This supplier has many other advantages such as higher margins than you on the same existing product.

Competing with them head-to-head is a waste of time and resource because most of the time, they win out all because they can afford to. You need to be creative and exploit other channels that they are not using to acquire the same target market and beat them. Relying on Google AdWords or Facebook Ads isn't going to cut it.

Capitolo 20 Market Research and How to Find A Niche

While you don't need a business degree, investors, inventory or millions in capital as a traditional business, you definitely need some resources and the right approach. You need to have the right idea of what you are going to do. It's unwise to go into any business thinking you just want to make money fast. If you want to make money quickly, a traditional job will suffice where you get paid within your first month.

We've already established it's going to be completely online and most of, if not all, the heavy lifting is done for you. As well, you don't need a lot of money to start. What you'll need is a plan; a step-by-step blueprint of things to do now, today, and what's going to happen next. That's why this guide is so important.

It's easy to show you exactly how to find products, build your store and offer these products up for sale. It's going to look amazing once you do, but it would be an outright lie to tell you that you are going to be successful in taking this approach. It is the fun part yes, but one needs to fundamentally understand how they are going to bring a high level of value to their potential customers. That's choosing a 'good' niche and hence the 'right' products that will essentially fill a gap. Half- heartedly going about this is not going to yield the desired results. Worst, you are not going to sustain a long-term business.

That said, don't worry right now about not having a niche, not knowing where to start and so forth because apart from having the resources and tools, which I will show you in subsequent chapters, you will know how to effectively deploy those tools and resources to gain maximum sales and profit.

Some people fail at dropshipping even with having all the tools, apps etc. simply because they are using the wrong approach.

Providing Value

It's the most important aspect of a successful dropshipping business. When thinking of value, there are at least three critical factors that should always remain at the forefront –

•What makes your company/business/product unique and different?

•What is it that your customers really want?

•Who are you going to work with to provide what they want?

Just because you're a dropshipper and reselling products, does not mean the products have to be cheaply made and don't do what they claim. If you have to rely on beautiful visuals and resorting to less than favorable tactics to get your product to sell or outsell your competition, then you're setting yourself up for failure.

Consumers aren't stupid. They're paying for something and they shouldn't get less than they deserve. Once you're able to see the benefits of a product, and you believe that it is something that will fill a gap in the market and the product isn't readily available and flooding the place everywhere you turn, you potentially have yourself a winning product that's going to provide value to the public. From there, you can build a reputation and it's going to mean more sales and profit for your business.

And it is actually doable. Some dropshippers will have all of these things in a product, but taking the wrong approach with no real strategy, is going to cause them to fail when trying to sell the product. I for one, have been able to sell products that were thought to be 'failures' because I was able to have a strategy in place, find and target the right audience and show them the benefits of and why they need it.

Think about any reputable and well-known business. They hardly, if ever, sell features. They sell benefits, experiences and they give value.

So, in starting your business, whether choosing a niche, product and your marketing strategy, always think about value. Always think about who you're trying to help, how to put your customers first and make them feel like they're number one on your list of priorities and choosing products that are of high quality and high perceived value (more on this later).

The Right Niche Market

Niche Market: A small sector or portion of a market for a particular product.

I love any and everything to do with phones and electronics. I'm always reading and I'm always watching videos on my devices. That's what I'm interested in. Ah, there's my niche. I'm going to sell phone accessories, tablets and other electronics because I love them. My store is going to look awesome.

It's true, the store is going to look amazing but that's absolutely the wrong method of choosing a niche and you're going to be doomed to fail. It isn't just true for online businesses but also brick-and-mortar stores.

Why would anyone want to go into a market that is already saturated with tons of the same types of products? If you do so, in this example, try to sell phone cases, for one, it's very general, everyone uses it and there are hundreds, even thousands of online and offline stores that sell these to no one particular niche. It's difficult to pinpoint, and you're going to have issues trying to target the right audience, their interests and so forth.

Here is a better example. A portable folding fishing rod that's not bulky but sturdy and strong. It serves the outdoors market, which, of course, is very broad. However, you can narrow it down to people who like to fish. You can also further narrow this niche down to fly fishing, for example.

So, your fishing rod is not a product that everyone uses, it has a specific audience, it may be unique to a lot of people in that area and there are so many benefits to it. Better, you're going to understand what they want (creating value) and how you're going to set out marketing the product to that audience. It is also going to give you an opportunity to discover and offer even more products in this niche that could be of tremendous usefulness to your core audience. It's going to be a lot less competitive and easier to be discovered than phone accessories.

With the niches that I have just listed above, which are only a tip of the iceberg, you can easily think of the vast array of those products flooding popular sites like Amazon and eBay.

Products Not to Sell

•Phone accessories (too competitive, it's going to be difficult to get noticed)

•Cosmetics (you don't want to go up against Maybelline and the like even though there are gadgets that sell insanely well once you find the right ones)

•Clothing (this is a very competitive market to get into, not to mention, hard to set up for first time dropshippers)

•Medical products (leave that to the experts, you don't need any problems)

There is hardly any real way of differentiating oneself and providing something truly unique in these spaces that will give value to your potential customers.

It isn't impossible however. But you will need to prepare for very stiff competition from other dropshipping stores that have been established for years. But if it is your goal and you have a strong foundation and have laid out a plan, there's no reason for you to turn your back on your goals.

With dropshipping, anyone can become a success story. An easier and more plausible approach however, is finding a niche that may not be that popular. As you can imagine, if a niche is not that popular, there may not be a lot of dropshipping stores selling products in that niche. There may be a high demand for certain products but limited suppliers, which is where you can step in, introduce products that you know the market will want and thus, make your mark in the dropshipping community. It's going to be less competition; you'll be able to differentiate yourself and you'll be the go-to for particular products because you've established yourself; you've been there longer.

Once you find this, always strive to stay ahead, always find ways of improving your store and looking for new customers.

The Right Product

You have not chosen a niche yet, but I hope you understand what goes into it. So, when you have chosen a niche, you'll need to select the right products.

Imagine you see an ad on your phone, laptop or other device for a pair of headphones. You get the product, it doesn't do what it says it will, it's cheaply made and it just doesn't look as attractive as it does in the video/photo that you saw.

What's going to happen is your ad is going to have a lot of negative reviews, more dislikes than likes and subsequently, you're going to have to deal with returns, customer service which

I previously discussed, lower traffic and sales. That's because you didn't do enough homework on the product, you didn't properly 'feel out' the supplier and you paid the price.

Worst case scenario, you're going to spend time and/or money on advertising but you're not going to see any returns on investment. So, trying to sell the most popular product isn't always the best way to go.

You need to be very selective and nit-picky about what you choose to sell. You need to once again, understand what your customer wants and need, and work with that to find products that will meet those wants and needs and yes, create value.

While choosing products that are already successful and popular is an excellent way to go (think of the fidget spinner where tons of dropshippers made thousands in sales) you need to consider how sustainable it's going to be.

Likewise, one should also be competent in analyzing trends and use that to establish yourself in a certain niche and become profitable while sustaining profit. For example, it's a no-brainer that backpacks sell extremely well in particular months, but it's not going to be so throughout the year. However, if you find a product that is at the beginning of a trend and only began selling a few months ago, you have hit the jackpot because most likely, they're selling well.

I will discuss in further detail how to find products that has a high potential for profit. A great deal of your time will be spent on finding the right products for your customers. Remember, a lot of the public are not aware of many products that are available out there that is going to have a positive effect on their daily lives. It's up to you to find them. After all, it's what you're going to build your business around.

The Right Suppliers

There is a huge misconception that products that come from China are cheaply made, poorly designed and doesn't give satisfaction. This couldn't be further away from the truth. For one there are hundreds of first time as well as seasoned entrepreneurs who have and continue to use suppliers from China with much success.

The key to finding a good supplier will be to look at the numbers, the reviews about the quality of the products and so forth. As previously mentioned, suppliers are dropshippers as well who owe it to their customers to supply the best.

One of the most popular and successful dropshipping supplier is AliExpress who has gained the trust and respect of many dropshippers worldwide. It's not a fly-by-night organization and there are reputable dropshippers who source products directly from wholesalers.

The thing to be aware of is, you need to know how to choose your suppliers and be able to differentiate a good supplier from a bad one. Once you have sourced a good supplier, you will then build a relationship with them which is going to make your life much easier and your customers happy.

If this seems daunting, have no fear. I will show you the methods that I and many other dropshippers use to obtain legitimate suppliers who you can come to rely on as your business grows and develops.

An Actionable Plan

It's worthwhile to have a plan or strategy of how you're going to approach your business in order to achieve your vision. Start by asking yourself first of all, what is the vision you have for your online ecommerce business.

To start with, it must be realistic and achievable. For example, where do you want to be in the next year? It could be that you want to earn a full-time income and quit your job. You can even get more specific, you want to earn $10,000 or over $100,000 per month. More so, you may want to be able to make claims like, 'I made six figures in my third month as a dropshipper.'

Whatever your goals are, you need to take actionable steps to make it happen. You'll plan your time wisely, knowing how much effort you're going to put into it. How much money are you willing to spend on advertising and learning? Are you in it for the short term to 'see what happens?' Or are you serious and in it for the long term and you're going to make it work for you no matter what?

These are real questions that need answers. Make up your mind and then you can focus with a clear vision on the more minute details that are going to help you realize your goals for your business.

As well, what are you going to do if you're three months or six months in and you don't get the results you were expecting? Are you going to throw in the towel and say dropshipping doesn't work? And trust me, many people do this, which I don't mind because individuals who think this way were never in it from the start or for the right reasons, they don't really care about what they put out to the public and give dropshipping a bad rap.

Or if you 'fail' which I don't believe in, are you going to take the mistakes you make and use it as a learning experience to make things better? As Colin Powell said, there are no secrets to success. It is the result of preparation, hard work and learning from failure.

So now you have a clear idea of how you're going to start dropshipping and some of the most important things you need: -

•A good niche

•The right products

•Choosing the right suppliers

•A clear-cut plan of what your goals are for your business.

Other Things You Need

PayPal, Stripe, Amazon Pay or any other type of financial institute is absolutely necessary for your Shopify store to collect payments from customers and also for you to receive funds. When you first set up your Shopify account, which is the best and easiest platform, in my opinion for first time dropshippers, you are given the different options to set up and verify your financial information.

Applying for any of these services are safe, secure and free. In my free Shopify 2019 Guide which you can download here, I show you exactly how to set up everything to get your store ready for your customers.

How Much Does Dropshipping Cost?

There is no standard amount for how much dropshipping costs. What may seem expensive or inexpensive to you can mean the direct opposite to someone else and vice versa. At this point in your business, you should focus on understanding how the process works, have a strategy of how you're going to get customers to your site and an idea of how you're going to scale and continue to make money with your store.

However, there are certain things you cannot do without when you're starting.

•Shopify – With Shopify, you get a two-week trial, so there's no cost there. After you have thoroughly gone through this guide; know your niche, know how to conduct product research, figured out your marketing strategy etc. then you can sign up for a Shopify account.

The reason is that you can then play around with the store, see how things work, add a few products, and make mistakes. After the two weeks, the basic price of a Shopify account is $29.

•Shopify Apps – Even though you pay for your Shopify account, you're also going to need some apps on your store. Luckily, the most essential ones that you definitely cannot do without are free of charge. When you start to make money or even before you start to make money and you want to increase your chances of making sales, you can purchase some apps.

Most of the apps do come with a trial, and to actually pay the monthly fee for an app will cost you the price of selling a single product on your store so it's extremely reasonable.

•Advertising – Social media, while it isn't the only way of advertising, has proven to be an excellent method for dropshippers, especially Facebook and Instagram ads which is my main strategy. There are literally more than 2 billion users on Facebook from all around the world at your fingertips. You have their demographics and psychographics and you can get them to click on your ad and go to your store.

Capitolo 21 The Dropshipping Process

Should You Start Dropshipping?

Now that we know some of the pros and cons of dropshipping, it is worthwhile to ask yourself if dropshipping is really for you before actually delving into the detailed process of it. It's certainly not for everyone. But if you like the premise of being completely behind the scenes, researching, doing absolutely everything online (nobody has to personally know who you are, you don't have to talk to anyone, you're an introvert like me) you like trial and error, you like to get things up and running yourself and you stick to whatever plans you devise, then it's for you.

On the other hand, if you're looking to get rich quick or just sell anything to anyone in hopes of making a quick buck, then that screams scam and your business isn't going to go anywhere anytime.

You're going to be providing products to consumers and you need to do the work to ensure that those products are of high perceived quality, they do what they were advertised to do and that they're providing some sort of value to your customers. This is a mindset that you need to develop if you are not already thinking in terms of adding value.

Once again, don't be bogged down by fears of not having any experience in any of this because for the most part, anyone can do dropshipping. Don't become stressed about not having enough time because you're not going to just quit your job and everything else and focus solely on this new venture.

Of course, you can do this if you would like to, that would be excellent because you know exactly what you want and where you're heading. But dropshipping is a step by step process. You can do it to your leisure as a side hustle because maybe you don't want to quit your day job, or you just want some extra cash. Maybe you're a college student and you want to earn some more money.

Maybe you want to approach dropshipping aggressively and make it your full time ecommerce business. It's still flexible, you can scale it up/grow it rapidly and continue to grow and retain a customer base. The goal here will be to grow while keeping your costs low.

Once you have figured out the ins and outs of how-to dropship and make it work in your favor, you're going to have so much time to yourself because you've mastered the art. That leaves you more time to do other business ventures to grow your wealth as many have done and are doing, or you can just spend more time doing whatever you want to do and love.

Anyone can do it. You don't need millions in capital and loans. You don't need to manufacture your own products without any real proof that you're going to make it in business.

The reason why thousands have been so successful in dropshipping is that it leaves a very clear footprint. It's like the fidget spinner (even though this was sort of a passing fad). There were ways to go about finding out if the fidget spinner was really something to start dropshipping. Through research, everything pointed to the fact that this product was a must sell product and as a result thousands of entrepreneurs made loads of money off of this.

There was no one supplier of this product. Likewise, there are so many products out there selling like hot bread, and with the right tools, (this handy guide included) you can be one of the many businesses providing products and making enormous profits.

The Dropshipping Model

The dropshipping process is a simple and uncomplicated one.

Step #1 – The customer is directed to your store and purchases an item at the retail price of say, $300.

Step #2 – The merchant (you) receives this payment and information at their store from the customer then purchases the item at a wholesale price for $200, giving the supplier the customer's name and address.

Step #3 – The supplier ships the product directly to the customer's desired address. Your store makes a gross profit of $100.

But while simple at the forefront, it is important to know how this works at the backend. Why? Because you need to understand how to make your business flow smoothly and be as efficient and effective as possible. It is also crucial to know what your customer will experience during the buying process. A bad experience for the customer will no doubt end in fewer checkouts and thus low sales for your store. On the other hand, a good experience will make for quick sales and customer retention.

So, first things first, let's see how the product moves from the supplier to the customer and everything in between.

•The Manufacturer – Manufactures the products and then sells them in bulk to either suppliers or wholesalers. So, they can sell to a supplier, for example in this case, someone from AliExpress. You, as the merchant, then buy from a supplier on AliExpress and the supplier ships the product to your customer.

You can also purchase directly from the manufacturer at a significantly cheaper price than a supplier.

•Suppliers and Wholesalers – Sell products they have sourced to retailers. The benefit to purchasing from a supplier is that it's easier and sometimes they specialize in a specific niche so once you find your niche and a good supplier, you make your process simple by building a relationship with your supplier. The downfall, not a bad one, is that the supplier will charge you more than a manufacturer. But you also charge your customers more than you paid your supplier.

•Retailers – In this case you as the merchant sells the products that you sourced from your supplier to the public where the supplier will dropship to the customer. To do all of this, you open an online ecommerce store and stock it with non-physical products, meaning images, descriptions and prices.

The above image is an example of a highly successful dropshipping store that rakes in 6 and 7 figures per month. Note that it has a very simple layout and offers basically one product. It is very successful because the product is in high demand, it solves a problem and isn't readily available in stores.

You don't need any experience and you don't need to know a single line of code. Everything is point-and-click, drag and drop. The free guide is more practical in that you already know how the business works, what you need to do and what you're going to sell. So, it would just be to get the ball rolling.

Note: Download the free step-by-step guide on building your Shopify store. You will learn how to customize your storefront to give it a professional look and feel, add products from trusted suppliers and much more. Click here to download.

The main focus of this guide is to show you how to become the retailer who purchases from suppliers and then sells to the public. I can't stress enough how important this is. Some first time dropshippers have a very basic and unfortunately poor understanding of what it takes to run a business like this, therefore they run into obstacles they weren't aware of and walk away believing that the model does not work rather than realizing that they have done things the wrong way and didn't take the time to learn and understand how it works.

The Process as the Customer Sees It

I'm assuming that you have made multiple purchases online in the past whether it's from eBay, Amazon, Newegg or wherever. Think about what your experiences have been like. Was it simple? Was it straight to the point? Did you encounter any problems that you just couldn't get answers to or couldn't find a customer service rep when you really needed one?

All consumers at some point in time, may encounter an issue while others may not. Your job as the retailer is to minimize problems and potential issues by making the buying process as simple and painless as possible because this is what the customer wants.

For example, you want to make the experience as follows:

•A customer comes to your online storefront and orders an item. They get instant email notification of their purchase and the cost.

•Depending on your shipping time, the customer then receives either a few hours or days after purchase, that their item has been shipped to the desired address. They also receive information on how they can track their package. (There are apps for all of this which I will cover in the free Shopify guide here.)

•The customer receives their item in the allotted time.

So, this has been a painless and convenient process for the customer. What it means for your business is a good reputation, trust building, and the customer does not have to interact with customer service which you don't want to have to deal with especially at the beginning.

As well, the customer has no clue that you're the middleman or that any other parties are involved. They bought the product from your store that has your name/name of your business on it.

The Process as the Retailer Sees It

•So, you notice that you have an order for one of your products. You're happy, it's just the beginning and you're motivated to say the least.

Your store, Cell Luxury, will receive the same email confirmation along with the customer's payment.

•Cell Luxury then sends an order to the supplier who then processes your order. You, Cell Luxury, will be charged for making that purchase. And say the entire amount, including shipping of the case will cost a total of $12.46. This means that your profit will be $7.49. Not bad at all.

•So, you ordered the cell phone case and the supplier packages your order. Well, the supplier is going to address the package from Cell Luxury and Cell Luxury's name will be displayed on the invoice and packaging slip. The supplier will then send all this information to you.

•Then last, but not least, this information will be automatically sent to your customer through whatever app you decided to download to do this for you. The customer receives their cell phone case, they're happy, you're happy.

So, you do two things in the dropshipping process. You make the orders from the supplier when you actually get a sale, and provide them with the shipping information of the customer.

That's dropshipping in a nutshell.

Note: When starting dropshipping as a small business/sole proprietorship, it is common to use one's own funds for example a credit card. Since platforms, example Shopify, doesn't pay immediately, you can use your own card to fulfil orders, meaning, buy the items from your credit card as orders come in. Therefore, it is a good idea to forecast how much sales you plan to make and have a budget to start with. Or you can wait a couple days to have funds from sales transferred to your account.

Capitolo 22 Setting Up Your Dropshipping Business

How to find a niche

W hen you are starting your business, there are multiple factors you need to keep in mind and it is up to you to create a balance and sync all these variables with one another. However, as it all begins with you settling for a niche, it is mandatory for you to invest time and effort into picking the best one for your business. When doing so, you should consider going for something that has sufficient demand and which you can be confident about selling a good minimum number per day. This is a good indicator for you to understand whether this niche will be a good long- term investment or not. The niche should not suffer from changes in season or climate. You should lookout for a product that is not in an overly competitive market. On the other hand, you should think more strategically and look for keywords that are not frequently used by your competitors. For a single product, you and your competitors may use the same search words; if you have different words, it can help you gain a competitive advantage over the others from the very beginning. You should remember to consider the size and dimensions of your product; you should opt for something small and light as it will be easier for your suppliers to ship out to your customers. In the end, running a business and putting that much effort in should help you make a profit and you should choose a product that will complement this. According to a lot of dropshippers, when you start out, you should set a target to have around ten sales a day, regardless of your product type. However, depending upon your niche, you can set the percentage of profit you want to make per sale.

How to find suppliers

After you have selected a niche, you should look out for suppliers according to your niche. You can start by looking for suppliers who are near you, however, you should be open to suppliers based in another state or even country. In most cases, you will notice that suppliers are based internationally and that you have to dropship from there. Try to keep in mind that the further your suppliers are, the higher the possibility of having delays in shipment times. Having said this, you should prioritize quality over quantity and go for the ones with more experience in providing products in your niche. You need to do extensive research to find the suppliers as you will notice that suppliers who have been in business since the beginning of dropshipping do not focus much on customer service and communication. They tend to have a very outdated website with basic information on it. You should be ready to expect hurdles like this and call or email these suppliers to talk about their pricing and policies regarding returns and refunds in detail. Besides, there are various online tools available that help you locate suppliers according to your niche; you can also opt for more personalized service.

How to choose a product

Choosing a product among so many can be a tough task and under no circumstances should it be done in a rush. If needed, you should take your time and have discussions with people face to face to gain perspective. There are a couple of factors that work together to help you choose a product for your store. Firstly, try to get help from other online communities and online stores that are in the same niche to help you brainstorm efficiently. Doing this will give you some ideas and allow you to compare these product ideas to your target price range. Doing this will help you narrow the list down even further. You can use online tools such as Google Trends to make comparisons on a local and global scale for these chosen products. You can filter out the results and see how well these products may work out for your dropshipping store. You should compare data obtained for the sales and profit margins of these products to help you cut down more from the list until you are left with the best one to match your business goals.

How to create your business

The previously mentioned processes of finding a niche, a supplier, and a product were just a few of the important steps of starting a business. However, before even thinking of getting involved with these stakeholders, you should be able to develop a dropshipping business concept that is marketable. This will help you draft out your long-term and short-term plans and help you assess your progress as you move along the way. In the meantime, you need to get registered with your government if you want to become a fully functioning enterprise and make everything legal and official. You need to have a dropshipping website that is the best representation of your niche and your product line. You should invest in this and hire professionals to work on building this store for you if needed. When your website is ready, you should be ready to add products to it. You should be careful when doing so and do prior research before settling on a niche. You should have direct communication with your supplier to check the availability of items before adding them to your store. Lastly, after you have a fully functioning website that has all the products you want to sell, you need to allocate some resources to promote your store and manage the day to day activities.

How to get permits and licenses

After you are done setting up your business, you need to deal with the legal aspects and think about getting permits and licenses. For starting a business in the US, the very first step would be to register your dropshipping business with your state where you should expect to pay around $150 to $300, depending upon the type of products your business is targeting to sell. This makes you eligible to obtain an EIN

(Employer Identification Number) from the IRS (Internal Revenue Service) - this does not require you to pay a fee and you should be able to receive the EIN smoothly. Afterward, you need to make a requisition in your respective state for a sales tax ID. This is also free unless your state is an exception where you need to pay a sales tax. You need to open an account to show that you are in an established relationship with a dropshipper, which should also be free of cost. Lastly, it is highly recommended that you get your website made beforehand as things will be much easier to verify if any legal issues occur. There are exceptions to this process, especially regarding total cost; however, for a dropshipping business, $400 is more than enough to get started.

How to choose a sales platform

There are various platforms that you should consider when choosing one for your dropshipping store. Firstly, if your main focus is to earn money within the shortest possible time frame, then it would be best for you to dropship on your own website. This will allow you to stand out from the crowd and have control over the operations. You will not be exempted to pay fees as you will have to pay them when you are dealing with Amazon and eBay. You can be sure to get more exposure for your products when you are engaged with Amazon and eBay, as customers will trust them more. You can even get access to Fulfillment by Amazon FBA (if you use Amazon). On eBay, the website is extensive yet easy to navigate for the customers, but the auction-style may not be fully suited to the dropshipping industry. On the other hand, it will take longer for you to gain a large customer base, so it might be better to go with Amazon and eBay. It totally depends on where you want to see your business in the long run and how the sales platform will bring more value to your customers.

How to create a payment system

Today, there are multiple methods of accepting and receiving payments and it is recommended for you to be aware of all of them. You should offer ease and convenience regarding payment methods for your customers and ensure that they feel safe with the choices you have given them. PayPal is the best choice in most cases and it is accessible anywhere. It is wise to use the most common platforms people use but you should look into the demographics of your target customers and see what would be the most convenient for them. If you need to accept bank transfers, you should make arrangements for that beforehand. You should also research what the most popular and respectable method of payment is in the region you are expecting to sell in.

How to set up a customer service system

Regardless of your niche or industry, customer service should always be a priority. The customers remember their experience, so if they had a positive experience, they will definitely share this among their peers, who in turn contribute to bringing new customers to your store. However, negative experiences have the potential to completely ruin your venture. You need to be careful when assigning any of your employees to handle the customer service department. You can set up a helpline or give the official email address of the company where they can make product requests. Moreover, you can offer live chat sessions with them at set hours with regular phone call facilities on toll-free numbers. You can think of email marketing in this case and can send forms out to your customers after they have made a purchase to get their feedback. Try to keep the form in the form of short answers or multiple-choice answers; filling out the form should be hassle-free and efficient for them.

How to create a list of offerings

Your niche is what you design your entire business around. Within that niche, try to find out what products have a higher probability to make sales. These are the ones you should target and try to figure out whether these products will be trendy in the near future or not. You can also try to analyze the proportion of profit you can make per sale among these products within your niche to make thorough comparisons. You may need to conduct surveys or study surveys conducted before to understand the nature of the market and to be aware of what is in demand. Considering all of this, you can start creating a list that will be posted on your website for customers to keep track of what is available and what is not. You can divide them into categories, in terms of price range or season for example. The information you acquired has to be relevant to your niche and needs to be updated at regular intervals. It is better to use online tools when you are starting out as the process would make it easier to keep track of additions throughout.

How to purchase the product from the supplier whenever you make a sale

When you have received an order from a customer, you are now sure that there is a specific buyer for this item and now you can go ahead and buy it from your supplier. You should not stock up on inventory because it gives you uncertainty and prevents you from investing in other sectors of your business. Dropshipping does not encourage you to buy products in bulk. The trends may change and customers may be more inclined to buy whatever is trendy. If you make bulk purchases, you cannot invest in other products as your money is already stuck with those orders. You should confirm with your supplier before confirming with your customer about the availability of the product. You should focus on using online management software that lets you keep tabs on the number of purchases made along with their prices and estimated dates of delivery. You can also keep a manual list and send your supplier a hard copy of the invoice.

How to find ways to market your business

Marketing your business is essential to be able to compete or even initially just survive in the industry. Due to not having any restrictions to enter the market, the dropshipping industry tends to become more and more competitive every day. Thus, you should do everything within your reach to make the most of the online platforms available to you.

Answering Questions

You can drive traffic to your store by paying more attention to your customers. You can assign an employee as a social media manager or you, yourself can be in charge of this. Platforms like Reddit and Quora are a great way to gain exposure where you can link back to a blog post you have written on your store or provide a link to your website each time you respond with an answer or leave a comment. This will attract new customers and also help you connect with the ones who commented on the post initially. For Reddit, you will find divisions or sections known as subreddits for niches that your store is related to. You can be part of multiple subreddits as long as they are related to your niche and product line. You can even get ideas from others who are adopting this tactic. On the other hand, for Quora, the system is more straightforward. As it is a question-answer based site, you can pose questions or answer any question that is related to your niche, but you should remember to link it back to your blog or online store. Lastly, there are separate forums available on various kinds of niches where you can apply the same tactics. Overall, your focus should be to add value through these platforms in the long run.

Affiliate program for your dropshipping store

This is a very unique strategy for when you have gained a solid customer fan base. For total newcomers, making this work will be a challenge since the very concept of affiliate marketing depends on whether you have sufficient traffic to your store for this tactic to work. The affiliate program motivates people to market the products in your dropshipping store. The higher the number of people involved in doing affiliate marketing for your dropshipping, the higher the probability of your sales increasing. These people get a certain share in percentage from the sales they are bringing in. The total revenue that you earn through the affiliate program is comparatively higher than that of other strategies. Here, you are paying the people not from your business funds but from the revenue they are bringing in for you. This helps you to thrive and acquire more customers.

Email marketing

This strategy is to increase your customer retention rate. The customers who have made purchases from you before can be significant, as well as new customers that you seek to sustain, both in the long run and in the short term. If they do not come back, it implies that your competitor may have been able to add that customer to their customer base; this becomes a setback for you. Initially, you can see it happening with one or two customers, but over time it can become a trend and it will be too late for you to recover. Hence, email marketing is suggested in order to keep them coming back. You can do it through sending various offers during holidays, or encouraging them to subscribe to your blog; this depends on your target demographic so you need to learn how to grab their attention.

Capitolo 23 Find the Right Products

The Basics of Selling Products Online

Every business needs a good marketing strategy to work. When you start out, virtually no one knows about your business, the products you offer, and your terms. Before customers can start buying from you, it is important that you start reaching out to them, making them aware of your business. In this chapter, we shall look at the different avenues where you can reach out to people willing to pay for your products and the strategies that you can use to do so.

When deciding to start advertising on either of these channels, you should consider the money you intend to use in your marketing efforts. You can then evaluate each advertisement medium and allocate a portion of your total budget based on its effectiveness. Starting out, a daily budget of about $10 spread between Facebook, Pinterest, is recommended. Henceforth, you can increase the budget on each platform based on the results of each post.

If you are a novice in the dropshipping business, you could end up wasting a lot of time trying to figure out the ins and outs of running the business. To enable you to hit the ground running and to get ahead of the learning curve, let's discuss how you should operate your business once it's fully set up.

First, you have to understand that things are going to get mixed up at some point—that is the nature of the dropshipping business. The fact that most logistical functions are handled by third parties (manufacturers, wholesalers, and suppliers) means that there are lots of things that are out of your control, and so you should be mentally prepared to deal with mistakes and screw-ups.

Your suppliers will occasionally mess up your customers' orders, and sometimes, they may even run out of stock. When this happens, you may feel frustrated, and you may be tempted to give in or even to switch to a different business model. We can't lie to you and say that there won't be any challenges, but we can guarantee you that you will be able to handle most challenges if you are adequately prepared, and if you have taken the time to establish rules and protocols for all types of challenging scenarios.

One thing you need to remember is that the dropshipping model is already complicated by its very nature, so you should try as much as possible to keep things simple on your end. Try to find simple solutions to any problems that arise, rather than wasting time and resources trying to figure out the perfect solution for your problems. Things move fast in this business, and if you focus too much attention on singular events, you are going to get overwhelmed. Have a simple structure for your business, and make sure that all your operations move along smoothly.

Since mistakes are bound to happen, you shouldn't spin your wheels too much when they actually do occur. Even the best suppliers will occasionally mess up an order, and the customer will end up getting disappointed by the package he receives. Whatever the error, don't waste time passing around blame.

When addressing a customer's complaint, own up to the mistake and apologize, then take quick measures to make it up to him by seeing to it that your supplier fixes the issue. Think of every mistake as an opportunity to learn and grow.

Most professional suppliers will own up to mistakes that are genuinely theirs, so you don't have to be too confrontational when you report your customers' complaints to them. It's important to maintain a good rapport with your suppliers throughout because your success as a drop-shipper depends on it. However, if a supplier makes a habit out of messing up your orders, it may be wise to conclude your association with that supplier, because he may drag you down the path of failure.

Even though drop-shippers don't personally handle inventory, one of the biggest challenges that you will have to deal with as a drop-shipper will be the management and coordination of inventory, given the fact that you will most likely be working with multiple suppliers (we've already discussed why it's important to build redundancy into your supply system by having backup suppliers for each product in case there is a problem with your primary supplier). Managing and monitoring inventory is quite complicated, but as you gain more experience, you will become much better at it.

Even if you have a supplier and a backup supplier for a given product, you should keep a list of every other supplier who stocks the products that you are selling so that you can monitor things like price changes or the introduction of new models of the product to the market. If you don't keep tabs on all suppliers in the market, you could miss major market changes that could either render your prices unsustainable or make your products less viable. For instance, if you sell fashion accessories, your suppliers may be late to introduce new trendy items, and you would be stuck selling outdated items while your competitors' cash in on the new trend.

If multiple suppliers are operating in the same niche, they may not all stock the same exact products, but chances are they all have the best-selling items in their catalogs. Always go with the supplier who offers you the best deal and don't be too hung up on loyalty—your primary aim is to increase your profit margin and make more money.

You should also exercise a lot of wisdom when selecting the products that you want to carry in your store. Try to select products that are readily available in multiple stores so that you can always have options when you have lots of order to fulfill. If you pick a product that is only available from one supplier, you run a much bigger risk of failing to fulfill an order if your supplier runs out of stock because there are no other sources of that product.

Find High Demand Products

Picking Products That Are Popular

The first and possibly most obvious thing that you want to do for your business is picking products that are going to be popular amongst your niche audience. You want to make sure that you are going to be selling things that people actually want to be buying. Picking products that are popular will help you with creating a strong shop that is filled with interesting, attractive items that excite people and encourage them to pay attention to your shop.

You can identify which products are the most popular in your industry by going to platforms like Amazon and Etsy and searching for keywords that are relevant to your industry. Doing this will take you to the category relevant to your business, which will then show you the most popular items that people are purchasing. Depending on what platform you are on, you may need to adjust your sorting settings to say "Top-Rated" or "Best Selling." Choosing these search parameters will ensure that everything that is being shown to you is what people are actually purchasing on a regular basis, and not just what has been posted or sponsored by the people selling said product.

After you have searched on these platforms, you will get a general idea for what types of products are selling the best. Then, you can use platforms like Google Trends to do research on said product so that you can begin to see whether or not it is actually popular enough for you to stock in your shop. Ideally, the product should have a strong uptrend behind it, but it should not be at its peak trend. Any product that is in peak search numbers, based on the parameters given to you by platforms like Google Trend, is likely to be too competitive for you to make sales in. You want products that are going to be popular, but not oversaturated to avoid having to attempt to compete with far too many brands that are already out there selling products to your target audience.

To help get your shop started, you want to identify about 30-50 popular products that you could sell in your shop. This may sound like a lot, but it will be narrowed down through the following steps to about 15-30 new products that you can stock your shop with. This is plenty for a new dropshipping company to start with and leaves you with space for growth over time, so avoid going much higher than this number.

Pricing Your Products Effectively

As you go through the most popular products that you could potentially stock your shop with, you want to make sure that you also jot down how much money you could charge per item. This is going to be helpful with determining what your profit margins would be later on, while also giving you an idea of how you can use your price points to position yourself in the market.

When it comes to price points, you want to look around and see what the exact same products are going for in other shops. As you do, seek to identify the lowest price point in the market and the highest price point in the market. Then, try to identify the most popular price point, which will be the price point that has made the most sales. You might expect that the lowest price point would be the one making the most sales, but the truth is most consumers consider products that are priced too cheaply to be cheaply made. In many instances, dropshippers that are pricing at the lowest possible prices are seen as companies that work with low-quality suppliers, resulting in people being skeptical about ordering through their business at all. For your business, you want to price around the mid-point or slightly lower or higher depending on what you want your positioning to be. If you want to be considered inexpensive or affordable, you want to make sure that you are using the lower end of the midway point. If you want people to perceive you as being a more high-end boutique shop, price slightly higher. This way, you leverage your pricing as your positioning as well by using it to help influence how others perceive your business.

Ensuring that the profit Margins Are Big Enough

After you have identified the ideal products that you can stock your shop with, you want to make sure that your profit margins are big enough. Your profit margins are calculated based on the amount of money that it is going to cost for you to stock items in your shop, versus the price that you are going to sell your products at. To calculate your true price points, you need to factor in the cost of running your business combined with the cost of the product itself when you order it from your supplier.

Ideally, the products you sell should have at least a 30% or larger profit margin as this will ensure that you produce enough money to pay for listing and selling the product, while also making a profit on top of that. Anything too far below 30% is going to likely prove unworthy of selling as it will not earn you enough to really run your business. Unless you are making a decent profit margin that covers the cost of selling that product and you are selling high volumes of it, there is no point stocking anything with a lower margin.

It is important to understand that the more popular your products are in the industry, the less your profit margin is going to be because you have such a large competition amongst you. This is why it pays to pick products that are popular but not overly saturated, as it helps ensure that you are getting the right profits and attention on your products for you to succeed with.

Analyze your Competitors

Use Tools Available Online

There are site explorers like SEMrush which help you in checking the domain authority and rank of a website using a URL. You can use them to get a clear picture of the amount of traffic that is driven to their website from keywords as well as from other links. You can also personally observe their sites and get an insight into the way they function.

Order Items from Your Competitors

There may be a difference between what appears online and the real things that take place. So, it is a good idea to order something from your competitor's website. This will enable you to become familiar with the peculiarities that make them a unique enterprise, or the negative aspects of the brand experience provided by them. You may even get some tips to improve your own enterprise.

However, there is no need to copy their entire process of working. Just observe if there are any flaws which you can avoid and improve your customer's experience.

Analyze Your Competitor's Social Network

The social channels of your competitor are an important means of getting direct feedback from the customers about his business. They also provide a basis on which you can analyze your rival's marketing strategy. You can check how well their brand is performing and what are the flaws. You can work on these to enhance your brand.

Capitolo 24 Working with Suppliers

Finding a reliable supplier is one of the biggest stumbling blocks for every dropshipper. That is why this is one of the most important things that you need to decide on.

You may be a great marketer but if your supplier screws up then you end up trying to fix things. And a lot of times the causes of these troubles were outside your control in the first place.

You should take every precaution to find the right suppliers. There are several strategies that you can use. With some practice you will learn to spot a reliable wholesaler and avoid the bad ones.

The Makings of a Good Dropshipping Supplier

The following are the characteristics of a great dropshipping supplier:

1. The Absence of Huge Per-Order Fees

Wholesalers and suppliers will usually charge what is called a per-order fee. This is a fee that covers for the time and resources necessary to get your order packed and shipped to your customers.

Some suppliers take advantage of this and will charge a rather high fee. So, how much of a fee are we looking at? It usually ranges anywhere from $2 to $10 (and sometimes higher).

You should factor that when you select products since this fee will be added to the actual product price that you need to display on your ecommerce site.

Sometimes the fee can get too high and you end up reducing your profit margin. Remember that $10 might not sound much but if your competitor can lower their prices by $5 because their supplier charges them less then you can bet customers will choose to do business with them instead.

2. Quality Products

Here's a rule of thumb. If you provide quality products then you should expect lower product return orders from your customers. It also translates to the following:

- Better product reviews, which in turn boosts sales

- Fewer returns

- More organic and word of mouth referrals

- Higher rate of customer satisfaction

Are there any downsides to finding a supplier that can provide you with quality products? Well, I can think of only one—possibly lower margins.

That means you can't jack up the prices of your products a lot higher. However, even if you don't make a huge amount of profit per product sale, you will end up getting more profit from volume sales.

The more satisfied customers you have the more potential repeat orders you will get. That can also translate to more profits from referrals and the increased number of customers.

Yes, you may get low margin per sale. But that is a lot better than getting high margin sales but low-quality products. It will not benefit you in the long run.

3. They Give You Access to Big Name Brands

Earlier it was mentioned that you should avoid big brand products. Yes, it is true. But that is a rule for beginners—hope that clarifies things. After your dropshipping business becomes a big hit you might want to look into selling big brand products.

Brand name products also represent better quality products. A good and reliable wholesaler is one that can supply you these products. If big name brands trust them then you can trust them as well.

4. Helpful Representatives and Years of Experience

Of course, it goes without saying that you should look for a supplier who has been doing it for a while. Their years of experience sending products to customers will be a big thing to lean on especially when untoward incidents happen.

That means if there is a botched delivery (e.g. damaged goods upon delivery, wrong delivery, missing items etc.) then you can coordinate with the supplier to amend the situation.

No one is perfect—we should all know that by now. And even the best suppliers and wholesalers who employ the highest standards will make mistakes from time to time.

Remember that these businesses manage hundreds if not thousands of orders every single day. Mistakes and blunders will happen every time that happens. You can chalk it up to Murphy's Law, I guess.

If there is one thing that can make up for that is rep from the supplier that you can talk to that can answer all your questions. Of course, you can't expect them to know all the answers but the really good reps would be more than willing to find out what happened to an order and get back to you.

They will know how to handle any issues that come along. They will also be able to answer any questions that you might have. And if they don't have an answer at that moment, they will go out of their way to find out and give you an update.

5. Fast Shipping

Delays will always make customers unhappy—and obviously you don't want that in your dropshipping business. If your supplier can't deliver the goods in 24 hours then they are not good for this kind of enterprise.

But you can give them a 24 to 48-hour window to get the goods delivered. However, do take note that a48 hour delivery window is pushing it.

Dropshipping is a very competitive business. There is no room here for delayed shipments. If your ecommerce store is known for delays then your competition will eat you alive.

However, if you do find a wholesaler or a supplier that delivers things on time every time, then you have just found a goldmine. You already have a competitive edge.

Customers will like that a lot. Now, you can test your supplier by creating a test order. Order something yourself and have it shipped to you.

That way you get first-hand experience at how fast the supplier gets the order delivered. And you also get to see the quality of their service. You can do this to test two different suppliers or wholesalers. The one that can get things done in record time should be the winner.

6. Technologically Invested

You're going to be running a store that will be cloud based. That means you need to partner with someone or another business that is also just as committed to technology as you are.

Your supplier should be one that also takes advantage of the latest technologies. That means that both of you should be on the same page when it comes to automation, scalability, and of course efficiency.

This will be increasingly important as your dropshipping enterprise grows and of course along with that comes an increase in the number of orders. The more customers you serve the more difficult it will be to manage these orders if your supplier is still doing things manually or on paper.

Remember that you may not be the only dropshipper that your wholesaler is serving. If it is a good wholesaler then chances are that other dropshippers will also take advantage of their services as well.

Now, how do you know if a wholesaler or supplier is also invested in today's technology? They should have at least the following:

- They have automated order placement and order cancellation.

- There are also options to place and also cancel orders via email

- Their product listings are updated as fast as their inventory listings

- The products on their website have updated and detailed information.

Note that not all suppliers will have all of that information readily available on their website. But if there is a number that you can call and the support staff can answer all of your questions then you might be looking at a good provider—their tech needs to catch up but they'll get there one day.

Note also that you shouldn't also judge a supplier based on how good looking their site is – if there is a secondary method to get you the info that you need then they're good to go.

7. Dedicated Support Reps

The sales rep that answered your call or product inquiry shouldn't be the same person you talk to if something goes wrong with your order. In fact, the really good supplier can assign a representative to you to help monitor your situation until it is resolved.

8. Order by Email or by Phone

This is a small thing but this can actually go a long way. There should be alternative ways to place an order. What if the supplier's website experiences a downtime and you have lots of orders?

If a supplier can accommodate other methods of placing and managing orders then you immediately solve a problem right there. At least you know that this wholesaler or supplier can manage and fulfill orders during difficult situations.

How to Find a Great Supplier

Again, the goal is to find a supplier or wholesaler that is reliable and also legit for that matter. One of the simplest ways to find a good dropshipping supplier is to do a Google search.

The easiest way to find a supplier is of course through Google. You just need to open your browser and use the following search term:

<name of product> + dropshipping supplier + <country or location>

Here's a sample search term I used:

socks dropshipping suppliers Australia

And that pulled up over a million results. I didn't know it would pull up that many search results. But if you look closely the SERPs provided by our favorite search engine really didn't give me purely a list of supplier websites.

Some of the websites listed on the first few pages weren't even in Australia. Some were lists of wholesale sock manufacturers in China, UK, and the US. I guess these manufacturers also ship to Australia, which is why they're on the top of the list—not sure though.

Of course with that many on the list it will be like looking for a needle in a haystack, right?

Attend a Trade Show

Trade shows don't happen a lot but when one does you should make the effort to attend it. This way you can find out who the manufacturer is. You can even come up to a rep or the manager and ask for information yourself.

Find the suppliers and manufacturers that provide the products you are interested in. You can ask for their contact info and introduce yourself as retailer interested in their products. You can then ask them questions like payment terms, warranties, and others (more about that later).

Order from the Competition

This is a good trick that you can do if you know that a competing ecommerce store is actually dropshipping their products. Here's how you do it.

Make a small order of the product that you are interested in. When the product arrives check out the return address. Look it up on Google and see which business is on that property.

Sometimes it works and sometimes it doesn't. This at least gives you an idea who the original shipper is—which may likely be the wholesaler or the manufacturer. The next step is to get that company's contact information.

Look for Dropshipping Supplier Directories

So, doing a Google search can give you an idea but you will have to fine tune your search. You need to use something better. So, what is better than organic Google searches?

You need to search for supplier directory sites. Using supplier directory sites is a kind of shortcut since the people behind these sites have done the background research for you. Here are some of the benefits that you can get from using them:

• Faster research – you can quickly find out the product offerings of each supplier. Some suppliers are listed by product type. Their contact information is already given.

• Easier searches – you can easily filter out the search by different category. You can filter the results by product, price range, and other specs that you need.

• Lowers your risk – the list provider has done the grunt work and has taken out the scammers.

List of Popular Suppliers

We have a list of the most popular suppliers below. The information about each of these suppliers can help you decide which one to choose for each particular product. Note that there are pros and cons to using their services.

Since they are popular and highly rated then you can be sure that they offer the best delivery and also have some of the best products. However, since they are popular you should know that you're not the only dropshipper that will take advantage of their services.

That means that there will be times when these guys will be overloaded with orders that they might have trouble keeping up. Some of the businesses in the list below aren't necessarily wholesalers. Some of them are online directories that will point you to actual suppliers.

1. AliExpress

This is one of the most popular dropshipping platforms and also a wholesaler. They also help connect dropshippers like you to actual suppliers. Take note that a lot of their suppliers are from China.

However, take note that their suppliers are a mix—some are good and some are not so good. If you want to make sure then run a test order.

The good news is that they have suppliers from more than 40 niche categories—which is a lot. You can find pretty much everything from apparel to electronics. The other good news about them is that they have free sign up.

2. Doab

This is actually a marketplace where manufacturers and suppliers are listed. You can search for suppliers and manufacturers by product or industry. They have done the research for you so can find good suppliers for your selected product. The downside is that their service comes with a monthly fee of $29 (minimum).

3. Worldwide Brands

This is a massive directory of bulk distributors and wholesalers. Their list of suppliers covers pretty much every niche you can think of. The best part is that they make sure that each company on their list is reliable and reputable. The downside is that there is a huge one-time fee to sign up with them amounting to $249.

4. Dropship Direct

This is a general supplier and they offer more than 100,000 products on their list. The products are all shipped from their warehouses. Other than a huge product list and an expansive warehouse system they also offer you data on the different products such as the number of orders, cancel rates, etc. on each product.

They provide you with a lot of metrics that will help you decide if a product will sell well or not. On top of that, they have free sign up.

5. Mega Goods

If you're interested in selling electronics then this is the supplier that you might want to check out. Their products include Bluetooth devices, TVs, kitchen appliances, cameras, clocks, and others. They charge a service fee of $14.99 per month.

6. National Dropshippers

This is a wholesaler that has more than 250,000 products in their warehouses. Since they are a huge warehousing company they can offer products at 50% MSRP, which can potentially increase your margin per sale.

The downside is that they have monthly service fee of $19.99 and they charge you $2.49 for each order they serve.

7. Dropshipper.com

This is a dropshipper platform and they connect you to more than 890 suppliers. They have a massive product listing of almost 2 million types of products. They have everything from electronics to beauty products.

They charge a one-time fee of $99. It's either that or you pay a monthly fee of $69.

8. Inventory Source

This is actually a dropshipping network that can connect you to more than 150 suppliers. They also connect you to dropshipping platforms such as Amazon, eBay, Shopify, BigCommerce, and the like. Their service plans start at $50 a month.

9. Sunrise Wholesale

This is actually a wholesaler that offers more than 15,000 types of products. Their product categories include garden decorations, jewelry, sports and fitness, home decors, and lots more. They also connect you to dropshipping platforms like Amazon, eBay, and Shopify among others. They require a membership fee of $39.95 per month or $99 each year.

10. Wholesale Central

This is another wholesaler or supplier directory. And the good news is that it is free to access. You can search their directly using different filters. You can also search by product niche such as pet supplies, candles, books, and eye wear among others.

Capitolo 25 How to Dropship with Shopify

Shopify is by far the best online tool for drop-shippers who don't have the technical expertise to create their own shops. It makes it possible for anyone to sign up and start his own online store in just a few minutes. It's great for people who want to start a dropshipping business but lack the technical know-how or the resources to build their own e-commerce websites from scratch. If you want a hassle-free experience as you start your first store, you should seriously consider using Shopify. The service offers free trial periods for beginners who want to test the waters before making a financial commitment. Here is a step by step guide to help you start your first Shopify dropshipping store.

Choose a Name for Your Dropshipping Store

When creating a Shopify store, your first task will be to select a name for your dropshipping business. You want to make sure that the name you select is simple, creative, and memorable. If you already have a niche in mind, you could try to find a name that is related to that niche so that people can have an easy time figuring out what you are selling. There are some online business name generators that you could use to come up with a list of possible names before you narrow it down to one.

When you find a few possible names that you may want to use, you must check to see if they are available. Google each of your shortlisted business names to see if they are already in use. If you use obvious sounding names such as "American Watches," chances are someone has already thought of that, and they are already trading under that business name, so try to think outside the box.

Create a New Shopify Account

Shopify has made this step extremely easy. All you have to do is go to the Shopify homepage. At that page, you will find a field where you have to enter your email address to start the process. Once you have entered the address, click the "get started" button. You will then be asked to create a password and input your chosen store name. Shopify will ask you a few questions about how much experience you have had in the e-commerce sector, and then they will ask you to provide a few accurate personal details. After you are done providing those details, your account will be officially opened, and you can then proceed to optimize your settings.

Set Up Your Account and Add All Necessary Information

You have to go through your new account's settings one menu item at a time, and you are going to input the information you need to configure your account before it can be operational. You have to put in place the correct settings to allow you to receive customer payments, to create your shipping rates, and to establish your store policies.

When customizing your account, your first task will be to add one or more payment options to your store. Unless you have this in place, there will be no way for your customers to pay you for the products they'll purchase. Go to your Shopify settings page and click on the tab that has the word "payment" on it. You will have the option to add a PayPal account or to use other payment solutions.

We highly recommend that you use PayPal because it's extremely convenient and it has a deep market penetration, so most people who shop online already have PayPal accounts of their own. You can also opt for other payment systems if you find them convenient or necessary given the particular nature of your products (for example, if yours is a store that mostly sells products to offices and other businesses, you may find it more convenient to add a payment system that allows for bank transfers.

After you have all your payment channels in place, it's time to set your store policies. These policies will govern the relationship between you and your customers, so you should make sure that they are clearly stated and that they are compliant with the law.

Shopify understands exactly what kind of policies you might need for your store, so they have created a tool that enables you to automatically generate store policies that are standardized. You can immediately generate a refund policy, a privacy policy, and even a set of terms and conditions that will protect your store from legal liability in many foreseeable situations. To gain access to the policy creation tool, you have to click on the "checkout" tab, the go through the page to find each of the fields that you have to fill. You can then click on the "generate" button, and your policy will be set.

When your customers check out after making a purchase, the full text of the policy will appear, and they'll have to accept those terms and conditions before the sale goes through. If you have your own conditions that you want to include in the policy, there are some templates that you can use as guides to create your own policy.

Finally, you will have to declare your shipping rates. Many e-commerce experts recommend that you should account for the shipping price when you mark up the price of each item in the store, and then, you should offer your customers "free shipping." This is a marketing technique that works pretty well because it makes most customers believe that they are getting a great deal, so they'll be more inclined to go through with the purchase. You can click on the 'Shipping' button and select your preferred shipping options for different zones, starting with domestic ones and proceeding all the way to international zones.

Launch Your Dropshipping Store

After you are done with your settings and configurations, you should proceed to launch your new dropshipping store. To do this, click on the "sales channels" option, and then click on "Add sales channel." When you are done with that step, you will have a real online business that is up and running.

Design and Personalize Your Store

Now that you own an online store, it's time to personalize it. Here, you have to consider how you want your customers to view your site as they browse through it and make purchases. The design of your shop is going to be crucial, and it may have a huge bearing on your level of success as a drop-shipper. You want to make a good first impression when customers visit your site, and you want to project an image of professionalism. The two most important design aspects that you have to consider are the theme and the logo of your shop.

Shopify has a large collection of themes in their inbuilt theme store, so you don't have to worry about finding a theme that suits your brand. You can use a free theme option, or you can pay a little money for a premium theme. If you are working under a tight budget, a free theme will do just fine. However, if you are very particular about your branding, you may want to go for a premium theme. Try out a few themes before you settle on one. After selecting a theme, you can customize it to make it more reflective of your brand.

Logos are important for branding purposes because they enable customers to remember your dropshipping store in case they want to make more purchases in the future. Your logo should blend with other design aspects of your shop because you want to create a sense of uniformity.

You can use tools like the Oberlin Logo Maker to create a high-quality logo in a matter of minutes. All you have to do is play around with colors, fonts, and icons. If you are a skilled graphics designer, you can create your own logo and upload it onto your Shopify account. You can also hire graphic design experts for cheap on sites like Fiverr and Upwork. After you are done with both the logo and the design of your store, it's time to add your products.

Add Products to Your Store

To add a product to your shop, go to Shopify Admin and click on "Products." You should then click on the "Add a Product" button on the top right part of the page.

You will then have access to fields where you can enter the title and the description of your product. Fill the fields by either copying and pasting the text from your supplier's website or adding a description that you have prepared on your own. Make sure that you use colorful language in your product description because your customers are going to make purchase decisions based on that description.

You should then scroll down the page and find the "Images" section. Here, you have the option of adding images by uploading image files from your computer. You can also use "drag and drop" to achieve the same outcome. Make sure you upload your favorite product image first because it's the one that is going to act as a "featured image," meaning that it will appear prominently on the sales page when your customers scroll through your shop.

You should then review all your product details, particularly the "visibility" settings to make sure that your product is set to appear on the online store. You should also review the "Organization" settings and modify them to make sure your product is properly categorized according to Vendor, Product Type, and Collections.

You then have to input the price of the product. As you do that, you can select an option that makes it possible for customers to compare prices, and you can also check a box that allows a tax to be added to the final price of the product.

When you get to the inventory section, you should add your SKU, your Inventory Policy, and a Barcode. Indicate whether or not your product has a shipping price, then select the weight bracket of the product. If your product comes in different sizes and colors, you should fill the "Variants" section appropriately, and put in the different prices for each variant.

Finally, you should edit your Meta Title and Meta Description in order to improve your SEO (search engine optimization) so that customers will have an easier time finding your product online. Ensure that you save all your product information correctly and that you view your product listing from the front end to see it from the point of view of the customer. You should repeat all these steps to add more products, or you can use services such as Oberlin which can help you add products to your account automatically.

Start Selling and Cashing in

Now that everything is done, you can start making sales. Remember that dropshipping is a competitive business, so you should do everything that you can to promote your products on blogs, social media, and other websites. Advertising is also an option if you have the resources.

Capitolo 26 How to Market your products

Nobody will see the items you have in your store as a dropshipper from Shopify unless you sell them vigorously. If you have to market, get ready to go out and let people know about the items you've got in your store. Now, you can advertise your store and drive or generate traffic in several ways. We're going to look at some of those ways in this section. We typically have two main ways to drive a store's traffic–organic and paid traffic.

This is a good example of organic traffic when you post on your social media timeline about the products you have in your store and leave a link to the store or product page. You don't care for it. When you make guest posts on blogs and include a connection to your store in the call-to-action section, you can also get free or organic traffic.

One issue with strategies for the production of free or subsidized traffic is that they require time to produce outcomes, and the outcome only trickles in like water. Unless you're a big influence on social media, it shouldn't be your best option to focus on sources of organic traffic. Rather, by paying for traffic, you should make your results easier.

Facebook PPC (pay per click advertising) is one of the main traffic drivers for dropshipping. What makes it great is that you'll get huge traffic in your store if you do it well. Facebook ads, as they are often named, encourage you to target individuals who are actively interested in the types of products you market.

It doesn't leave you space to blindly speculate–within a certain group; you can target people; you can target people residing in a specific area. You can also hit anyone who, in the last few months or weeks, have purchased something online.

On almost any other online platform, Facebook captures user data, and that's the info they use to enhance their advertising plans. Another great feature of Facebook ad is that when someone views or clicks on the message, you will still be paid. It's not liked some other forms of advertisement where you are paid whether or not viewers see the advertisements.

Facebook won't charge you if people don't see your ads, so it's a win-win for you. Interestingly, running Facebook ads is cheap–you can run high conversion ads with as little as $5, and send a lot of traffic to your store. You're going to spend on the advertising and the big traffic you're going to get when you compare the amount, so Facebook ads are worth it.

Here are the measures you can take to operate Facebook ads: Note: making strongly transformed Facebook ads is a path on its own–and this topic is not something we can cover. If you are interested in learning more about how to operate successful advertising, consider getting some materials on the topic. What we're trying to bring here to you is just the help you need.

Stage 1: Build a Facebook page – for operating Facebook ads, you need a Facebook page. You can't use your personal Facebook page to run ads. Make sure that the page name represents the type of products you market while designing a website.

Step 2: Go to your page, and click on "Ad center," then "create ad."

You will be required to give a name to your advertisement and mention what you want your ad to achieve. There are choices for you to choose from–would you like to increase your page's exposure? Would you like to direct traffic to an outside channel such as a website or e-commerce store? You will see a lot of options from which you can pick.

Step3: Choose your target audience – you can set up your ad to only see viewers in a certain place. You can also set up advertisements so that advertising can only be seen by people who earn a certain revenue limit.

Step 4: Creative ad and ad copy – ad creative is the image or video that accompanies an ad. People prefer to use videos as a creative ad–the logic is that videos have a better conversion ratio than images. You can use photographs as well. Make sure that whatever you use as your innovative ad is relevant to your business. Yes, if you use an illustration, it should be a picture of the product you advertise. To have the frustrated Facebook user swipe down their page to pause and check, it should be enticing enough.

The text that follows the ad picture is your ad copy–you use it to illustrate to the audience what's in it. If your ad text isn't compelling enough or you don't have a lot of Facebook user benefits, they won't bother clicking what you're advertising.

A good way to learn how to write ad copies is to start watching some of the various Facebook ads that show on your Facebook timeline from time to time. Look out for ads any time you click through Facebook and see how the marketers produced their copy and the kind of creativity they used. This will help you learn how to make your own ad copies to create the best artistic ad.

Step 5: Set your budget – Facebook allows you to set or determine how much you would like to spend running an ad every day. If you want to spend only $5, you can set it. Facebook will not charge you more than your daily budget.

Once the ad has been set up and personalized, post the ad and wait for the Facebook team's approval. The ad would usually be checked to make sure it follows all requirements. If you followed the instructions, your ad should be accepted as soon as possible.

You can then sit back and watch the traffic coming to your store once the ad has been approved. Use different ad sets to create more ad campaigns and learn the one that performs better. This is also single checking of A / B. Stick to it once you've found the ad sets that give you the best performance.

Remember, the above steps are just an overview–learning how to run effective Facebook ads, as mentioned earlier, is a course on its own. To broaden your knowledge, you might consider getting some materials on the topic. You'll also know more about how to tailor and automate the ad for better results while you continue to run your ads.

Other means of driving traffic to your store

Using Instagram influencers

Instagram has progressively moved from being a platform for photo-sharing to a powerful marketing tool. Since then, companies have found that they can draw more clients simply by sharing on Instagram about their business.

What makes Instagram perfect is that a number of monthly users are getting in. Over 800 million people are currently visiting the platform on a monthly basis. Will you know the meaning of that? Several people will be revealing your business.

One thing that makes Instagram unique is that the secret value of Instagram as a marketing tool is still to be seen by other business owners. Many of these advertisers still see Instagram as a photo- sharing platform that is only suitable for sharing pictures of their holidays.

Many advertisers are still searching it out for Snapchat marketing purposes on WhatsApp. But if you're going to take your business to Instagram, you're going to be among the early birds that will use the site to log huge sales.

There are three approaches you may advertise the store on Instagram:

- Build a huge following

- Air Instagram advertising–close to Facebook ads

- Pay Instagram influencers to endorse the brand

This takes time to build a massive audience on Instagram—you may need to spend months to do so. Often, to maintain your audience, you will need to regularly post useful content. This may seem like a long process to the typical dropshipper who just wants to send traffic to their store and make money. For such a dropshipper, the other choices are to display Instagram ads.

Although it takes time to grow a following on Instagram, and it won't give you instant results, you still have to do it. That's how to do it—whether operating Instagram ads or partnering with influencers, make sure you create your own follow-up at the same time. By the time your following has expanded to a reasonable number, you could stop working with influencers and start posting content for ads directly on your website.

While waiting for your audience to expand, start with Instagram advertising—it's just like running Facebook ads. You pick your target audience, you set up an innovative ad and replicate them, you set your schedule, and you're ready to go. Instagram ads are growing, if not stronger, just like Facebook ads. It can be a huge source of traffic to your store if it is set up correctly.

You should partner with an Instagram influencer to help you drive traffic to your store apart from the two solutions above.

Who's an Instagram influencer?

An Instagram influencer is just an Instagram user whose content they share on the platform has grown considerably. Influencers also record huge commitments on their posts—so it's clear that you'll get good results if you pay them to market your product. Anyone with up to 50k followers might typically be considered an influencer.

Influencer marketing, which involves paying influencers to sell a business, started to become common as many people's lives began to focus on social media. Influencer marketing is now perceived to be a legitimate way to market a product or service. In the coming years, it will also continue to be relevant.

Another thing that works well for influencer marketing is that people who follow influencers see them as a leader and would be able to do something that they were requested to do by the power. Influencers are seen as more knowledgeable people on a topic, and their followers obey their advice when they suggest a product or service.

Use the search feature for Instagram to locate an influencer in your niche. Check for users with a huge following in your niche. Observe their patterns of posting and how many people are involved with their posts. Go through their posts and see if, in the past, they helped people post sponsored content. Write a direct message to the influencer and let them know that you'd like to partner with them.

You need to be vigilant when looking for an influencer, so you don't pay anybody with fake followers for money. How do you know a follower of someone? It's easy—considered the number of their followers interacting with their articles and juxtapose them with their number of followers. For, e.g., if someone has 100k followers and less than 100 people are interacting with their posts, it goes to show you that most followers are created by a bot.

You don't want someone whose posts don't record a lot of commitment to pay money. Many unethical people are paying money to get bot-generated followers on Instagram—make sure you're not working with people like this, it's a waste of your time.

Give them a direct message if you've completed your due diligence and picked an influencer to partner with. Let them think that you want to give them a yell. Negotiate with the influencer with the quality following and give them the promotional profile you want to advertise. In order to get the advertised product, the influencer will include a connection to your store to their bio and encourage their fans to click the link.

Make sure that the influencer does not make the ad post sound too salesy when collaborating with an influencer. Alternatively, you'd like them to build the article in a manner that seems they're only trying to suggest a product they've used before.

The shootout post can stay on the influencer's page for a day, week, month, or several months, based on your agreement with the influencer.

The price you'll pay for the ad to live for one day on an influencer's page will vary from the cost you'll pay for the one-month post.

How much is paid by an influencer? There's no fixed amount for the influencer. The price you're going to pay hinges on so many things like your negotiation capacity, the influencer involved, how many days you want the post to stay up, and even the type of product you're selling. The expense of influencer marketing is not going to dig a hole in your pocket on average, and the findings can be quite promising. Most dropshippers utilize marketing power to drive traffic to their stores.

Capitolo 27 Tools That You Need for Your Store

In this rapidly changing world, no business can survive without using certain online tools. These provide assurance to the business when trends change and act as a backbone whenever any support is required. The convenience that using an online tool provides is incomparable to other manual forms. Whether it is making calculations for inventory or to make business expansion plans, technology plays the biggest and most significant role. Productivity and efficiency have increased by a lot, especially in the past decade as businesses of all sizes have had the opportunity to update its online services. The constant need to be updated with changing technology is essential for businesses to be able to attract new customers with ease.

Creating your e-commerce store

To explore the potential of your store, you need to be ready to adapt to all the available platforms, which will ensure the sustainability of your business. Before even looking all of the options available to make your store stand out, creating an e-commerce store is the first step. It is a necessity to have sound knowledge in technology and the online tools that are out there to start. There are professionals who can set the store up for you, as well as websites solely dedicated to help out beginners like you. Do not hesitate to seek help! These platforms are very well suited to e-commerce entrepreneurs who are just starting out. Moreover, these applications can guide you through steps to manage almost everything when launching your store.

Picking a theme

Now comes the part where you need to focus on particular and intricate details of your niche that will define your e-commerce store. However, before this step, you need to have good knowledge of the type of products you want to work with. The very inspiration for having a relevant theme that portrays your vision comes from your product range. If you are seeking help from a professional website or application, you will find a lot of preset themes there already. These can help you in brainstorming ideas and making decisions if you are unsure where to start. More importantly, think about customizing your store and giving it a unique touch. In a lot of cases, generic designs can be a turn off to consumers, while innovative ones can entice high-end customers and turn them into returning customers in the long run.

Designing an e-commerce store

Whenever customers visit your store, the theme, color palette and the design are the first things that they notice. At times, you may wonder, "Why do I need to put an extra effort into making it pretty?" or "Isn't having a great range of products enough?" Well, the answer is simple - if consumers are not interested, they will not bother going through whatever your store has to offer. Having an aesthetically pleasing e-commerce store entices customers and also validates your business as a professional one. With word of mouth, more people can become aware of and take notice of your store. If it is unorganized or shabby, it would be very difficult for you to attract them. Hence, to have and maintain loyal and potential customers, investing your resources on building a good e-commerce store is a necessity.

Online Logo Makers

After you have designed and set your store up, now is the time to brand it. This helps to gain recognition for your products and creates a lasting first impression in the minds of the customers. It can be anything from a simple tree to an intricate design; this should depend on the type of products you are selling. It is better to be more open to ideas and new designs instead of being adamant on one. Having a professional store can do wonders and help create a buzz among customers. Hence, a logo is the simplest and best solution for you to put your business out there. If you want to experiment, do not shy away from creating your own design but if you are not proficient enough, do not shy away from help from online logo makers. Hiring graphic designers or outsourcing can be great options too, depending on the budget you have for creating the logo.

Payment processing

Due to globalization, we have access to faster services, much faster than those in the past. The systems for making online payments have developed immensely and have made it easier for us to make daily purchases. You do not need to carry cash around all the time. Their personal information and details are encrypted and have protection from credit card frauds for when businesses are willing to adopt such models. You should do research on the most common online methods of making payment among your targeted customers and make sure that you provide them with those payment services. PayPal is one of the most efficient systems in the most recent times. You can also be open towards offline payment services but the online payment methods are much more convenient in today's time.

Online business plan services

If you are happy with your strategies and find that they are working for your business, this should not be a tool you need. However, it is recommended that you explore these services. An outside perspective is necessary for you to be able to work on your shortcomings. For entrepreneurs, these online plans for your business guide you in designing a feasible and strong plan when you are making the transition from great idea to a profitable business venture. The inbuilt features and tool templates of web-based applications help you generate charts on performance and goal achievement. Your financial status, depending on investments made for the business, can be studied carefully. You can be in charge of and keep track of the progress that you are making. Once you learn about what the services offer you, it would not be a surprise to see that you have started to think more critically and that your ideas for your store and product line go beyond the surface.

Using social media for your store

Whether you want to focus on Facebook, Instagram, Twitter, or any other social networking website, engagement with your customers through this platform is one of the most effective ways to draw and drive traffic to your store. Using social media is attractive as you do not have to invest a lot of money into it and you can utilize it to broaden your reach. Millions of people all around the world can engage with your store. Specialized tools on individual platforms are available to make social media users aware of new products and you have the flexibility to promote your products and content related to them. This also helps you to create a brand for your store. The best part is that as more time passes by, these platforms continue to grow and once you can get comfortable with social media, you should expect to look at great numbers!

Web hosting

The pace of the business world is much faster than what it was ten years ago. You cannot expect to apply those same strategies for attracting customers today. Hence, if you have not explored the internet yet, you will lag behind and before you realize, you will already be out of the game. A web hosting service allows you to start a website and run it. The files that makeup the website on a data server can be stored through these services and these files are uploaded to the web automatically from your web hosting service. The use of email marketing and installation of one-click supported applications are some of the many features that you can use when building your business. You can also be assigned an email address that includes the site's domain name.

Shopping cart software

When you have set up your website, there are some additional things which you need to offer your customers when they make a purchase. Shopping cart software is necessary to be able to make payments through your website. This is not only beneficial for the customers as it can allow them to feel safe when buying something online, but it is an advantage for your store too. Tracking inventory gets easier and you can keep tabs on which product to promote or communicate with the suppliers if a surge is predicted with the latest trends. This will also help you produce reports based on this data through your website's services. This software can be connected to multiple platforms for making payments. PayPal or credit card services can be offered to customers and this makes their experience more familiar as well. The purchasers can also be aware of the amount of tax they are paying and how much they are being charged for shipping costs. You promote transparency and convenience through these services on your store's website and it will help you gain a good reputation among old and new customers.

Webinar services

As your business grows, you may think of expanding and gaining new customers, both locally and internationally. Webinar services can help you connect and take orders faster and most importantly, they can help you monitor your day to day operations, especially if you have multiple offices. This will help you out if your employees are working remotely and if you have multiple working locations. Training sessions, meetings with all of your employees, either within a specific branch or all together, can be conducted much more comfortably. Webinar services are a great fit for you when you want to present your sales online and make product demonstrations for your clients too. Becoming more proficient in this helps you connect with your customers faster and you can respond to their queries in real time.

Anti-virus software

When you are using your computer, it is highly likely that you are storing information through a variety of applications. Whether you are dealing with storing personal information or you are processing orders, you need to keep all the data in an organized way. The information stored here is valuable and not having any protection programs on your computer puts you and your business in a lot of danger. Apart from the technical issues that your computer will go through, you could experience data theft, which would be a very big loss for your business venture. All businesses should have anti-virus software to guard the computer network against viruses, malware, Trojans, worms, or spyware. Since the platform of dropshipping is online where you have to constantly be in touch with your suppliers and customers, having a good antivirus software is a necessity and it is equally necessary for protection.

Receiving payments from customers

In order to deal with customers from various backgrounds, your knowledge in different modes of payment platforms is required. It reduces hassle if you can connect to multiple platforms that your customers will feel safe using. There are additional charges when you want to use these online payment platforms, ensuring to keep you safe against business fraud. You will be charged a fee for every sale you make and an additional amount to ensure protection for your store. You should check out different platforms apart from PayPal to make a sound decision, however, it is and has been the most trusted and convenient one in the market. Apart from this, there are built-in features to provide you protection if you are using platforms like Shopify.

Online data storage

Due to the ease of an online platform, storing data has become much easier than it used to be. Online data storage acts as backup storage if anything goes wrong with your computer. Of course, you can access your data online even if no problems arise instead of relying on your computer's storage. Data is stored on a cloud server which is convenient and safe. You can access the files from any part of the world at any time. Also, if you want to free up space on your computer, having online data storage is the best way to go about this. It is wiser to have online storage as hard drive failures, theft, and file erasure can occur and make these files extremely difficult to retrieve.

Business tools that you should know how to use

Google AdWords & Analytics

Google is the place we think of going instantly whenever there is something we want to know. From getting instant information about the most complicated technologies to doing the most basic spell checks, Google is our one-stop solution. For your business, you need to learn to make the most of this platform. Whenever you want to know about anything, this search engine can give you around 40,000 results per second and is definitely the most reliable search engine today. You can focus on getting on the first page of the search list and witness how this changes your income. Use an SEO (search engine optimization) strategy to try and make it on the first page. It may take a long time, maybe even months or longer, but you should keep at it. This will ensure you benefits in the long term. However, there is another way that can help you attain a first-page position faster, and this strategy includes using Google AdWords. This is a scheme of paid ads where you pay every time a visitor clicks on your advertisement. Additionally, you need to invest time into how to utilize Google Analytics and understand its importance for your website and your business. This tool allows you to understand the types of mediums through which your visitors come from and this could be a huge advantage when you are starting out or are struggling to reinvent your line. Overall, this will assist with things that are working and not working, guiding you towards better execution and expansion plans.

SurveyMonkey

Now that you have set your store up and are getting ready to attract customers to your niche, you need to know about the current market and what the trends are. This is a surveying tool available online that helps you connect with your audience. Survey Monkey already has a lot of preset questions along with built-in templates to give you a thorough insight when analyzing data. The best aspect is that the tool gives unbiased responses which can help you modify your strategies or help you create new and improved ones. The free version of this tool still provides you a lot of information through the surveys but the number of features is limited. Give it a try and see how much it helps improve your product line. If you are finding it useful, go ahead and get a subscription with a paid plan. The paid plan will provide many more useful tools for surveying.

X-Cart

For newcomers who do not have a lot of money to start out but want to give dropshipping a shot, your e-commerce website still needs to stand out. This tool is cost-effective and will not put a strain on your funds. X-Cart has a free version if you want to give it a try and see whether you find it suitable for your business or not. It helps you build your website and you can explore its various features. Moreover, free extensions will allow you to create shipping labels, slideshows, and do so much more! Your business can access these facilities and prioritize what will be more beneficial to get started on in terms of harnessing technical skills. You can get acquainted with the different themes available online and customize them wherever you feel necessary.

Tableau Public

This is a marketing tool that helps you to conduct research and lets you make a thorough analysis of your business data. You learn to make better predictions on what will work and what will not and this helps you make better decisions for the future. This tool is very effective because it sources out data from CSV files and Excel among many others. When the business venture is new, investing in high profile marketing research tools is important but expensive. This is where this tool is handiest as it can give free access to up to 15 million rows in one workbook and provide data solutions for free with up to 10 gigabytes of space.

BuzzSumo

In the modern day, social media has been the best platform for marketing. Social media is perfect for if you want to understand demographics, connect with influencers, find out what the most shared content is and much more. BuzzSumo is the best influencer marketing tool that allows you to find out what content is performing the best on any social media platform. You can choose a paid subscription but there is a free trial period too which you should definitely make use of before making a purchase. This application helps you understand what sort of content will work well with your product line; this in turn will help you connect with influencers who can help you in expanding your marketing strategies.

Capitolo 28 Create your brand and build your audience

Assuming you already have a website and an audience, you can skip this chapter. Otherwise, it is vital that you continue reading to make sure your brand is aligned with your business model and the product you are selling. A good start-up point is to ask what exactly a brand is. A brand is much more than a simple logo and is rather an ethos, a mission and a commercial approach. That logo simply tells people that the product or service they are receiving meets the same standards as anything they have used in the past. Start your brand by choosing why you do what you do. Why should people care about your company? How is it different from other companies that offer the same? How do you want the world to change, after your company is part of it? This is what allows a company like Apple to capture the imagination of billions of people and create such loyal customers.

Apple not only cares about selling hardware but also about creating beautiful, personal, and highly targeted hardware for creative people who break the rules compared to large companies. When the first Apple computer was launched, the only competition was IBM and by taking this position, Apple was able to differentiate itself a lot and excite many followers accordingly. The same is true for many companies that want to create a greener planet. These companies are doing more than just making money and their fans love it. This is enough for people to choose their products instead of the same products offered by another company. These two companies could sell exactly the same product, but the way they do it is completely different. And if you can convey this mission statement, you will find that the right type of customer will go absolutely crazy about your brand. This is the type of customer whose vision is aligned with his. Don't try to attract everyone who will never work. Instead, try to attract more to the right kind of person.

Create your logo

You can do it in two ways, designing it yourself or hiring someone to design it for you. The goal of a great logo is to communicate what your business is about. You are trying to tell people what you sell and why you sell it as soon as they look at your business. Suppose your company focuses on natural and health products, so you could create a logo with a tree or a heart. It would probably be green and have an edifying and healthy name. On the contrary, if your business is to punish gymnastics workouts, your logo may include an image of a handlebar and have the word iron somewhere. The idea is that the combination of your logo, company name and perhaps blog posts is enough to tell any visitor to your site immediately that this is a company that runs them exactly and they will love it. This should also extend to site design. In the meantime, make sure your logo is designed using a vector file (which means it is made in Illustrator or similar software that simplifies editing and resizing) and avoids the use of clichés. Again, this is a good place to invest some of your money in advance that you will pay largely in the long term.

Build your audience and build trust

This is the basic concept of content marketing to create an audience of people who love their content and trust their opinion so you can convince them to buy the products you recommend and so you can continue to attract people to your site from time to time. From time to time, offering you more opportunities to make a sale. The way to do it is to start writing high-quality content and publish it on a blog on a regular basis. The more you write and the more you research your topic and make it different and interesting, the faster you will create a dedicated audience to which you can sell. Show that you really know what you are talking about, that you only recommend things that you sincerely believed in and that your audience can rely on you as a resource for more useful ideas and information. Similarly, try to build your mailing list and your presence on social networks. Firmly incorporate your brand into all social media pages and anything else you create, so people know they are dealing with the same business. Making someone follow you on social media when they think they are interested in your brand is much easier than letting them buy you a product and spend money! Meanwhile, your social media accounts will help you attract more new customers to your site by allowing people to share with your network. You can also help by providing buttons to share on social networks that will allow people who like your content on Facebook or Tweet on Twitter. Only after you have generated a large audience of people who regularly visit your site, you should start thinking about introducing products on your page. If you have really created a brand that you believe in and if you have provided real value to your content, you should discover that you have real fans. And true fans will be desperate to buy your products when you start selling them!

Other ways to promote your products

Of course, there are many additional methods you can use to send more customers to your products and market your store. One option is to create your own affiliate program and encourage more people to help market your items. Another method is to pay for advertising if it's a pay-per-click campaign through Google AdWords or if it's a highly targeted Facebook ad for your specific demographic. Both will be explained vividly later in this book, so don't worry too much about it now. It works well in scenarios where it sells from eBay or Amazon and is not trying to create an audience. If you intend to pay for advertising, you must calculate the LCV (Customer lifetime value) of each customer. This will allow you to ensure that, regardless of what you spend on your ads, earn more, and see a solid ROI.

Capitolo 29 Mistakes to Avoid When Starting the Business

Here are some common mistakes that many novice drop-shippers tend to make. We will discuss why people find themselves making these mistakes, and what you should do to avoid making them:

Starting Without Learning the Ins and Outs of Dropshipping

There has been much hype around the topic of dropshipping, and a lot of misinformation came along with it.

Many self-proclaimed "dropshipping gurus" have been telling people how easy it is to start a dropshipping business, and this has led a lot of people to assume that you don't need to learn any technical aspects of the business to succeed. The truth is that the dropshipping game is evolving pretty fast, and there is stiff competition in every niche, so you should avoid jumping into the business without taking a little time to learn as much as you can about the trade.

Choosing Bad Suppliers

Many newbies fail to look into the history of suppliers to find out if they have a reputation for unreliability. They assume that in order to maximize their profits, they need to go with the supplier who offers the lowest prices, but the truth is that the quality of service and the reliability of a supplier is much more important for a drop-shipper than saving a few cents on each order. If a supplier messes up and makes a lot of excuses during your first few weeks of operation, you should drop him and find a more reliable one before your business gets stuck with a bunch of negative reviews.

Lacking Faith in the Dropshipping Model

For you to succeed as a drop-shipper, you have to stick to the model. Some first-timers make the mistake of doubting how the model works, so they try to blend dropshipping with other forms of retail e-commerce. This often happens when newbie drop-shippers worry about their suppliers running out of stock, so they go out and use their own money to buy some inventory. If you have chosen to be a drop- shipper, you should stick with it and concentrate on scaling your business, and you should avoid complicating things unnecessarily. Have faith that the system will work.

Expecting Money to Come Easily

Again, the notion that dropshipping brings in quick and easy money comes from the so-called experts who misinform people because of their own personal agendas. As a drop-shipper, don't assume that you will set up a store, launch it, then sit back and start watching the money flow in. Success in dropshipping requires hard work, proactivity, and a competitive attitude. Customers don't just come to your shop, you have to go out there on the internet, find them and bring them in through advertising and content marketing. Dropshipping is not a get rich quick scheme.

Failing to Retarget Your Site Visitors

Retargeting site visitors is probably the most effective marketing strategy out there in terms of the sales that it generates. If you don't take advantage of retargeting ads on Facebook or Google, that's akin to throwing money away. People visit a shopping site or a sales page because on some level, they really would like to buy that product, so if you keep reminding them about it, one day, as soon as they can get some money, they are highly likely to come back and make that purchase. If you have limited marketing funds, make retargeting ads a priority in your marketing strategy.

Using Low-Quality Product Images

First-time drop-shippers are encouraged to use free photos as a cost-cutting measure, but that doesn't mean that you should use low-resolution product photos. If your supplier provides low-quality photos, try to find better photos of the product elsewhere online, or you can order a sample of the product and take your own photos of it. Online shoppers don't get to see the products they are buying beforehand, so they rely on photos to make purchase decisions. To be fully convinced about the quality of a product, most of them would want to see lots of high-resolution photos from different angles so that they can zoom in and study the product in detail.

Misleading Your Customers About Your Shipping Time

Many new drop-shippers are afraid that the customer might go elsewhere if they think that the shipping time for a product is too long. Some drop-shippers are tempted to either conceal the real shipping time or to straight up lie about it. If you can't guarantee fast shipping for a certain product, you should be honest about it, and offer an explanation as to why it's taking longer than expected (perhaps you are shipping it from abroad). Misleading customers about your shipping time counts as terrible customer service, and if a customer has to wait longer for a package that he was promised, he is highly likely to take his business elsewhere.

Being Afraid to Reinvest Your Money in the Business

When dropshipping novices make a little money from their businesses at the beginning, some are usually afraid of putting the money back into the business for fear that they could end up losing it all. However, the right approach is to reinvest at least some of the money you make into the business through adverting or SEO. There are lots of ways to advertise one's dropshipping business—you could hire influencers, buy PPC ads, etc. Your business won't grow if you take every cent you make out of it. Use your proceeds to scale your business in order to make more profits.

Failing to Work with Instagram Influencers

Right now, Instagram is one of the hottest platforms if you are looking to advertise any kind of product. People follow influencers on Instagram to an almost religious extent, and you would be surprised at how many people will be willing to buy a product just because one influencer mentioned it. You can easily find an influencer within your niche who is willing to give your store or product a shout out for a bit of cash. The bigger you dream, the bigger you'll grow, so don't be afraid to spend a lump sum of cash for an endorsement from a few powerful influencers.

Using Complicated Shipping Fee Structures

First-time drop-shippers tend to publish complicated shipping fee structures on their websites or to display shipping fees under the price tag of every item in their shops. This can be confusing and off-putting for many customers. Customers don't need to see your cost breakdowns; they just want to know how much the whole thing is going to cost them. Instead of having separate shipping fees for all listed items, you should just set prices that account for shipping costs and then offer free shipping. This is a neat marketing trick that can make customers think that you are offering them a great deal.

Creating Unclear Policies

Many novice drop-shippers make the mistake of thinking that store policies are mere formalities, so they fail to make them as clear as necessary. You should avoid having unclear policies. If you don't know how to create such policies, you can borrow ideas from other similar businesses, or you can use online tools provided by industry players such as Shopify. For example, if you don't explicitly state in your policies that a customer has to include a tracking number when returning a package, and then the customer claims that he sends back the package without producing a tracking number to prove it, you won't have any recourse if the package "gets lost in the mail."

Mishandling Product Returns

Product returns are complicated and frustrating for drop-shippers because they require a lot of correspondence, and they cost money. However, they are also an opportunity for you to deliver good customer service, and they help you learn the weaknesses in your system so that you can fix them. Many first-time drop-shippers mishandle product returns by trying to shortchange the customer or by taking their frustrations out on the supplier. You have to remember that returns are part of the business and in the end, they are inevitable. You should prepare for them by outlining clear rules on how they ought to be handled and by sticking to those rules even if things get frustrating.

Relying Too Much on One Supplier

Many drop-shippers make the mistake of counting too much on a single supplier. This leaves them unprepared in case anything unexpected happens. You should always have several backup suppliers for every product in your store. If something happens, say your supplier runs out of stock or hikes up his prices, you can count on your backups to fill your orders. If you are in a situation where your business could live or die depending on the actions of a single supplier, then you are not managing your risks properly.

Failing to Test Several Products

You may have a niche in mind when you start your business, and you may select great products that bring in a decent profit, but that shouldn't be the end of it, you should keep testing new products to see if you can make money off of them. If you are inflexible about the products that you carry in your store, you could wake up one day to find that there is a universal shortage of your best-selling product, so it's good to have backup products. By testing several products, you can identify those that may come in handy when you want to scale your business.

Focusing on Price Competition

Many first-time drop-shippers make the mistake of thinking that they can beat out the competition by setting their prices lower than everyone else. While it's true that customers like bargains and low prices, there are other more sustainable ways to make your store stand out from the competition. If you start a price war, you will be digging your own grave. Whenever businesses start undercutting each other, it's the ones that have few resources that end up losing. You cannot undercut dominant online retailers because they are always willing to match the lowest price, so you have to differentiate yourself by offering great service with a personal touch.

Selling Products That Violate Trademark or Copyright Laws

Just because a supplier has a product available in his inventory doesn't mean that it is entirely legal. There are many cases where suppliers stock knockoff products that are often imported from Asia. You may also see clothes or accessories with nice logos from popular Western franchises and decide to sell them in your store. You should be extremely careful in these situations because some of those products may violate the legal rights of other businesses, and you could get sued by the companies that own the trademarks, copyrights, or other intellectual properties that were used to make those products.

Capitolo 30 How to Scale Your Dropshipping Business

S caling is vital for the success of a dropshipping business. Without growth, your business will stagnate, and that is the beginning of the end of any business. No matter what your personal goals are for your business, whether you want to become a business mogul or settle in and have a comfortable and sustainable business, you have to scale. The whole concept of scaling can be unnerving as you will be moving out of your comfort zone and taking on more responsibilities. However, if you go about scaling your business step-by-step and use all the tools and strategies available, it becomes easy to do and exciting to see your business grow.

Scaling is not a single option only way of growing your business. It is very flexible and if one particular form of scaling does not work for your niche, you have a variety of other options to try out and implement those that fit your particular dropshipping business the best. That is what makes scaling so successful, you can add all the different options that fit, there are no limits.

Are You Ready?

Premature scaling is the phrase used in commerce for expanding your business without first putting into place a solid foundation to build your scaling for your business. It is not only startup businesses that fall into this trap, even long-established companies and this invariably leads to failure.

Before you can be ready to scale, you must work through several steps for your scaling efforts to be successful as follows.

Cash Safety Net

Build up a cash safety net for your business before you scale to allow for any setbacks during scaling. This will allow you to change strategies during scaling and have the cash to back you up if one strategy does not work out. Without a cash safety net, you won't have the means to try more than one strategy to get the perfect product and market fit.

Logical Steps Forward

You need to take the steps from the start to the implementation stage of scaling in the correct order. Starting at the wrong end of your scaling will result in a lot more work, money spent needlessly and opportunities lost.

Once you have committed to the scaling process you become less flexible to maneuver as you have started spending money on products, hiring a person or people to help run the business and advertising.

To avoid all the problems of premature scaling is not difficult. Do not spend money on non-essentials, save all extra cash to enable you to progress without getting into a cash bind in the middle of scaling. Once you have that set up you make very sure that you know exactly what your customers want and have all the ways to reach potential customers and have set up strategies and advertising to reach all of your potential customers in the target group of your scaling effort. The last step is to test whatever products you want to scale, or new products you want to add to your business. You must base your scaling on proven test results, not guesses or what people say are the latest trends or fads. Once you have all the above in place, you have eliminated the possibility of premature scaling and are indeed ready to start scaling your dropshipping business.

Scaling Vertically

Traditional vertical scaling means you add more products in your niche or expand on the categories in your niche. You also increase your budget for advertising for existing ad sets that are doing extremely well. In short you offer more products, increase your ad spend, but do not focus on finding new audiences to target within your niche. This is a good, solid way of scaling with a proven track record.

Scaling Horizontally

Scaling horizontally give you several options, or combinations of the horizontal scaling options to implement, whichever fits your business best and you find the most comfortable to use. Basically, instead of scaling upwards with your existing products, you scale by introducing your products to new audiences – you scale wide.

Become Your Own Franchise

You duplicate your existing business and online store to open up the opportunity to sell to clients in your niche who speak another language. If you speak more than one language, you can manage this yourself by simply translating everything on your existing website to the target language.

If you do not speak another language, go into partnership with someone who speaks your target language and share profits for the new franchise website on a 50% basis with this person.

Duplicating your business in another language has greater appeal to people where the official language is not English. Shoppers in Europe, the Balkan countries and the Far East prefer to shop online in their own language and prefer the Euro as payment currency.

The benefit of duplicating is that you will have a higher conversion rate, but you also take on a lot more work and you will be limited in how many countries you can target in your scaling efforts.

Keep It English and Go Global

Scaling globally and keeping everything in English has the drawback of losing potential clients who do not want to do business in English and use USD as the currency for payment, giving you a lower conversion rate.

To offset this drawback, scale globally for the countries where English is the official language or one of the official languages.

This form of global scaling is a lot less work than duplicating your website, freeing up time to concentrate on other areas of your business.

Scaling into Neighboring Niches

This is a great way to scale your business, by investigating the niches that borders on your own niche and look for any products in these neighboring niches that would complement the products that you are already selling. Look for products that the customers in your own niche would be interested in buying and test the reaction to the new products by offering a few at a time. Your sales statistics will clearly show you which products your niche customers like best and then you can make adjustments to the products you offer from neighboring niches.

You can do this form of scaling indefinitely without spending extra on advertising before you are sure that any neighboring niche products are viable to be added permanently.

Facebook Lookalike Audiences

Facebook offers a segmentation tool that creates lookalike audiences based on the followers that you currently have. The tool takes the interest and demographics of your followers to create a lookalike audience that you can target. As the demographics and interests of the new audience closely match that of your current followers, this form of scaling enables focused marketing and finds you groups with a very high potential conversion rate.

Facebook uses its massive user base to look for similarities to create a lookalike audience that would never be found without the user data stored within Facebook. This tool works as long as you have a minimum of 100 people in your client group, but the larger your total is, the more effective this tool becomes.

You can create your lookalike audience from your customer lists, your website traffic and the fan page you have and select different types of lookalike audiences.

Specific Demographics

You can refine your demographics for the lookalike audience by setting certain parameters such as specific location, gender, and age group for an even narrower focus to target your advertising.

Audience Size Selection

Select the large audience option to maximize the number of people you reach that similar to your current audience gives you a much broader audience, but there will be less similarities shared than your fans and current customers have in common.

When you select a smaller lookalike audience, it will result in a smaller number of people seeing your ads, but those people will share far more characteristics with your fans and clients.

Facebook CBO

In September 2019, Facebook introduced a new feature for optimizing how your advertising budget is distributed, the campaign budget optimization (CBO) feature. This algorithm now does real time optimization of your ad budget across your ad sets. It targets the best opportunities separately, optimizing them one-by-one on what it deems to be the least expensive cost per result. Once done with an opportunity, it moves on to the next best opportunity. It does not take into consideration the amount spent on the previous ad set. The benefit of CBO is that the algorithm targets your top performing ad sets and you no longer waste money on opportunities that are much less likely to lead to sales and conversions by intelligently optimizing your campaign budget to target the ads that perform the best and the audiences that respond the best.

Google Similar Audiences and Customer Match

Google offers several tools that assist you in re-engaging customers and scaling your business.

Customer Match uses your data, both offline and online, that customers have shared with you to enable you to re-engage customers across Display, YouTube, Search, Gmail, and Shopping. This tool can also target other potential clients similar to those you already have.

The Similar Audiences tool from Google, works on the same lines as the Facebook Lookalike tool. The searches for Similar Audiences most often use your marketing's lists, first-party data information to target new users who have share similar characteristics, and interests of your best performing website visitors' groups.

Estimate and Plan

Planning ahead is crucial for scaling to be successful. To enable you to plan with accuracy, you must do two specific forecast evaluations. It is important to be as thorough as possible with as much data as possible to give you the best realistic results.

A customer growth forecast, broken down into categories with specifics such as number of new clients, estimated number of orders and broken down by different months.

An expense forecast on similar lines as the sales growth forecast as to what systems you have in place and will need to cope with the extra number of orders. Also, what changes will be needed to your infrastructure, what upgrades in technology you will need, and the extra manpower needed to cope with running the business during your scaling period.

Suppliers

A vital part of scaling your business is your suppliers. You must be able to trust that your suppliers are able to scale with you and that you will not find yourself in the middle of your scaling operation having to deal with a supplier who cannot keep up with your increased orders. Make absolutely sure your supplier can keep up, especially if your scaling involves custom products or new products on the market. Should you have doubts about the supplier's ability, it is wise to search for a new supplier or a backup supplier.

When you start scaling communicate with your suppliers, you bring them into the picture. Suppliers are totally aware of the benefits your scaling will bring to their own business. They would prefer that you stay loyal to them, so negotiate the best prices for the products you are scaling. If you have built a solid business relationship with your suppliers, the majority of them will be open to negotiations.

Support Staff

As your business grows and orders increase, you need support staff as you will reach a stage where you can no longer handle the orders coming, customer queries and placing orders on your own. No business can afford to have a bad relationship with clients and especially new clients. You need to have a competent person or persons in place who will be able to help you deal with customer queries and communicate with and place orders with your suppliers.

A cost-effective way to have the needed support staff in place is to outsource by hiring a virtual assistant or virtual assistants for your specific business requirements. You can train and introduce your virtual assistant to your suppliers and you do not have to spend money on extras such as office space and equipment. This means you can use the money in your cash safety net for other needs within your business.

Technology and Automation

Automation is top of the list for the smooth running of any dropshipping company, and doubly so during the process of scaling. There simply is no time to do tasks manually as it is too time consuming, leaving you with little or no time to concentrate on the many extra tasks that need to be done to scale successfully.

Two forms of automation to put in place before you start scaling is to automate order fulfilment and auto order tracking. These to automation options keep orders being placed going and keep customers happy as they can track the progress of their orders. Tracking is especially beneficial when you are dealing with first time customers who may be uncomfortable dealing with a company they do not really know.

Make sure that you integrate as many of your systems as possible to prevent communications problems. The more unintegrated systems you have, the higher the chances are that the systems will not function well together, so prevent problems further along the line by integrating your systems to the greatest extent possible

Capitolo 31 Growing Your Business to $10,000+ / Month

Note that Facebook is the biggest social media channel there is. However, it can be costly. The next place you want to setup your marketing is on Twitter. It is cheaper and you can always start for free.

Finally, you can move on to Instagram and Pinterest maybe after you have seen the numbers and results in either Facebook or Twitter. Check how many conversions you're getting, how much web traffic is generated (how many people visit your site because of your ads), and see how many leads are generated (how many new accounts, add to carts, and checkouts are made).

Check if your market is on Facebook or if it is on Twitter. Remember that these are pay per click methods. You will have to pay these platforms for the amount of traffic they are able to generate on your dropshipping store.

Note that Twitter is seen by many ecommerce marketers as a very reliable social media platform as far as conversion is concerned. According to one study, about 52% of its users tend to buy products that are advertised there. On top of that they have 5 times more customer engagement, which increases your chances of conversion.

This page has a nice info graphic to show you some very interesting numbers:

https://www.webfx.com/blog/social-media/why-twitter-matters-to-marketing-infographic/

However, that doesn't mean that you should forget about Facebook and the other social media channels. Facebook actually reports some pretty good ROI for digital marketers. Consider the following:

Scaling Your Business

Scaling your business means that you need to move forward and grow. At first you will be a one-man team. If you can manage that then it will be great to do it by yourself. There won't be that many tasks to do at first.

All you need to do is to create your customer personas, do your research, setup your dropshipping site, register your business (i.e. sole proprietorship at first), pick and post your products, advertise in your selected medium, and then watch the analytics.

You need to determine where your customers are actually coming from. That will take a while. You will also need to craft ad campaigns, which means creating images, videos, slogans, and what not.

To scale your business, you need to do the following:

- Add complimentary products

- Use the power of email lists

- Increase your market spend

- Hire a virtual assistant (you can't do it all your own anymore)

- Go multichannel

Add Complimentary Products

Find out which of your listed products sell. You will then go back to Amazon or some other online retailing portal (like eBay for instance or a competing dropshipping site).

Look for your product there. You're not the only one selling it, remember? If you're product is unique then you should look for similar product. For instance, if you're selling waterproof Bluetooth speakers, then look for Bluetooth speakers that are also waterproof and are about the same price.

And then look at the "People who viewed this item also viewed" part of those product pages. Another section is the "often bought together" section that shows which other products were also bought with that Bluetooth speaker.

That will give you a good idea of the complimentary products that you can sell on your site as well.

You can also brainstorm things too. Think of other possible products that will complement your product. If you're selling a Vitamin D supplement, your customers might also be interested in Calcium and Magnesium supplements as well.

Why? Well, you need a balance of all of these three nutrients so that you can get the most of the benefits you get from all of them. Do your due diligence—do some research.

You can also just create a different offer—a competing product perhaps. And then see if people buy that instead or just head off to their own choice of complimentary product. The goal is to make people make their move and observe how what they do on your website. Make use of the analytics tools provided to you from the different social media channels and Google as well.

You're Going to Get Busy with the Problems

Here's a bit of fair warning. As your sales increase expect to get more returns and customer complaints. Big Hint: deal with it as fast as you can and as efficiently as you can or else your reputation will suffer.

Returns

Customers will return products for one reason or another. You should immediately check the return policy on that product (30 day or 45-day money back guarantees etc.). Base your next move on that policy provided by your supplier.

Chargebacks

Sometimes you will get chargeback motifs. More often than not a chargeback is actually fraudulent. However, the bank won't give you a lot of time so you better act quickly. You need to provide proof that you actually delivered the goods. Evidence come in the form of packing slip, tracking information, and the exact order that was made.

Shipping Type

Most dropshippers will offer free shipping and just work the cost into the list price they display on their online store. How are they able to do that? Well, they opt for flat rate shipping. It's the same charge for all items you sell.

But that is not always available. Sometimes you will have to use per type rates especially if the item being shipped is heavier or larger. If you're shipping larger packages your best carrier options are FedEx and UPS. They give better rates.

If you are usually shipping smaller items then USPS is the go-to carrier. They can charge less than $5 per package.

Customer Support

Expect to do some customer support yourself at certain times. A lot of dropshippers use support software to help them manage customer complaints and provide support options. Here are the top 3 choices for many dropshippers:

• Desk (operated by Salesforce)

• Help Scout (go to option for personalized service and it has a pretty good support ticket system)

• Zendesk (has lots of pricing options—great for beginners with smaller budgets).

Email Lists

Email lists are still a staple for ecommerce. If you already have your own website and your own dropshipping site then it makes sense to create an email list. You can offer discount coupon codes, product guides, brochures, create discount events or anything that you can provide for free in exchange for your customer's email address.

You should also indicate that you will be sending them promotional items on their emails when you ask for their email addresses.

You also shouldn't pepper your subscribers with emails every day. That will be annoying. You should schedule your emails like maybe once or twice a week. Email them whenever you have a sale coming up.

Here are some of the types of emails that you might want to send your customers:

- Welcome email

- Help email

- Answers to inquiries

- Unexpected freebie email

- Newsletters

- Important events email

You will want to use an email marketing service later on. It's easy to send out those emails to 25 or even 50 of your close friends and relatives. But as your customer base grows and as your website gains popularity, expect your list of emails to grow to the hundreds (or even thousands).

That is why you need the help of an email marketing service to help manage all of that. Mailchimp is the popular email marketing brand out there. However, there are other alternatives such as Benchmark, Mailer Lite, GetResponse, and others. Check out their rates and see which ones fit your budget.

You will also want to spend time to learn more about email marketing. Again, it's a huge subject and it can't be covered comprehensively in this book.

Increase Your Marketing Spend

After a lot of fine tuning (i.e. mistakes and blunders) you will find out the best practices and the best products for your dropshipping store. You will then need to increase your marketing spend.

That means increasing your marketing budget. You already know your niche and your market. Now it's time to get more sales and in order to do that you need more aggressive marketing ergo more funds spent on ads and analytics monitoring.

Hiring a Virtual Assistant

As your success grows your market grows. That also means you will get more customer complaints and experience more problems. You will end up getting so busy it can drive you crazy.

That means you have grown your business to a point where you can't do it on your own anymore. Then you have to delegate some of the repetitive tasks of your business to someone else and focus on the important stuff—marketing, sales, and advertising.

This is where a virtual assistant can come into play. Alternatively, you can hire someone in the neighborhood but that might entail some legalities which can drain more of your funds. Maybe you can do that later when your business has grown a little bit bigger.

For now, a virtual assistant who will work part time will have to do. You can delegate the following tasks to a VA:

- Graphic design

- SEO work

- Website maintenance

- Creating blog posts

- Writing newsletters

- Updating inventory

- Processing invoices

- Social media management

- Customer service

So, where do you hire your prospective VA? There are lots of platforms where Vas post their professional profiles. You can hire them from Upwork, Zirtual, or Freelancer. Those are the top 3 nowadays but there are others too.

Note that sooner or later you will need to assemble a team or several teams. Some VAs and in-house employees will be in charge of marketing. Some will be tasked with customer service (you'll need help dealing with hundreds if not thousands of customers), and others will be tasked with site management, product research, and other tasks as well.

Capitolo 32 Social Media Approach in Dropshipping

A successful business does well marketing on public streets but the truth is since we are entering a new age of electronic future businesses must make haste for their change if they haven't gotten to it yet. This next change is to discover the new world of social media marketing. You are going to be reaching out online in many different ways. If there has been any previous advertisement experience had for the Business then one knows the power the word of mouth can bring.

Having social interactions with others build a great rapport with the individuals engaged. This kind of behavior is going to promote the global presence that the e-commerce shop has. Bringing in social media to an already online and trending topic is going to make with e-commerce a perfect pair. A business might have more than half of their following on a social media scale and thus in great odds will also make it easier to combine them into some good business marketing.

Bring the business to the front lines and where more than half the customers are; that's online. The web is going to be a strong motivator for content you are going to design your product line. Release a post about your new inventory and be descriptive when you tell the world that is going to pop and be a strong reminder to the visitors why they are going to visit your shop and ultimately why they will buy. Get started now and try making a social media account if you do not have one already.

There are tons of providers and many of them you will be able to market your business with. Create a login and finish editing the personal information on the account and everything that the business will be displaying to the public. Make the business account look nice and professional and it will attract business-like followers ready to see your catalog. Choose a provider that fits your needs or open two or many accounts to see which is going to work best for the business. The business owner may choose one social media outlet over another and this could give the business presence edge.

The only way to tell the right fit is to just jump right in and start designing. Social media has strong sources of the population that are willing to third-party market and this is why it's important to establish a bond with the community that surrounds. It can city-based or global to give back in many ways as long as you make the connection with your audience. Make their time worthwhile since they are spending so much online searching. Supply an online incentive that will encourage your audience to come back and share the content with other friends and family that are with them on these accounts. Find important partners that can also give you mentions and that will give you credible posts about the business you run and for many to see.

The question is canning the e-commerce website survive from only social media marketing. This is not going to be a likely route because the only option the business has could lose it and have nothing left for support. If the company only dedicated their marketing budget to social media marketing, they are going to see the expensive cost burn through the budget quickly. Popularity is so important when it comes to running an efficiently visited shop but the company needs to take advantage of its capabilities to obtain followers from the social media sites that they could also be using, some of them even being free.

The more popularity you have the more profitable the business can be. The business can create very engaging motives towards their audience and they could attract more and more attention to the sites that are trickling into the shop daily. Keep gaining more followers and see what this popularity can do for the business.

Facebook Ads

Facebook ads are great and they are for any age range with a company structure. With Facebook as a company can market themselves from the bottom up and with little to no cost at all. Running Facebook ads can become costly if there is no following audience to broadcast to. If the company has no following on their web-sites then they are going to be paying money for company promotion and not for product promotion depending on how far we have gotten already.

These social ads are great because it engages thousands of people together for a common focus on the marketplace and this creates a strong playing field for posting products on any page. A company can pay for personalized ads that are going to air for the community to see sponsored posts on their pages and feeds so that they cleverly run into company products posted for great values. These advertisements cost the company upfront but they will also give great exposure to the presence of the shop.

The shop can post an ad about its new items or maybe marked down items that the company has extra inventory of. If the company can make an ad about the marked down items that are full in the inventory ware-house then products can be efficiently moved off of the warehouse shelves and into new revenue that is going to have the company break even with its assets. There has to be a balanced routine when it comes to paying for Facebook ads because not only can they get pricey but there will also be other ads that bring competition to the playing board.

It is in the best interest of the company to know exactly when to place an ad on the market. The company is going to need to be ready for any turnover and sales to skyrocket if necessary because if there is the right product niche the success is going to come pouring out. Customize ads with the company logo and titles that entice the customers to come on in and visit for the new sales.

There is going to be opportunities to make a catalog or a flip advertisement and get creative with the cover flow when putting up an advertisement for the week.

Advertise on a good schedule so that none of the customers see the posts as spam and give the audience a chance to respond to the advertisement and give feedback about the current promotion. Utilize these ads when holidays come around and make an advertisement that speaks out above news in the Facebook place. This Facebook marketplace is going to create a level opportunity to see your posts and engage with the shop site that you like to involve in the posts. Ads can also be placed on the Facebook marketplace and this could include single items or bulk items.

This is a not usually the case because there are at times selling restrictions under certain sites but with Facebook ads this allows the company to list any variety of products. The company will be able to list products that can be sold as common goods or rare goods that are even handmade and at a limited source. Take advantage of the market diversity within Facebook because it will create a great opportunity to post and post again even when the product may not have sold the first week. If the product does not sell the first week through a Facebook ad markup the price and make the product bio look spiffier.

When the customers see that ad again, they will have a new take on it and they will dedicate more time to considering visiting the shop site and picking out something that encouraged them to get there. With Facebook ads, it will be easier and easier for the average product supplier to have a global reach for the line in their shop. Global diversity is important so that every market genre can be tapped into and the company can take full advantage of selling their products to everyone around the world never missing a sale.

Google AdWords

With Google AdWords, there is going to be great diversity in search engines to bring plenty of crowds to the consumer website. With Google, AdWords google is going to place ads for the company on several landing servers and it is going to create ad space for all sites that are affected. AdWords is going to display ads for the company that relates to the company's mission or its makeup so that when someone is shopping or researching a site low and behold there will be an ad for the company and its product. This company ad is going to replace any space that may not have had an ad in the first place and this will create brand marketing for anyone who sees this ad.

AdWords control the ads that individuals see when they conduct searches like google searches for a specific product. This search is going to bring up many trending topics and depending on how much money the company decided to spend with AdWords the trending topic could the shop on a seasonal weekend. If the company is just starting AdWords is going to make a great opener for a company that has not built any brand advertisement. Lead a great advertising campaign by setting some money aside and spending it on advertisements every quarter to create a better-defined presence online.

This is going to maximize the reach the company makes on all of the audiences and this is going to ramp up production for any customers that have not seen or purchased from the shop yet. If product awareness can be brought to attention for the viewers all at once there could be a high spike of customers that come in to purchase all at once and this could send the company into a new stratosphere of sales. One of the main consistencies is the crowd flow and the amount of advertisement money spent which could be with Google AdWords.

Dropshipping Conclusion

D ropshipping has been around for nearly two decades, yet it still proves to be a highly effective business model for turning a profit online. These days, if you want to be a dropshipper there is plenty of information out there about how you can get started and what you need to do in order to turn your business into a success. The key for you is to ensure that the information you are reading is relevant and high-quality so that you can find yourself amongst the top earners in this industry.

I hope that through reading Dropshipping for Beginners you were able to identify a strong approach for you to get into dropshipping and earn a profit. By giving you some insight as to what this industry is and a clear strategy for how you can get started and grow your business, I hope that you now feel confident in generating your own success. If you really want to make the most out of this information, you need to be ready to apply it with consistency and confidence every step of the way so that you can generate a huge income through your business.

The next step after reading this book is to research what industries are the most successful for dropshipping and then find yourself a niche that you can build in. After that, you can begin to create your brand and grow your business through developing an online presence for you to reach your customers with.

Make sure that you start small and grow out, as this is the best way to ensure that you test your niche first so that you can validate its profitability. If your results are promising, you can use this information to help you increase your sales and grow your business out even further. As well, don't forget to check out my other titles like Amazon FBA so that you can further grow your knowledge in this industry!

Knowing exactly what you can do to grow your business through strong sales channels is going to help you get your name out there and maximize your success in this industry.

You also need to make sure that you pay close attention to the tips and advice that I have given you, as this information can help you succeed even faster. The information I have provided you with here is intended to help you quickly grow beyond many beginners' mistakes and challenges, whereby you can step into mastering your dropshipping business right from day one. Avoid underestimating this advice, as it truly can help set you apart and guarantee your success in the industry!

Blogging Introduction

Blogging is not a walk in the park, it is a job and can be a rewarding one, but it takes dedication. Please do not enter into the career with expectations of only doing a very light workload for a great living. In truth, it takes many hours of research and writing/rewriting to produce a great blog post that people will read and share. But as well, it is one among the most rewarding ventures out here. Jump in with all you have, dare yourself, and see how much you can pour into a blog and how much great information you can centralize and give to people in a concise manner. It is a system that rewards hard work, dedication, and creative endeavor. But what are some good strategies you can employ from the start to help keep your blog and the information it gives on top of your niche? This will also keep you on the top of the desired sites for advertisers and make sure people think of purchasing your product or service above all others.

You have not just a blog, but a community of peoples, across many platforms that requires your input and direction. I know, "I can't afford help", but you can use websites like Upwork or Fiverr with a multitude of freelancers that work for reasonable prices. Also, you cannot afford to let things fall behind, that will cost far more than the couple hundred dollars per month it takes to hire help. You have to develop a workspace that will churn out work that is needed, but that will not make your audience feel the shift. They have to think it is you answering them and writing your blogs, so to hire carefully is paramount. At the end of the day, the goal is to offer the same great value they come for in your blog in your daily interactions.

Your work and salary now match the many years of creativity and good writing.

As the company expands, a team of creatives and general helpers will go a long way in ensuring you keep your edge in the marketplace. You will have to let go of the "I got this" attitude and learn to delegate; this is true of any business that is successful.

Capitolo 33 Getting Started

T he first thing that comes to mind when blogging is mentioned is the definition of the term blog. Many people have interacted with blogs without knowing what they are. So, there goes the first concern, what is a blog?

There are many ways in which we can look at the word. First of all, the term blog is a shortened version of a weblog. This term is used to describe websites that have ongoing records of information. This term can also be viewed as an electronic diary on the web, which has comments and links to specific articles or websites. The links are, in most cases, presented as a list of entries in reverse sequential order. Blogs can sometimes be personal and focus on a specific subject or line of information. At times blogs can be political, or something of that sort, and delve into a broader scope of information concerning various topics.

Many blogs are mostly focused on a single topic. For instance, there are ones that are solely about web design and development, sports updates and news, or technology and smart devices. Some are more wide-ranging, presenting various links to other websites with a wide range of information. In other cases, you will come across blogs that are mostly designed like personal journals with the owner's (author's) thoughts about life and everything that happens daily around them.

In general, blogs do share some common aspects, although there are some exceptions here and there. Some features that you will come across in almost every blog are:

• Feeds and pop-ups such as RRS or RDF files.

• Blogrolls, which are links that lead readers to other sites with additional information.

• A comment section after every article for readers to share their thoughts about the publications.

- A home page, which the main content area that has articles and publications. New ones are always on top and organized into categories.
- An archive of older publications.

Some blogs come with extra features, while some may not have the features mentioned above at all.

What is a Blogger?

A person who owns the blog and runs or maintains it is called the blogger. He/she is usually the one who posts articles, publications, news updates, cases, reviews, and any other information worth sharing. All the posted information is called blogposts.

Blog Content

Content is the entry on all websites. For instance, a school website will have information about their curriculum, the institution, and all relevant news concerning learning and programs. A news site will have the latest news updates and archives of the previous report. A personal blog will contain opinions, observations, or case studies. A retail website will have a list of products and their prices, etc. The bottom line is, there must be some updates or information on those sites for people to find a reason to visit them.

In the same manner, a blog must have some content; and that comes in the form of articles posted by the author (blog posts or entries). There are some blogs with multiple authors, and some even have an allowance for guest authors to make their contributions. In typical fashion, these authors write their articles in a web-based interface, which is inbuilt in the blogging system. In some cases, authors may write their articles offline and post them later on their blogs. Such a feature is called the stand-alone blog client software.

Comments

For an interactive session on the websites, the blog comes with a feature that allows visitors to leave their comments, tips, and views at the end of every article posted. This feature enables the sharing of ideas and thoughts about the blogpost.

Almost every blog has this feature to enable people to share their opinions about the articles posted. Some blogs also have nifty ways that other authors may use to comment on articles without visiting the blog. These features are called trackbacks or pingbacks, and they ensure that bloggers communicate among themselves easily through their websites.

The Difference Between a Blog and a Content Management System (CMS)

CMS is software that provides a way of managing a website, and a lot of blogging software programs are categorized as types of content management systems (CMS). The CMS offers features that can be used to set up, manage, and maintain a blog. At the same time, they make Internet publications simple, just like writing articles with titles and having them arranged according to their categories and specifications. A primary CMS blogging tool should provide a simple interface that enables authors to write and post their content. At the same time, it takes care of the other logistics, such as making the posts more presentable and readily available to the public. In simple terms, the blogger is given ample time to concentrate on their topics of discussion while the tool helps in the entire management of the site. However, some CMS are very complicated with sophisticated features. An excellent example of such a blogging tool is WordPress that comes with a range of features. The device has an Administration Screen that allows bloggers to set up options that control how their websites behave and present their blog. Through the feature, an author can easily compose an article and publish it online with a simple push of a button. WordPress goes a long way to make sure that blog posts are beautifully presented in the right fonts, and the HTML codes are generated following the standards of the website.

Terms That Bloggers Should Know

In addition to having the necessary knowledge of how blogging software works, bloggers should also understand some terms and concepts related to blogging. Here are some:

Archives

A blog is one way that a person can keep track of significant events and articles. Some blogs come with the archive feature, which is based on calendar dates. For instance, yearly archives. Some have daily files on the front page of the weblog. Archives can also be presented based on specifications and categories of articles on the site. Posts can also be archived based on their authors or in alphabetical order. There are endless possibilities when filing content. A blog becomes a personal tool for publications and presentations of ideas, views, and other relevant information because of the ability to have the content arranged and presented in a systematized fashion.

Feeds

A feed is a special function in a website that allows people visiting the site to access the new content and then post the same content on other websites. It is a way that users can keep track of the latest information posted on the site. Feeds may include RSS, RDF files, or Atom.

Syndication

As stated above, a feed is considered a machine-readable content that is published regularly on a web. Weblogs update their feeds for users to access information all the time. There are tools (feedreaders) that check specified blogs to see if there are new feeds posted or when there are any updates on the sites. If so, the tools display those updates with a link and part of the post (or the entire post). When going through the feeds, the feedreader checks if there are new items that can be downloaded for users to read, which saves them time visiting the blogs they like. All that is there for readers to do is adding links to the RSS feed of blogs that they would like to visit. The feedreader then informs the user when there are any new items posted. These feeds are called syndication feeds.

Managing Comments

As said, comments are one of the most exciting features in a blogging tool. They make the blog interactive and allow users to share their opinion once there is an update on the site. Users can also share links to your post and recommend them using trackbacks and pingbacks.

We are going to discuss how you can manage and moderate comments posted on your blog. On the same line, we will see how you can handle comment spam on your weblog.

Trackbacks

Initially, they were designed and created by Six Apart, the developers of the Movable Type blog package.

In general, trackbacks were created to provide a better way in which there can be notifications within different sites. In simple terms, they are a way in which X can communicate to Y by telling them about something they would like on X's website. In that case, X would send a trackback ping to Y.

Let us take a better look at it using an elaborate example:

• X posts an article on their weblog.

• Y intends to post a comment on X's blog about the article and, at the same time, wants her readers (Y's) to see her opinion and get the chance also to comment, but on her site.

• Y posts her blog and sends a trackback ping to X's weblog.

• X's blog receives the trackback and put it on display as a comment to the initial post. The feedback has a link that leads to Y's post (on Y's site).

The basic idea that brought about by the setup is that more readers are introduced to the post since both followers from X and Y sites are both able to follow the link to the article. The trackback also brings some level of authenticity to the post as it comes from another weblog. However, there are no ways that a person can verify any trackback, and that might pose the risk of fake trackbacks.

In most cases, trackbacks only send a section of the article to X of what Y has to say about the item. This setup acts as a teaser to make X and his readers click the link leading to Y's site and read the full comment.

X can edit the comment of Y in his site, which also compromises the whole idea of authenticity.

Pingbacks

Pingbacks are meant to solve some challenges posed by the trackbacks. And that is the reason for the pingback documentation: to act as a description of a trackback. Let us take a look at an elaborate example: A write an article on her blog. B reads the article and comments on it while creating a link to the initial report. By the use of pingbacks, the software of B will automatically notify A that there is a link created to her original post. The software of A, from her side, then includes the information on A's site. This feature will only work if both A and B have pingbacked enabled blogs.

The best way of looking at it is by thinking of a pingback as a remote comment, which is generally displayed on a person's blog as a link from another person's post. There is a general misconception that unlike trackbacks, they do not send content to the initial article. But that is not true because when a pingback pops, there is always an excerpt from the other blog displayed on the comment section on the original post owner's dashboard. However, there are very few themes that show such parts of the post from the pingback. For instance, if using WordPress, the default theme will not display any excerpts.

There is only one feature that differentiates pingbacks from trackbacks, and that is the technology that both uses. Pingbacks use XML-RPC while trackbacks use HTTP POST. The difference is, however, useful in the sense that pingbacks cannot be targeted by spam since it has an automatic verification process. To some people, trackbacks remain the better of the two because readers of X can take a look at what Y has to say about the post and may decide if they want to read more by clicking on the link. And some may think about the verification connection between the two blogs as the feature that makes pingbacks the superior one of the two.

Using Trackbacks and Pingbacks

Comments posted on the comment section of a blog has often been criticized as lacking authority and moral standards since there is no way that they can be verified and regulated. In that sense, people get to say anything and use any language in giving their opinion about the post and may even go overboard to some irrelevant issues. That is where pingbacks and trackbacks in the equation to offer some way of verifying the blog comments.

Select the two options since selecting one may not go well with the other one. Once you have both of them enabled in your blog, all trackbacks and pingbacks from other sites will appear in the administration screen the same way other comments appear on your posts. In the case of blog pages, the two will appear depending on the theme design of your weblog.

Anytime you publish a post, a pingback will be sent automatically without any further actions (as long as they are enabled). But in the case of trackbacks, you will have to find the trackback URL in the post that you want to link to. If you are not able to find any URL, then the site you are trying to connect to may not be supporting trackbacks. But if the site does support the feature, then you will have to copy and paste the URL into the field that allows you to send trackbacks (it is usually found on the "Add New Post" screen). If the field is not available, then you can go to the screen option and select the "Send Trackback" option. It is worth noting that selecting the send trackback option does not automatically send a trackback. It only brings you the send trackback field. Every time you post something new, the trackback is sent to the URL you have pasted in that field. O your Edit Post screen, the field will display for you the statuses of you pingbacks and trackbacks.

Moderating Comments on the Blog

Comment moderation is a feature that allows bloggers to monitor and regulate the comments posted on their articles. The same can also help in dealing with the issue of spam comments. In other words, it helps in the general regulation of the comments. For instance, you can delete some comments that are offensive and sensitive; you can approve good comments and let them appear in the comment section, and make any other decision you deem fit concerning people's comments on your blog posts.

Comment Spam

The term is used to describe comments that are deemed useless and irrelevant. The feedback may also include pingbacks and trackbacks to the blog post. These spams are always not related to the article posted and may go out of context and sometimes do not reflect the value of the post. They can have links to other websites that do not relate to the blogposts.

Spammers are always notorious in using comment spams to get higher page ranks for their websites and domains in Google to sell the domain names at better prices or to have a more top search ranking. Due to the large amount of money that is involved, they become relentless and may go as far as building automated tools to submit the spam comments rapidly to numerous blogs and websites. And for a beginner in blogging, this issue may be overwhelming.

WordPress has a solution to the nuisance created by spammers. They have generated many tools that are aimed at combating comment spams and ensure that bloggers can manage them effectively.

Capitolo 34 How to Create A Blog?

After you've determined your niche, and you've managed to narrow down the kind of content you'd like to create, it's time to move to the next step. This step is the peak of it all, because this is where you will create a blog. There's a lot required in order to successfully execute this step, and we've managed to break it down into several sections that will help you understand everything you need to know.

Choose the Right Platform

This section will give you the pros and cons in using a certain platform. This will also help you to choose what is the most ideal platform for you to use in creating your blog.

Blogging Platforms

1. WordPress.com

There's a reason why the ".com" was included. When you Google the word "WordPress", you'll find WordPress.com and WordPress.org. Is there a difference between the two of them? The answer for this is Yes. Wordpress.org is a software platform that allows you to build a blog or website on your own. While it offers bloggers the opportunity to have total autonomy over their blog creation process, it is not advisable for first-time bloggers. That is why WordPress.com exists. It's a blog hosting service that offers elementary blog hosting service for free. It also offers additional options like a custom domain name, extra storage, and access to different theme designs – but most of these features can only be accessed through WordPress' premium plans.

If you're starting out as a blogger, it's advisable that you start with a free plan, understand how it works, and then later consider opting for a premium plan. The platform has differently priced plans with features that can cater to the needs of personal bloggers, small businesses, and enterprises. This platform comes highly recommended because of its reliability and affordability.

However, there are several benefits in using .org over .com. The paid platform allows you to have full control over your website, while the free one only allows you to use the free themes. WordPress also has 54,000 free plugins which you can use to make your blog stand out from the crowd. It is even search engine friendly which you can use to create categories and tags for your blog entries. For the domain name, it is around $14.99/year and $7.99/month for the hosting.

2. Wax

Wax is another popular platform that you have probably heard of. It's a hosted platform that is used to build custom websites. One of the reasons why it is a popular option is because of the easy ways it provides users to create a website. Wax offers drag-and-drop options to make the creation process straightforward and user-friendly.

A great benefit is that you have many templates and third-party apps to use when customizing your site. The free account, however, is very limited and a lot of Wax branding and ads appear on your site. The platform also offers you an opportunity to add a custom domain – for a fee of $8.50/month which can go up to $24.50/month.

There are premium plans that you can choose from as well when creating your blog.

Also, one good thing about Wax is that no coding skills are needed since it is quick and easy to use, which is really an advantage for beginners. However, one disadvantage of using Wax is not being able to change the template one you have chosen it.

3. Blogger

Blogger is a free platform that was acquired by Google in 2003. The point of this platform was to offer non-technical users, who were relatively clueless about setting up a blog on their own, an opportunity to blog freely and easily.

These were the major advantages of this platform such as: only Google Account is needed in order to start a blog and in addition to the fact that it could rely on Google's secure platform and reliability as well.

The disadvantage with this platform, however, is the many limitations it comes with – basic blogging tools, limited design features, and no option to receive frequent updates or new features. Third party templates for this website are often low quality, which is not advisable. Google can also cancel your blog anytime, especially when they have detected that your projects have been abandoned, without a warning. If you want to try creating a blog without a hassle, you may use this website and switch to another one when your blog grows.

4. Tumblr

Tumblr is another popular option that has a significant difference from other typical blogging platforms. People actually refer to Tumblr as a "microblogging platform" because of its social networking features – e.g. relogging, sharing tools, etc.

Tumblr is free and extremely easy to use. Its social aspect also makes it a lot more enjoyable for users who are looking for an interactive experience. The plus side of Tumblr being a microblogging platform is that users can easily blog interactive media like videos, GIFs, and audios. However, the disadvantage of this platform is that Tumblr has a limited set of features that cannot be altered if your blog grows. You also have to purchase a domain separately and link it yourself. You may also face difficulty in importing your blogs to other platforms and backing up all your blogs.

Medium

Medium is relatively new to the scene in comparison to the other platforms. This platform is easy to use and requires no setup or coding schools. It works like social networking sites where you sign up, enter your interests, and you can start blogging immediately. A major advantage that comes with Medium is that you don't have to worry about design – every Medium blog appears the same way. This is to help users focus on reading and writing the content available. You also become exposed to an online community that already has the same interests as you. No coding skills are needed for this blog site since it is also easy to use like the other platforms. You may focus particularly on your writing since you won't have problems in designing it yourself.

The major downside with this platform, however, is that you can't run your own ads to make money and Medium also owns your audience. So, if you lose your blog, you'll lose all the followers you attain. In terms of designs or building a brand, Medium has very limited features. You cannot even have your own domain name for your blog since it runs like a social networking site, you can only get a link of Medium with your name at the end of the link.

Hosts & Domains

Before we proceed in discussing about hosts & domains, we must first look at the of platforms, hosts & domains. Platforms, as you can observe from the early discussions, are pre-made websites which you can use to create your own blog, but it doesn't mean that it is yours. Platforms are like a trampoline in the blogging world so you can produce your blog for a limited amount of money or even for free. Hosts, on the other hand, serve to maintain files for one or more websites. It works like a storage facility that allows you to store things and letting other people see it freely. Meanwhile, domain allows you to have your own identity online. If you decide to change your webhost, you can do so since you have a domain name for a certain period of time, depending on your registration.

Most major blog service providers have a feature that allows you to host your blog and secure a domain through them; but some people prefer to use an alternative web hosting service to get their domain.

There are a series of web hosting sites you can choose from. They all come with the option for you to purchase a domain and other features. Each platform has a different pricing plan, various features, etc. There are dozens of web hosting services to choose from and that can become very overwhelming for you.

When you try to Google web hosting services/providers, your results page will be filled with a varying number of ads and review posts –

that are often sponsored. To make the search process far easier for you, we've listed (in no particular order) the top three providers you can rely on:

• GoDaddy – This is both domain registrar, and at the same time, a website hosting company. It's a two in one provider which allows you to build a website and put it on the internet all in one place. As of now, GoDaddy has 18.5 million customers worldwide. The price for using GoDaddy depends on the plan that you are going to get. It may range from free-$300 per year. The price may also be influenced by the number and type of themes, the bandwidth, diskspace, search engines and mobile devices packages that you are going to get.

• Bluehost – Like GoDaddy, Bluehost is also a web hosting company that also offers domains hosting. Today, the company offers 4 hosting subscription which you can choose from ranging from $2.95 to $13.95 per month on the initial 12-month contract. However, the subscription increases from $7.99 to $25.99 per month after the expiration of the initial contract. The four-subscription plan gives you one free domain for a year, which is a good deal. The features depend on what plan you are going to choose. The higher the plan, the more features and benefits you can have.

• HostGator – Among the three famous hosts & domains, HostGator offers the lowest cost for plans. In fact, HostGator offers $2.75/month in the initial contract, and increases to $6.95/month after renewal. You must pay $12.95/year to have your own domain.

Customize the Blog Design

When it comes to your blog, appearance is everything. Yes, the content you produce needs to be great quality, but so does your blog's design. When users come across your blog, the first thing they are going to pay attention to is how it looks. If your blog appears to be basic, with no form of aesthetics whatsoever, you'll lose up to 75% of potential viewers and subscribers.

You don't need to channel a lot of money into making your blog look good. Most top blogging platforms offer free themes and tools that will help you create a blog you would be proud of. Before launching your blog, you need to put a significant amount of planning into the process. The last thing you want is to reduce the value of the content you produce, with an unattractive blog. In order to know first how to customize your blog, we must differentiate those good and bad blogs. Examples of good blogs that you can visit and look into are:

- Evernote
- Wister
- First Round Review
- Mos.

If you look closely on one thing that they do have in common, these blogs are simply designed! Despite being famous blogs with thousands of readers, these blogs chose to remain simple. As you also read through the posts of each blogs, you can also observe how the contents are well organized in a manner that you can understand well what the topic is all about. You may also notice how the blogs use simple fonts and colors to highlight the contents in their blogs. We will get through with that later on.

Choose the Right Font and Font Color

An example of simple customization of your blog is choosing the right font and font color. Choose a font that is simple and is easy to read. Avoid choosing cursive fonts that would make your content harder to read. Font color is also important in creating your blog. Some people use bright colors, which makes it hard to read. Always remember to consider your audience in creating your blog. You may want to show your design first to your friends and get their opinions before publishing it. This may limit the bad reviews you'll receive from your audience.

Do Not Mislead Your Readers

One common mistake that bloggers do is that they do the click-bait style rather than being honest with the content that they create. Don't get me wrong, there's nothing wrong with creating an attention seeking title. But the problem here is that, some people uses a different title to the blog content that they actually have. This actually doesn't work in the blogging industry. Focus on what your content is all about.

Avoid jumping into different topics into a single blog content in order not to confuse your readers on the topic that you are discussing.

Create A Content Skeleton

The key to providing a good blog is actually not only in the design but also in the content. It is important to think carefully about how you will write it in order to gain the attention of your audience.

You may follow this structure in order to organize the content for your blog:

1.   Title
2.   Subtitle (optional)
3.   Brief Description
4.   Introduction
5.   Body Content
6.   Conclusion

You must also remember not to make the blog content too long. This is because some readers get lazy to read long blog contents.

Limit Ads

It is also more practical not to have ads when you are still a beginner. Monetizing is more advisable when you already have a large audience for your blog. You must also remember to place the ads on the place where it doesn't annoy your readers. Going easy on ads doesn't mean that you'll have less income, but rather a strategy to attract viewers. You may increase your ads later on when you've already stabilized your blog website.

You may also use bulleted lists when creating blog content. Remember that some viewers may just have stumbled on to your blog accidentally. Some of them may just be wandering around the internet and looking for some good reads. Summarizing your blog content in a good way can attract the eye of the viewers which can make them read the whole content.

Capitolo 35 Investing in Your Self

Blogging is like creating a present and giving it to someone, whether you know them or not. Of course, you want to make it as presentable as it can be in order to make them happy. One problem in creating a blog from scratch is how you will step by step organize all your ideas into one. You must also have the need to begin with the end in mind as mentioned by Stephen Covey. This means that your main goal is to generate money and before you can do that, you must first do the basics. Making money as your goal would help you package your blog successfully.

What do you want to write about?

The first step is knowing what you want to write about. The best topics to blog about are topics that interest you; topics that you have sufficient knowledge in. Writing on issues that you are knowledgeable on will make your content more authentic, and it also makes planning your content a lot easier. It's also important that you actually understand the topic. If you create your blog posts based on copy- paste information you found on the internet, the audience will lose their interest in reading. Viewers always know when someone doesn't truly understand the blog topics they're discussing – and you do not want that.

So, think about the topics that come best to mind and note them all down. By the end of the chapter, you'll take a look at all the potential topics you can use for your blog, and you will narrow them down.

Knowing the topics, you are good at will help you have ideas on what you want to write about. Finding the right content to write about will become a lot easier when you have specific details to work with. You'll find these in your niche, which will be further discussed. The niches are the most lucrative for those looking to monetize their blogs. You do need to keep in mind, though, that most profitable niches are very competitive. So, you need to pay extra attention to developing a strategy that works.

Find Your Niche

One term you're going to hear of often is the word "niche". "Niche" is a common buzzword in the online industry; the sooner you understand what it's about, the better. The word refers to a particular area or space you want to focus your blog on. Within that particular space, you will find an audience that is interested in the same things you'd like to blog about. In this current Digital Age, it is important that you find a niche of your own. With millions of bloggers trying to carve out the same kinds of space that you are trying to form for yourself, it's important that you stay away from trying to be generic. This will help you develop content that viewers will find useful, valuable, and/or relatable.

Finding a niche isn't an easy task, though – especially if you are a first-time blogger. You most probably have a series of ideas that you would like to share, and you aren't sure where or how to start. This is what leads most aspiring bloggers to ask, "What kind of blog should I start?" To help you with your dilemma in finding your niche, here's a list of the 5 most profitable niches that can help you in thinking about your blog topic.

Lifestyle

A lifestyle blog is a visual representation of the author's everyday life, interests and activities. The blog will be very personalized – since the content comes from your thoughts and your actions. You will typically find quotes the author will relate to or find inspiring; pictures of areas they visited; pictures of their homes and workplaces; and reflections on the activities that went through their day. Lifestyle blogs are often created to inspire people on ways of living.

The lifestyle blogger's goal is to be seen as a go-to person when a user is trying to make decisions regarding their daily lives.

Travel

A travel blog online is often dedicated to showcasing the different destinations, across the globe which the author of the blog visits. A travel blog is more effective when pictures are used. This is why most travel blogs found online consists of various pictures of the author's adventures. A travel blog can also be used to inform the audience on efficient ways to travel to certain destinations.

The blog doesn't have to be based on international destinations. One could start a travel blog that depicts their locality. The blog could be dedicated to giving viewers from different parts of the world an inside look into what the author's town, city, or country looks like. It will inspire the audience to consider visiting that place – which should be the goal of the blog in the first place.

The blog could be dedicated to showcasing the sights and scenery of one location in particular. For example, one could set up a blog dedicated to showcasing the sights in Switzerland, in which the blogger would upload high quality images of the scenes they came across as they traveled across Switzerland.

The purpose of the travel niche is to encourage the audience to travel to the destinations the blog covers. It can also be used to help the audience in their travels. Some blogs cover topics about trip expenses, how to travel on a budget, and other tips in traveling.

Fashion

According to a study in 2010, 50.9% of blog readers online are women. Thus, blogs about fashion have boomed as time goes by. Fashion is a major niche with diverse expressions. It is a type of blog that can showcase clothing and accessories from different type of brands. A fashion blog could be dedicated to displaying the latest fashion trends.

A fashion blog could take a personal approach as well. There's a significant number of online users who utilize their blogs for exhibiting their fashion choices. With every photo they upload, this includes the details of the clothing and accessories they are wearing – promoting the brands that they are wearing. Fashion bloggers with large followers often end up becoming ambassadors for popular clothing labels, which is also a good way to generate money.

Some fashion blogs are dedicated to showcasing clothing, accessories and trends from one particular brand. Designer labels like Christian Louboutin, Chanel, and Louis Vuitton have blogs where they promote their latest releases and their most popular products.

For someone who is thinking of using this niche as their foundation in blogging, it would be advisable to start as a fashion blogger or as someone who is promoting clothing that they have been designing and selling before they started blogging.

Health & Beauty

Topics about health and beauty became one of the most major niches in the online community. In fact, 53.3% of blog readers are 21-35 years old. People in this age group are more health conscious than other age groups. Thus, creating blogs about this niche has a large chance to create a larger audience. There are different spaces to explore in this field, especially because the health & beauty niche has a wide range of topics to talk about.

There are commercial beauty blogs that are dedicated to advertising beauty products from one particular brand or from several brands. This type of blog includes the experiences of bloggers in using the product itself.

Blogs about make-up are also a good topic to talk about, especially because a lot of brands are in the market today. Make-up artists use their blogs to showcase their skills by posting the work they have done on clients. Some make-up artists use themselves as models, applying their skills on their own faces. Others use this as a way to promote cosmetic products as ambassadors for a particular brand.

Skincare practitioners also make use of the platform to promote their products and offer advice on skincare. There are also blogs that contain tips on how to use organic products for their skin.

Blogs about health are really relevant nowadays. As mentioned earlier, people are health conscious and using this as an opportunity to create a blog is really an advantage.

Especially if you are a medical practitioner who wants to start your blog, you might want to share your knowledge about health by giving tips to readers on living a healthy lifestyle. Health topics are wide too. Using this as one of your niches may allow you to create various content for your blog since it has a wide range of topics. Just make sure that you are knowledgeable in this niche in order not to mislead the readers.

Food

Food blogs are popular with Web users – since everybody loves a picture of good food. You must remember that pictures play an important role in this niche. In order to attract readers, you must first catch their eye by convincing them about the taste of the food, whether it is good or bad.

On the other hand, restaurants have resorted to use blogs as a platform to exhibit their best creations. This is with the hope that it will attract more customers. Some individuals use food blogs to exhibit their culinary skills. Such blogs are usually created with the intent to find clients, employment or to build their brand as a personal chef. Some just want to share their experiences and give tips to readers about what to eat at a certain restaurant, or where is the best place to eat on this particular place.

These are only few of the many niches you can find online. There are other niches like Sports, News, Entertainment, Business & Economics, etc. which you can also consider when thinking about the topic for your blog. It is also necessary to focus on one niche in order to make your viewers know what you really want to talk about on your blog.

Find an Inspiration

Finding an inspiration is also helpful when you don't know what to consider in creating a blog. You may find successful bloggers online and try to study how they package their blogs. Finding an inspiration doesn't mean that you will copy these famous bloggers, but you must remember to still create your own style in order to attract an audience. If readers notice that you are just copying someone's style, you may get into trouble in the future. Find a blogger that is successful in the niche that you have chosen and use this as an opportunity to develop your own style of blogging.

It is also important to remember that finding an inspiration doesn't necessarily focus on looking at other bloggers, but also looking at the niche as a whole. To elaborate this, you may read the latest updates about the niche you want to work with. Thus, this will give you an idea on what is the trending topic that people are interested in right now.

Choose the Blog Name

The blog name plays an important role in your success. Choosing the wrong blog name, in fact, can create a tremendous effect later on. Bloggers sometimes think of random names without further considering the topics that they will publish under it. This is why choosing the right blog name is important. You may use these several tips when creating a blog name.

1.   It Should Not Be Long

Long blog names are hard to remember. Blog names should have a recall to the audience in order for them to remember you for a long time. Keep in mind that your main goal is to generate an income, and you can get this when you have a large audience for your blog. When viewers don't remember your name, they might have difficulty finding you in the internet.

2.   Don't Be Too Specific

Being too specific in your blog name might also affect the stories you want to publish. For example, if you named your blog "Travel in America", and decided to move to France after two years, your blog won't publish the right posts for your blog name, which can confuse the readers.

3.   Make it Catchy

Catchy doesn't mean that you are going to use numbers or special characters just to get attention. Being catchy means being cool and creating unique name that will make a recall for your audience.

4.   Ask Your Friends or Family

Sometimes, the best ideas are from the closest people in your life. They might give you an idea of a blog name that you are not aware of. You may also share your ideas to them and take note of their opinions about it. It might be useful in the future. Remember, more brains are better than one.

5.   Use an Online Name Generator

If you think that the first four tips are not working, you may consider using a name generator or the dictionary itself. A name generator can help you to come up with the right name for your blog.

Create Your Own Blog Calendar

One basic step in creating a blog is knowing how to organize it at first. You cannot just create a blog randomly for an unknown reason, but you have to think ahead of it. Remember that you are creating your blog package and we want you to make money from it. The benefit of creating your blog calendar is to make you consistent in blog posting. This will help you to organize your thoughts and schedule when creating an entry for your blog. You may input how many blog posts you want to create in a month and how many days you are planning to write them. You may also include the topic you want to write about for that certain month.

Creating a blog calendar is a very useful for a blog beginner. You may create simple calendar depending on how you would want it to look like. Here is an example of a blog calendar.

Capitolo 36 Creating and Cultivating A Blog Community

earch Engine Optimization (SEO)
What is SEO?
SEO stands for Search Engine Optimization.
When people search for a certain word or phrases relevant to the content on your site, it can ensure your website ranks on a search engine's results page (SERP), like Google.

Traffic Generation Tips

Here are six search engine optimization tips to improve your ranking.

Do your keywords research.

Keyword research is essential for on-page optimization. There are a variety of tools for finding related keywords relevant to your post that you may not have noticed.

Utilize keywords throughout your article. Once you finalize the valuable, relevant keywords, it is essential to place them where they will have the most impact for readers and search engine crawlers indexing your blogging.

Try to include the keywords in the following places of your posts:

* Title
* Headings and subheadings
* Introduction
* Paragraphs
* Anchor text (that is the text you hyperlink to other related pages on your site)
* Meta descriptions & Title tags

Optimize all your images. When you upload a photo to your blog, be sure to include keywords in the file name, and fill out the alternate text, keyword-rich description of the images.

Recommend other bloggers/pages with links. When you mention some content or article in your blogging, you can include a link for your referencing information. Not only is it a proper blogging etiquette, but you may also get lucky and receive a link back. Quality links are valuable for site ranking on Google search engine pages.

Allow readers to subscribe to your blogging. Include prominently placed RSS or Feed Subscription Buttons and offer viewers the ability to subscribe to your posts via email. This allows your followers to have instant notification of your latest posts without having to check your site for new content periodically.

Use social media to reach more audiences. To get more online exposure, you may be utilizing Twitter, Facebook, Google+, or other social media networks to create connections with potential and current customers. Free programs like Hootsuite make it easy to post links to your latest blog post on all of your social media sites with just a couple of clicks. You can even schedule your posts ahead of time!

Google Advertising

Question 1: What Are Google Ads (AdWords)?

Google offers paid advertisements that appear in search results on google.com.

Question 2 Which is the benefit of advertising with Google Ads?

The main benefit of advertising with Google is that you can choose how much you spend, the audience you want to target, and you only pay when someone clicks the ads. It can work faster than search engine optimization, access to comprehensive analytics, and reach more customers.

Question 3: Google Advertising Cost

The cost of Google advertising varies based on many factors, including the competitiveness of your keywords, the industry, your geographic location, the quality of the marketing campaigns, and so on.

The average cost for Google search advertising is $2.30 in the United States. In other countries, the average prices for Google ads are often much lower.

Question 4: How to set up Google AdWords Account

There are eight steps to set up an account and create an ad on Google.

Step 1: Sign Up. Simply go to the Google AdWords website and sign up with your Google account.

Step 2: Set Your Budget.

Step 3: Select Your Target Audience.

Step 4: Choose A Network.

Step 5: Choose Your Keywords.

Step 6: Set Your Bid.

Step 7: Write Your Ad.

Step 8: Create your Ad.

Question 5: What's the difference between Google AdWords and Search Engine Optimization (SEO)?

SEO is a longer-term marketing tool, and it contains different factors of your website and online presence. Ultimately bring you more organic search and referral traffic. SEO is free and organic traffic. You need to pay your time and effort working on it.

SEO should always be an essential digital marketing method during the whole process. While Google AdWords is a quick way of bringing in targeted traffic to your website. It is straightforward to set up, and a far faster way to generate traffic than SEO.

Both SEO and Google AdWords are essential. SEO will help improve the quality of your AdWords campaigns. It is crucial to understand that running paid advertising with Google will not make any difference to your organic search rankings. However, it may improve the clickthrough rate of your organic listings.

Question 6: Is Google AdWords Only Search Adverts?

No. Google AdWords is an advertising platform that you can make advertising with different networks and campaign types. It includes the Search ads, Display ads (banners you see on websites), YouTube (banners and video), and Gmail ads, etc.

Google AdWords has many different ad formats from text display ads through to static banners, animated banners, videos, and lightboxes.

Question 7: How much do I need to spend on Google Ads?

It's up to you how much you want to spend, and you will only pay when people click on your advertisement, and the more money you invest, the longer your ads will display. With the right strategy, you can earn big money from it.

People recommend you would need to spend at least $1,500 a month, and you will need a few months to get real results from their campaign.

Question 8: How do I rank on the top of Google Ads?

The Ads position depends on various elements, and you can't buy it directly to the top. We suggest you analyze the keywords you use. High-quality ads and great landing pages are crucial to Google Ads' success. Landing Page is a webpage to attract people to click to get your marketing goal.

5 Tips for creating an effective Landing Page:

- Get an eye-catching headline
- High-quality image & Design
- Make value
- Social proof
- Call to Action

Question 9: How to pay for Google Ads?

Google makes this one super easy. You can choose a payment method that's available to you. To make one, follow these steps: sign in to your Google Ads account. Click "the gear" or "the tools"-- "Billing & payments" --"Make a payment."

You can choose from one payment method already associated with your account, or you can add a new payment method. Accepted payment methods include bank accounts, credit cards, and debit cards.

Question 10: Where is the Google keywords tool?

You're going to be using the Google Ads keyword planner tool A LOT, so bookmark it now. You will need to sign in as you would your Google Ads account, so Google can take a look at the information you've already provided in your ads and campaigns.

4.3 Social Media Marketing

Social media marketing is the form of using social media platforms and websites to sell or promote products or services. Social media marketing includes the management of different marketing campaigns, setting the scope, and the establishment of a website desired social media "culture" and "tone."

There are seven benefits of social media marketing:

- Instant Communication

Customers can reach customer service support and more accessible on social media platforms.

Businesses can receive, review, and respond to customers' grievances faster and easier.

It's faster than before to get in contact with the right people without picking up a phone, and they can use social media platforms to keep in touch with the people that matter most to their business.

- Increase Website Traffic and Improve the Ranking on Search Engine

Social media can reach different audiences in a pleasant, useful, quick, and entertaining way. Also, it may refer to a lot of potential customers to get to know and try your products or services.

This works well if you get everything done correctly. Social media can create massive sharing, and all the sharing gets more visibility for your content, which links to your blog. It will be a great benefit in getting a high ranking on search engines. Meanwhile, it will surely help your brand get more exposure.

- Brand Building

It's important to stress the brand as one of the most valuable capabilities of different social media platforms. You may not see a higher conversion rate via social media platforms as you do on other marketing platforms, such as Google Ads, SEO, etc.). But your social reputation and impressions can be built through social media networks.

During a business's branding journey on social media, you may talk about what's essential to the brand and its customers. Tell your brand's story; build the royal audience for your brand.

Share your passion and let your audience understand and support your brand.

You can share your brand culture, unique and personality, stand out among your competitors, and attract new customers and further improve your business even more.

- Competitor Research

Social media is an excellent method to keep an eye on their competitors. Social media can help you research your major and competitors. You can use identity who are your competitors and which platforms they are on. You can see how your competitors are interacting with their audience, the type of content they post, the frequency of their posts, and much more critical competitors' analysis information.

- Reducing Cost

Social media platforms are one of the most cost-effective ways to do marketing. First, signing up and creating your profile is free on the majority of the social networking networks. Besides, the paid promotions on social media are affordable when compared to other marketing methods. And you can get a higher return on investment (ROI).

As a startup, you may have limited marketing budgets. Social media network gives you both organic and affordable ways of reducing the advertising budgets. Using the right strategies, you will do marketing on social media and grow your business without spending a lot of money. But social media is time-consuming, it is an increasingly important part of a company, as people spend more time socializing on social media, and they prefer to purchase via social media. Your social media will be a gold mine for your business.

- Generate leads

For example, you can use content to get leads, and it can draw a lot of attention. It's an excellent way to gather emails.

- Learn more about your customers

Social media generates a massive amount of data about your customers in real-time. You can use that information to optimize your business. All of the major social networks offer marketing data analytics. Or you can use social media analytics tools to gather data from your accounts and campaigns. It can provide demographic information about the people interacting with your account, the page views, posts, age range, followers, impressions, profile visits, etc.

This can help you to track and improve your marketing strategy and maximize your return on investment.

What are the leading platforms for social media marketing?

In this chapter, we will talk about the features of different social media networks, such as Facebook, Twitter, Pinterest, Instagram, and LinkedIn.

Facebook

It's one of the most popular marketing platforms to reach your audience.

It's founded in 2004 by Mark Zuckerberg.

Facebook Demographics:

The monthly active users of Facebook are 2.45 billion at the end of 2019.

The average Facebook user has 155 friends.

84% of users are among 30-49-year-old.

Around 69% of users are US adults.

The number of active mobile users is 2.26 billion.

43% of users are female, 57% male.

The users created their personal profile on Facebook, and we can target based on their details, such as demographics, job title, the age of a user's kids, their location, the hobbies, their activities, etc.

Which businesses should be on Facebook?

We recommend all small businesses should be on Facebook, no matter what category your business is in.

Tips for Facebook marketing:

* Know and communicate with your audience

It will be challenging to engage your customers on Facebook. You can use some ways to improve efficiency. First, you can use Facebook Massager to connect with visitors. They receive a popup from Facebook chatbot to start a conversation. This can broaden your audience, get more leads. Second, add value to the conversion your customers talked about, no matter trends, news, or topics under discussion. Third, set up live streams for your customers and create engaging content or questions to reach more users.

* Share high-quality content

Post the organic content on Facebook, don't share the same materials that you shared on Twitter or other social networks, and continuously post the creative content that interests your customers. Make sure to add a call-to-action in your post.

* Join the right groups

Facebook groups bring together people with a common interest. Select and join the right groups which match your target audience. It will have multiple chances to increase your brand awareness and your audience.

After joining the group, you can answer the questions that demonstrate your expertise and professional skills. People need solutions to their problems. Then share useful blogs, or you can post some FAQs for your potential customers.

* Optimize your performance

Check your Facebook ads "likes" and "shares," then optimize it, identity the right campaign goals, always A/B test your ideas, optimize the ad placement, create eye-catching visuals.

* Post videos to attract more viewers

The Facebook video includes two types: live stream video and recorded video. Both of them are very effective ways to grow your audience. Try to keep your video short and sparky, add value to them, choose a compelling thumbnail, and post videos timely.

Twitter

Twitter was founded in 2006 in the US. It's a global platform for public self-expression and conversation in real-time. It provides an international network that connects users to people, ideas, opinions, and news, and the services include live commentary, live connections, and instant conversations.

Demographics:

The total number of monthly active users: 330 million.

34% of Twitter users are females, and 66% are males.

22% of US adults use Twitter.

80% of Twitter users are affluent millennials.

The top three users' countries outside the US are Japan (35.65 million users), Russia (13.9 million), and the UK (13.7 million).

Marketing Tips for Twitter:

* Create an amazing profile

Your profile will show the first impression to other people. Use your business name and images on your Twitter account.

For your bio, you can describe your business, includes your location, link to your website, business type, etc. Make it accurate and exciting. View your profile as a business card and access yourself. Use keywords and show confidence.

* Implement hashtags

Hashtags are used to index words or expressions, with a pound sign # in front of it. When people click on a hashtag, Twitter will automatically search for other Twitter account. So, it would be easy and quick for users to get topics or events.

Before you twitter, check the hashtag first, search it to see if there are any search results, and focus on your brand and keywords.

Keep it short and easy to remember. Meanwhile, promote the hashtag with other channels. You will get maximum exposure for your brand and business.

* Tweet mind-blowing contents

Write a great headline before you tweet it. For example, problem and fears, fact, truth, how to, best and worst, etc.

Capitolo 37 The Most Effective Method to Make Content Creation Plans or Strategies

To assemble and keep up a fruitful blog, you have to have a settled content plan. It ought to incorporate every one of the subtleties identified with future blog posts, distributing ideas, audience improvement, and considerably more.

Without this stable arrangement, it is challenging to keep up the ubiquity and true nature of your work. Underneath, we'll show you precise advances you can take to arrange your blog content. Utilize this model as a layout and alter it as indicated by your needs and capacities. A decent blog content system should address three questions:

- Why would we say we are making content in any case?
- What content do we need?
- How do we get that content to achieve our objectives?

We should begin with why.

Characterize your objectives. Having a characterized objective will set you up to push through the various advances, every one of the long periods of composing, and every one of the hindrances bound to appear.

Your objective is your why, and the more grounded it is, the more achievement you'll have. You'll be sure whether you are benefiting from blogging if you haven't set objectives for your blog. Is your goal to profit? Find another line of work? Discover individuals to interface with about a specific subject? Characterize your blogging objectives and intermittently inquire as to whether your blog is helping you meet them. If not, ask yourself how you can improve your blog to achieve the goals. How would you characterize your blog objective? These inquiries are essential to describing or finding the purposes of your blog. Would you like to:

- drive pedestrian activity to your shop or office?

- increase deals or produce leads?
- educate possibilities and clients on what you do?
- update your clients on what's new with your business?
- attract possibilities from outside of your neighborhood, as customers from abroad?
- build a brand?

Pick close to a few of these targets for your blog content methodology. Any more and your blog will become unfocused and won't prevail at anything. Be explicit about your objectives. Just saying, "get more traffic" isn't sufficient. You have to incorporate how a lot of traffic you need and in what period. A superior objective would be "Increment deals by 15% in a quarter of a year". Unmistakable.

When you have your reason, it's an ideal opportunity to make sense of what sort of content you need. Play out some objective statistical surveying. A minimal quantity of exertion can make something go from moderate to hot. You've heard this previously – it's known as the extra mile. This step is that little centimeter change that will take your blog from unremarkable to extraordinary.

All in all, how would you do target statistical surveying? Ask yourself a couple of reasonable inquiries:

- Where does my audience hang out online? (Certain blogs, online networking stages, gatherings, Facebook gatherings, and so on.)
- What is their most significant problem at work? (Perhaps they despise their drive or their chief, or they're exhausted, or they aren't getting enough traffic to their website.)
- What kind of content or articles do they most appreciate perusing? (Take a gander at your Google examination for your blog, if you have it. Which posts did the best? You can likewise utilize Bozzuto to perceive what your rival's most mutual articles are.)

Pretty much every organization thinks about their client's socioeconomics (for example, what their identity is). In any case, they know besides nothing about their psychographics (for instance, why they purchase). Compelling blog posts pursue the old Problem Agitate Solution (PAS) copywriting guideline. They start by presenting the root issue audiences are confronting. At that point, they foment those issues by diving into the manifestations and torment focuses. At last, they offer an answer (regardless of whether that is a thought, tip, hack, or just situating their item/administration as the arrangement).

In any case, you can't do that viably without getting (1) what your audiences are attempting to accomplish, (2) what's keeping them from doing it, and (3) what will transpire if they don't achieve it. Find the responses to those three inquiries (utilizing overviews, interviews, and so on.), and you'll have the option to make blog content that does one serious parcel something other than rack up social offers.

There you have it – the mystery is to discover the hidden inspirations of your objective audiences, at that point helping them accomplish those objectives.

When you have a thought of who you're composing for, next up is:

Make the rundown of themes, ideas, and watchwords to target. By this point, you comprehend what your blog will be about, and you picked a niche. Making a rundown of spots may seem like a confounded procedure, yet in all actuality, it's most certainly not.

The simplest method to construct that rundown is to the thought of various focuses for your niche and blend them up. By utilizing this methodology and embracing different mixes, you can, without much of a stretch, make many points.

Subsequent stage, you can begin posting things that would be longer, inside, and out bits of content. Additionally, called foundation content (we will discuss it in the following stage).

Watchwords are the bread and butter to a robust blog content procedure. Without them, you will be unable to rank well on web indexes. Without positioning on web indexes, you'll have a much harder time getting a great deal of steady traffic. Regardless of the over-burden of data from affirmed "Website design enhancement specialists," catchphrase research and SEO (site improvement) isn't too troublesome.

•   Find a few catchphrases you need to rank for that have high search volume and low-is rivalry.

- Write mind-blowingly excellent blog content that remembers your fundamental catchphrases for the title, body, headers, and picture alt message yet don't try too hard.
- Work on getting backlinks to that article with your primary watchwords as the stay content (for example, if your fundamental catchphrase is "promoting systems," you need the connection to your site to be associated with the content "advertising techniques"). In any case, be mindful so as not to overcompensate this either. Too many streamlined stays may incorrectly trigger Google.

There are a lot of different complexities like page load speed, time spent on-page, and (for Bing, in any event) the number of offers the article got. Be that as it may, on the off chance that you ace the three things above, you'll be end route to the first page of Google. You don't have to put together the entirety of your subjects concerning watchword explore. Catchphrase explore is an extraordinary method to concoct new thoughts and open doors for content, yet SEO ought not to drive your whole content technique. It should factor in, yet not wholly control, the subjects and message of your content. You may discover an open door for a particular catchphrase, yet you should then join that data with your insight into your objective market and personas to write the ideal content. Continuously attempt to target catchphrases, yet don't give them a chance to prevent you from composing on an extraordinary subject.

Pick and get ready foundation content.

Your principal aides will be your foundation content. The content will be utilized as an establishment for your website, and littler blog posts will be composed around that center.

If you don't know how to think of points for the foundation content, here is the thing that you can do:

- Use Google Keywords Planner apparatus to get the thoughts. Sign in to your Google account or make another one on the off chance that you don't have it. Under the area "Find new catchphrases and get search volume information." open "Quest for new watchwords utilizing an expression, website or classification" tab, enter the catchphrase into the case, and press "Get thoughts" button. You will get the rundown of catchphrases with their hunt volume.

• You can likewise utilize apparatuses like SEMrush and check what watchwords contender's website rank for to get the thought for themes. It's a paid apparatus, yet you can get two weeks free preliminary. Sign in to the instrument, embed URL of the contender website that you like, and hit the investigate button. Next, select the "Top pages" area on the left-hand side and check the "Top catchphrases" section to get watchwords thoughts for your subjects. This activity should assist you with discovering watchwords that are well known, and you can think of the things for your leader content. Make a publication schedule and start posting.

To help keep up your consistency, make sure to utilize some publication schedule. You can utilize Google Calendar, Outlook Calendar, or even a basic spreadsheet. Use it to deal with your thoughts and plan your content subjects for every month so that blogging is something you center around, not something you do in your extra time. You don't need to distribute each day, pick the posting stream as per your calendar. For instance, you can post your foundation content one day, display the first blog post the following day, and continue posting blog posts once per week.

A content schedule keeps you on track and makes a framework to guarantee your content is continuously first-class and distributed on schedule. The best plans likewise have social sharing and email advertising data prepared to make things sorted out and dull. An extraordinary content schedule gives you a 10,000 foot see and has your group's publication procedure heated into it. It enables you to make continuous updates, sort out every single content resource, and have started to finish placement into who is dealing with what, when each piece is expected, and which persona and phase of the pipe each bit of content is for.

You can likewise utilize a free instrument like Trello or Google Calendar to make your blog content schedule, be that as it may, in case you're searching for a wholly committed schedule with additional highlights to assist you with developing your blog, a device like Schedule might be increasingly useful.

Content Strategies to Drive Traffic to Your Blog

Make intriguing headlines for your blog posts: Features matter such a significant amount that there are whole books devoted to techniques for making them. They decide if an individual will snap to peruse your article. Features determine whether an individual will read your blog post or not.

At the point when an individual goes over your article via web-based networking media or an internet searcher, the feature is your one opportunity to provoke their advantage. To assist you with taking your function to the following level, utilize the free Schedule Headline Analyzer: This analyzer gives your feature a score dependent on different measurements like character check, article type, and word utilization. It likewise gives you proposals on the best way to improve it.

The most effective method to write the ideal features:

The feature, or title, of your blog post, needs to catch the consideration of potential audiences. Individuals may see it in their web-based life news channel or list items. At the point when you write a feature, focus on its tone and appearance:

• Choose a solid typeface
• Size your features to stick out

Standards of viral features

The feature you use will assume an essential job of getting more visits and social offers. Great features make individuals make a move since they show one of the accompanying's:

• Social cash

The more extensive use something or, the more compelling individuals use something, the almost certain individuals will emulate it.

Useful esteem: Helpful things to get consideration. Feature the profit and vow to pick up something if the individual makes a move.

Danger: Individuals frequently make a move when they have to shield themselves from some risk.

Make your meta description compelling

Your meta depiction is significant because it shows up in Google list items and as a component of the review when sharing via web-based networking media. (Like, the content that shows up with refreshes on Facebook.) If you're a WordPress client, modules like Yoast SEO enable you to redo your meta portrayal for each new page and post.

Like your feature, this scrap is an early introduction that decides the probability of an individual clicking to peruse the remainder of your article. So, make it fascinating! It ought to likewise mirror the content of the material itself, going about as a review of sorts. If you can, attempt to fuse a few catchphrases that identify with what your blog post or page is about.

Utilize relevant imagery

Articles with significant pictures store up 94% more complete perspectives than items without images, as indicated by Jeff Bullas. This is because we are generally attracted to symbolism. Besides, pictures go about as a pleasant method to separate enormous squares of content and outline ideas. You can incorporate free stock photographs, screen captures, or photographs you make yourself.

Besides pictures inside your post, additionally, utilize an engaging element picture. Included figures show up when you share a post on Facebook, Twitter, Google+, and even LinkedIn. On the off chance that you are a sorry creator, it is no issue.

Improve as a writer overtime

Be conversational: This isn't a literary composition! You need individuals to have the option to identify with you.

Keep your composition at a low understanding level: Stay away from intricate language, since you need everybody to have the option to comprehend your writing (without feeling like they're reading jargon words for the SAT). Additionally, remember that you may have audiences from various nations who know English as a subsequent language!

Keep away from cushion: Get to the point, and abstain from jumbling your sentences with superfluous words.

Remain on the subject: It's simple, particularly as a beginner, to veer off. However, they remain centered.

Recount stories: When they're applicable and identify with your subject, stories draw in your audience and make you increasingly relatable. They make your blog progressively charming to peruse.

Focus on arranging: This doesn't identify with composing as such, however, relates to how individuals will expend your composition. Maintain a strategic distance from enormous squares of content. Use records when fitting. Use blockquotes and bolded content, when applicable. While we don't care to consider individuals skimming our content—they do. Also, you need to ensure your material is edible for skimmers.

Be deliberate about improving as a writer.

Luckily, there are apparatuses accessible to assist you with improving as a writer. Some are:

1.   Hemingway application: a piece of free in-program equipment (there is likewise a work area application) that lets you know whether your sentences are hard to peruse or not and gives you pointers on improving. It additionally provides your content an understanding level.

2   Grammarly: a superb Chrome augmentation, in-program apparatus, and work area application. The equipment encourages you to become a superior writer by pointing out your missteps and offering arrangements, going past regular spell check to address things like comma situation and word utilization. I utilize their exceptional mechanism, however, they have a free alternative, as well.

Acing the specialty of writing requires some serious energy. The more you do it, the better you become. But at the same time, it's essential to turn out to be better after some time by utilizing apparatuses (like the two referenced above) or working with a supervisor who can give criticism on your work.

The Most Effective Method to Create Great Profitable Content

Presently it's an excellent opportunity to make the content. You'll peruse a great deal about improving your content for web indexes, and keeping in mind that that it is significant, on the off chance that you don't enhance your content for people, at that point you'll never pick up the presentation that it takes to get connections and rank well in web search tools. On the off chance that you write content that individuals love to peruse, at that point, you will get traffic, social offers, and connections as your readership develop.

Research your subject before you start composing

Investigate other contents in your niche. Attempt to make sense of what is working for the foremost idea pioneers and think of an approach to make the far better content. The best spot to begin is by directing a catchphrase investigation. You can utilize Google Keyword Planner to make sense of what catchphrases other individuals in your niche are using. Start by dispensing with watchwords that are not pertinent enough, have no pursuit volume, or appear to be dreadfully aggressive to rank for. The rest of the catchphrases on your rundown are the ones that you need to target.

Capitolo 38 Working with Brands

I deally, individuals won't pursue cash. They would be satisfied with whatever they have and go on with their lives. Be that as it may, it isn't so. Cash has picked up this fundamental significance throughout everyday life; in addition to the fact that it is vital for our extravagances our day by day needs. So, I could continue forever about how everybody should simply cherish what they do and life will be loaded up with rainbows and unicorns yet then I would lie. You have to acquire cash from your blog, and you will, however ensure it isn't the main explanation you blog.

Here's the reason I am so against on lucrative destinations: Suppose your solitary objective is to make $500 this month, presently regardless of whether you are working in the field you adore, defining an objective that rotates around a number tops your potential and the real cash you can make.

Give me a chance to expound with a model: Suppose I am a photography blogger, and I have increased a following of 10,000 individuals on my blog. Presently if my lone objective is to by one way or another make $500 this month, at that point this objective of mine will make me need to take alternate routes any place fundamental, what not I can consider is the means by which I can utilize these 10,000 individuals to make me $500. So, I may prescribe a camera I haven't looked into inside and out and post it on the blog saying it is the 'Best Camera Ever', to make sure I can pick up offshoot commission from it. Presently the supporters of my blog trust my decision so much that some of them will wind up purchasing the camera since I am prescribing it. Also, when these individuals discover the camera isn't extraordinary all things considered, they won't confide in my decision any longer, and soon they will tell different supporters of my duplicity.

The outcome is me nearly losing all that I've buckled down for, all since I needed to profit snappier.

Regardless of whether I made $500 that month, I denied myself of my devotees' trust and the potential cash that I could have made, had I been straightforward. Additionally, had I been straightforward, these 10,000 individuals would have prescribed the blog to various others, and my legitimate suggestions would have made me enough cash some place down the line.

For what reason did I shoot myself in the leg? Since I was pursuing cash, and I needed it speedy. Presently, I will disclose to your various approaches to profit from your blog. In the event that you pursue just cash however, no measure of intelligence will prevent you from fizzling. Comprehend the strategies I let you know, practice their execution, and you will profit from your blog. Persistence is the key here, take a gander at it along these lines, would you need to make $200 this month immediately or make $100 every month for the following 6-7 months and arrive at a point where you can procure $500 per month. Have the persistence to see the master plan.

The rundown isn't in any request, and a few techniques are simpler for certain specialties than others and vice versa, so read and get them, and through execution, you'll realize what works for your specialty and what doesn't.

Affiliate Marketing

This strategy is the best method for profiting from your blog when you are simply firing up. Think about an affiliate as this center man that elevates items to individuals, and if individuals purchase those items through the affiliate's reference, the affiliate gets a commission from it. Numerous individuals think Affiliate Marketing is sales rep marketing, which isn't valid in any way. A sales rep attempts to sell you items, their lone activity is to induce you to purchase their item, and as much as I value their abilities, you don't need to do that as an affiliate.

At whatever point you need to purchase an item on the pricier side, how would you choose on the other hand that you will get it or on the other hand not? Indeed, first, you check the audits that different purchasers have left. For what reason do you do that?

Indeed, you don't confide in the marketing contrivances that makers attempt to force, and you search for an assessment. Indeed, its visually impaired trust, yet it is more ameliorating than perusing arranged lines of advancement. We look for human counsel, and it sits as the fundamental factor in our purchasing choices. How often have you approached your loved ones for purchasing exhortation? A great deal I am speculating, since we confide in their assessment.

The perfect method to utilize Affiliate Marketing is to give genuine audits of the items in your specialty and afterward give your group of spectators a simpler decision to purchase the said items through an affiliate connect. First however, you should win your group of spectators' trusts and mind you, it is the hardest to gain.

So how would you gain this trust? You should consistently give a fair-minded feeling on an item, news, or hypotheses. When you continue making such content, your group of spectators confides in you and considers you to be to some degree an Authoritative figure in your specialty.

Your specialty has items, regardless of whether Physical or Digital, and these items are sold at commercial centers. You as a blogger need to approach these commercial centers and search for their affiliate programs. In the event that you don't discover a connection on the landing page, keep in touch with them an email, and you will get an answer.

There aren't numerous prerequisites for an affiliate program, yet it likewise relies upon your specialty. On the other hand, that the commercial center rejects your application saying you need more traffic on your blog, search for other confided in commercial centers and apply there. In the event that no commercial center acknowledges you at this minute, don't stress. Concentrate on improving your content, and you will arrive at the traffic necessities for the said affiliate programs.

When you are acknowledged to an affiliate program, you are presently qualified to make a commission.

Nonetheless, you can't simply duplicate an Amazon connection and glue it on your blog and hope to make a Commission from it. Affiliate connections vary from ordinary connections, and as an affiliate, you gain admittance to an interface where you can make these affiliate joins, which you can glue on your blog.

One significant thing to recall is that the commercial center you are an affiliate of should be dependable. They may offer the best limits, yet do they convey on schedule? How would they handle item returns? Is their client assistance adequate? You have to look into in light of the fact that you are underwriting them to your supporters.

In the event that one of your devotees were to have a disagreeable encounter, they would feel let down, and you will be a piece of the fault. No commercial center is flawless. I've seen a lot of bungles from somebody as large as Amazon, yet the likelihood is less, so I more often than not suggest items from Amazon.

Do your exploration and rundown great, reliable destinations, and after that apply for their affiliate programs. In the event that you don't get in, don't take a stab at sub-par locales. Pause! You can generally concentrate on expanding your traffic. It is unmistakably progressively valuable to pause, increment your traffic and attempt again than making due with an average commercial center.

So, you've gotten into a dependable commercial center, what next? All things considered, search for items in your specialty that you can audit. They don't need to be new. Take a gander at your storage room, see what you can find and audit it on the blog.

On the other hand, that innovation and contraptions are my specialties and suppose I have a two-year-old Bluetooth speaker, I will make an audit on it and call it, 'How my JBL cut 1 endured me through 2 years of utilization'. Imagination is the name of the game. You need not purchase extravagant new items and audit them, acquire something from your companion, associate or family, use it for two days and compose an audit on it.

Affiliate Marketing will test your respectability however, suggesting a decent $300 cell phone which gives you less commission is superior to suggesting an unremarkable $1000 cell phone which gets you twofold the commission. Keep in mind, backing and survey items as though you are doing it for your friends and family in light of the fact that there isn't a lack of individuals needing that brisk buck, furthermore, I genuinely don't need you to be a piece of that circle. The Internet is an open book, so the majority of the individuals think about Affiliate Marketing, and I'd suggest you express a note toward the finish of your articles that state something like this:

"The above connection is an Affiliate connection and obtaining through the connection gives me a percent of the benefit which encourages me keep up this blog. I'd truly value it in the event that you made your buy through the above connection. Much appreciated.

The above message is authentic and warm. Your guests will welcome the straightforwardness and will eagerly utilize your connections at whatever point essential. Commercial centers have characterized commission rates for items, tech items have a littler commission yet cost more while garments offer higher commissions yet are less expensive.

Commercial centers like Amazon and so forth showcase certain items more, when they do, they dispense the affiliate cash to marketing, thus on the other hand that you sell an item like that, you don't get a commission for it.

This doesn't mean you quit prescribing an extraordinary item. According to the Amazon Affiliate Model, when a client taps on your affiliate connection and arrives at a commercial center, a session starts, whatever the client at that point purchases in the session is enlisted as your deal, and you get the commission for it.

CPC, CPM and CPA Ad Network

Ever observe those Ads on the page you are perusing? These are called situation Ads, furthermore, the odds are, and you have seen them as of late. Additionally, these arrangement Ads by one way or another as it were show Ads significant to your perusing history, and no it is anything but a fortuitous event, yet that is a story for another page (see what I did there!).

Here is a case of situation Ads (checked red) on a blog:

Situation Ads can enable you to procure cash, however your blog needs extensive guest traffic for them to work. In any case, I should enlighten you concerning them, for when your blog arrives at huge guest traffic; you should execute them.

Some of you might need to actualize these immediately however you shouldn't and here's a model why: There is this vehicle magazine that has recently been discharged, and as an early on offer, it is accessible for least cost. Inquisitive about what's inside, individuals get it and to their shock, the content is amazing, the magazine here has not many ads in the middle of which makes the experience more flow than different magazines in a similar specialty.

Having not very many Ads gives the pursuer a smoother experience, and they don't feel like the magazine is simply forcing Ads on them. This grows better trust with the pursuers of the magazine, and thus, the magazine gets various enrollments.

Thus, when your blog is new, you need minimal measure of interruptions, which makes for a better guest experience which will give you additionally returning traffic. So, for the present, center around traffic, furthermore, when you increase a respectable after, at that point read the beneath segment once more:

To begin with, let me reveal to you why these arrangement Ads appear to be so pertinent to your perusing history:

When you visit a commercial center like Amazon or perform look on locales like Google, these sites keep up a little document about it called a 'Treat' which has little data on what you've scanned for. So, whenever you visit a site that has situation ads, these ads are given the Cookie which makes them show Ads important to your hunts. Presently, this may feel like an interruption of security, and somewhat it is, yet that is the expense of utilizing administrations from these organizations.

On the other hand, that you need to run position Ads on your blog, you have to approach an Ad Network. These are administrations which help interface the blogger with the promoters, and they do take a portion of the benefit, yet with all that they accomplish for us, it is a little cost to pay. So, before you approach an Ad Network, you should think about 'Income Models'.

Income models were created as a standard for bloggers, sponsors and Ad Networks the same, so you should think about them. Here are some prevalent income models:

CPC (Cost per Click) Revenue Model

In this income model you are paid as per the quantity of clicks enlisted on a specific advertisement. As I've said previously, these are directed advertisements, so the odds of somebody tapping on it are higher than expected. Keep in mind, you are paid per click, regardless of whether the guest winds up purchasing the item/administration or not. As a blogging beginner, this model is incredible for you, as you needn't bother with tremendous measures of traffic to get clicks. The Ad-systems characterize a Cost for every Click rate, which could be anything between $0.50 furthermore, $3.

Cost per Mille (CPM) Revenue Model

The CPM model pays the blogger as indicated by the quantity of guest Impressions on a specific Ad. These are typically estimated on a for each thousand impressions premise. At the point when a guest drifts their mouse over the Ad, without clicking it, it is enrolled as an impression.

The CPM rate is fixed by the Ad-arrange and can be anything somewhere in the range of $2 and $5 per 1000 impressions. This model works incredible with progressively huge traffic, so when you arrive at a greater group of spectators, this model will suit you better.

Cost Per Action (CPA) Model

As the name proposes, the CPA model works just when a client clicks on a promotion and finishes an activity. The promoter characterizes the activity, which can be anything from filling a couple of subtleties to finishing a buy. The CPA rate at that point relies upon what activity the publicist requires, the more drawn out the activity the better the CPA rate. CPA model pays a great deal of cash for an effective activity. Be that as it may, the likelihood of guests tapping on a promotion and finishing further activity is low. To prevail at this model, your blog needs a huge amount of traffic as the likelihood of the finish is low.

The above were the diverse income models, and now I'll show some well-known Ad Networks that you can approach. You don't need to do a lot, simply pursue a record first, and enter the subtleties of your blog and you are a great idea to go:

Keep in mind, you don't need to pick just a single income model, you can join to three distinctive Ad Networks and send all the three income models together. Be that as it may, as another blogger, you would squander a great deal of Ad Space in the event that you execute CPM and CPA Ads immediately, so my advice is start with conveying CPC ads, and as your traffic develops, you can explore different avenues regarding CPM and CPA Ads. It's critical to analyze however, when your traffic develops then you change between diverse Ad- networks and Revenue models and see what works best for you.

Renting Ad Space

You can sell Advertising Space on your blog to individuals ready to advertise. This technique gives you the opportunity to charge as you wish and gives you unlimited oversight. In any case, to execute this strategy, your blog must have extensive traffic, and you have to demonstrate these insights to advertisers ready to partake.

This strategy isn't productive enough for another blogger. When you have an impressive sum of traffic that is the point at which you can make the most out of this technique. You can compose a message like the one underneath to tell your crowd that you are willing to lease Ad Space:

Need 10,000 month to month guests to see your Product or Service?

We are leasing Advertising Space on our blog, on the other hand that you are intrigued, Contact Us Now.

The advantages of this technique are enormous, you get the opportunity to keep all the cash, you choose the expense, and what's more, you have full power over it.

Above were some simpler and moral methods for profiting from your blog yet these techniques will be powerful just when you make significant substance. Also, the best way to make incredible substance is to concentrate on it and not on the cash.

Capitolo 39 Use Social Media

Blog Traffic: The Whys and How's
When you set out to create a meaningful and profitable blog, you are going to invest a lot of time into it. What you want to know is that this effort is going to be worth it. While there is no guarantee, there are things you can do to help determine if your work is going to bring in the people you need to make the money you want. Bringing people to your blog is the best way to generate revenue. After all, if no one reads your words, no one will pay you for it. So, a great measurement for the success of your blog is to monitor how many people visit it. This is called "traffic". The minute you set up your blog, you should be tracking what is coming to it and track it often. One of the benefits of doing this is that you can curate your content to your readers and not waste time on topics they are not engaging with. You can use analytics tools to help monitor the traffic and how your readers are engaging with your content. These analytical tools identify what posts readers are spending time on and who they are. The analytics also show where on your website your readers are clicking. Using this information, you can spend time on a strategy that is informed. One of the most popular ways to track your blog's traffic and review the analytics is with Google Analytics. Many hosting sites offer their own built-in analytics, but those that do not generally offer a plug-in for Google Analytics. Even if a platform offers its own analytics, you should consider adding in Google Analytics by using the website for it. This is primarily because Google is the monopoly in SEO, so it only makes sense to get their information to improve your blog's performance. In addition, if Google does not recognize your blog, it is going to have a very hard time showing up in front of anyone you are trying to reach.

If you are not sure about how to add Google Analytics to your platform, get onto Google and type in, "How to set up Google

Analytics on *insert your platform here. *" Once you get it set up, do not worry if it is a little confusing or intimidating. To begin, start with small checks and balances. Measure a few things just to get the hang of the tool. Once you figure out how the tool works, you are ready to look at the big picture of your blog.

Another important factor to consider is the pages for your blog. Your blog should and probably will naturally end up with more than one page. You will probably start organizing content into different pages like an "About Me" or "Contact" page. You may also chunk up your blog content into different headers and have different kinds of posts that appear on different pages. For example, Lifestyle Bloggers may want to put cooking tips and recipes on one page while DIY tutorials for the home go on another. When you have multiple pages, it is easier for your readers to find your information quickly, but you also need to make sure your analytics are set up to handle this. With Google Analytics, it is easy. This report in Google Analytics is called "All Pages".

The steps to generate this report in Google Analytics are as follows:
1.   Open Google Analytics and log in
2.   Identify the section "Behavior" located in the menu on the left side
3.   Click on "Site Content"
4.   From the options, select "All Pages" to generate the report
Once the report is created, the information will be scattered all around for your pages. You are going to want to filter and move the information around to figure it out. For example, you may not want to gauge the success of your blog on the traffic heading to your "Contact" page. This means you will want to remove this from the results you are seeing. You can remove any page from the report that does not directly relate to your blog. For example, if you have a "Products" page, you can filter them out in relation to the performance of your blog. You can always bring that information back in at a later date if you want to. To filter, the first thing you need to do

is determine your blog post URLs. For example, your posts probably have a URL like www.website.com/blog/post#1, etc. Every time you create a blog post, "/blog/" is used in the URL. That is what you will use to filter your report by typing it into the "Search" field of the report. The process of filtering your results is rather simple. You enter the common path or word into your search field and then click on the magnifying glass icon to perform the search. This will then trim down the report to show you data only on the pages that contain that field in the URL. When the report adjusts to your new parameters, the blog posts will be listed out under a nice graph and various metrics listed out for each post.

The metrics in the report are important to understand. Below is a breakdown of what each item means:

1.   The first field is the URL for a particular blog post. There is a small square icon in the bottom right corner of the box. This opens the content of the analysis in a new window if you click on it.

2.   The second box shows "Pageviews". This tells you how many people have looked at the page during the time frame you told the report to run. For example, if you wanted to see just one day's performance, you can narrow down the report, or you can look at it for the week, month, quarter, or even year.

3.   The following column indicates how many people visited the blog post specifically during that same time frame.

4.   The average time spent on the page is valuable information. It tells you how long you captured the attention of a reader. Do not get too hung up on this information though. Google can easily misjudge it, especially if you have a high bounce rate.

5.   "Entrances" refers to a reader that arrives at your blog post directly. From there, they can engage with your site in another way, like reading another post or visiting another page. This does not refer to a reader that came to your site from somewhere else and then engaged with your blog post.

6.   "Bounce Rate", as mentioned earlier in this list, refers to the percentage of readers who entered your site through your blog post directly and then left after engaging in it. These readers do not go to another page or another part of your site after interacting with your specific blog post.

7.   "% Exit" is a similar metric, but this refers to the people that came to your blog post from other areas or engaged differently before leaving after engaging with this specific post.

You can use this information to look at the performance of just one blog over a span of time or you can compare your blogs to find certain topics or information that stands out. While this information is very important, you need to recognize that it is not always perfect and accurate. There are always little factors that can throw off your metrics or weirdly skew your data. This means you cannot count on it 100%, but it is the best tool to really gauge what people are doing on your blog. Now that you understand the information in the "All Pages" report, you need to know how to interpret it. What numbers are "good" and what performance indicators show it is "bad"? This may not be the best way to approach it since all blogs and traffic are different and change drastically over time, but you can start to determine the following:

1.   What is the most popular post or posts? Why do you think people liked these specifically? Check comments or contacts you got based on the post to try to put your finger on why your audience engaged with these the most. It could also be the length of the post that was attractive, the topic was trending, it was shared a lot on social media, or it was shared at a specific time. See if you can find something that stands out, especially if you are looking at a couple of popular posts. What is common about the two of them that you think made them more popular than the rest?

2   How can you use this information to develop a content strategy around these successful traits? If you see that your most popular posts are ones that have a short video clip and are about 500

words, can you replicate this format more often? Or were your posts shared by readers on social media after you posted on Facebook at 4 PM on a Wednesday? Can you make sure your promotion strategy includes posting at this time more often in the future?

3. In addition, you can play with your posts that are successful by adjusting or updating them in some way. This can potentially get more life from the post and show you valuable information about what your audience is interested in. For example, if a popular post is already successful, what if you added more information to it or an integrative feature, like a survey or quiz? Can you see an increase in activity again or do your readers move on?

4. Look at the length of time between your popular posts. Is there a certain amount of time between the two that you could replicate? If you increased the number of posts in a certain time frame, which means you post more frequently, do you increase traffic to your blog? If you find a "sweet spot" for frequency, can you keep up that frequency long term? To determine this, sit down and look at your calendar. Be realistic or even overestimate how much time it will take for you to create a post. Can you do this every week? There will be more information on this later; however, it is good to start considering it now.

Beginning to understand your blog's traffic and what it means to your future strategy is vital to your growth and success. This introduction is just to "get your feet wet"; however, you can begin to formulate your approach to understanding the performance of your blog and how you plan on using your metrics to reach your audience better.

Social Media Is Your (Marketing) Friend

You want your blog to generate traffic. This means you want to use social media to your advantage. People congregate on sites like Facebook and Twitter more than any other place on the Internet. When they are looking for information, one of the first places they start is through a social media outlet. It is also where these people share their opinions and experiences openly. The people you want to reach are probably on one or more of these sites regularly. This means it is an ideal location to launch a marketing strategy. Instead of hoping that people eventually find your blog, you can design advertisements and strategy to connect with your audience.

To help you in general when using social media for promotion, consider the following tips that can be applied to just about any form of social media:

1.   Always add a link to your posts. Get in the habit of always linking people back to your blog, even if your post is not about a recent blog post. This leads people from your quipping posts to your content-rich blog topics.

2   On your blog are social buttons linking to your various social media pages. At least have a link to Facebook. Add other social media platforms that you use regularly. This leads people to follow you through social media and not just through your blog.

3.   Enable others to share your blogs on social media. Most platforms have an easy feature you can add to your blog site to promote sharing of your content across a variety of social platforms.

4.   Include a clickable link in your blog post to your social media. In addition, if you have a video on YouTube that you want your readers to engage with, embed the video directly into your post, right in the middle, so they can easily see it when they load your blog post. The last suggestion brings up a good topic to review briefly; using video in your blog posts. It is a growing medium and influencer. Many people still discredit YouTube as a social media site, but it really does fall into this category. In general, because of its ability to share visual information with anyone, it is one of the most popular social media sites. Often, the majority of the video you find on other sites is cut from YouTube or can be found in a longer form on YouTube. In addition to embedding video in your blog posts, you can embed your video in a Facebook post easily. The platforms work nicely together, and the process is pretty seamless. It is a valuable tool that can be easily maximized and provides evergreen content.

Taking the time to develop your content marketing strategy through social media is worth the time and effort. You have to compete with all the other information out there, and having a strong plan on how you will do it will help you stand out from the crowd. You can also boost your impact on different platforms that already have a huge audience with constant views. Below are suggestions on how to plan an effective strategy for social media and your blog:

1. Offer a teaser and boost it. On Facebook, you can hint about what your upcoming blog is going to be about. Once you create the post, you then pay to boost it to a wider audience. This option allows you to pay for the engagement you get but only up to the dollar amount you are prepared to spend and for the length of time you want it to run for. Your boosted post can include anything from words to a video. Develop anything that you think will attract the attention of your audience and get them wanting your upcoming blog post.

2. When you post a video on YouTube, add your blog's homepage link in the description of the video. If your video is related to your blog post directly, add a link in the video and a recorded call- to-action asking people to go there.

3. Create cross-links on different platforms. For whatever reason, people seem to hesitate about cross-linking content. It may be from past algorithms in Google, but in reality, Google has never cared about cross-linking as long as it is above board and the content is pertinent to one another. You can also bring people from one platform to the next to learn more about a certain subject or expand information on a topic.

4. Create fresh content daily on Twitter and even Facebook. The more often you post, the more hype you can generate. Of course, the content needs to be valuable, but also short. If you can keep posts fun and easy to engage with, people are more likely to enjoy them. Instead of posting a long post on Facebook, for example, consider chunking up the information into little bites that you can share over a few days.

5. Now and then, offer a giveaway. This attracts people to your blog and your social accounts. Most social media users like to get something for free when they read or engage with your material. The main objective of this strategy should be to offer quality content, but

the secondary objective should be to show that you appreciate their readership and loyalty. Most of the time, the free item you choose to giveaway does not need to be elaborate or expensive. Offering an eBook or something digital like a checklist of some sort can be just as valuable to your readers as something physical.

6.   Do not discount less-popular social media sites in your strategy. Using social media for marketing does not mean you are exempt from the social part of it. People go to social media for more personal interaction, not to engage with business marketing messages. This means you need to show people the personal side of your money-making blog, like you doing things, your family, adventures you have been on, etc. This can be done well through the less popular social media accounts for marketing, such as Instagram. The influence of Instagram as a marketing platform is evolving, but it is still not the most commonly used platform. To capitalize on this platform for your blog posts and connect to your audience, consider adding images of personal pictures related to your blog and your life. For example, if you are a food blogger, post pictures of the great food you have made or eaten, and also the not-so-great experiences or attempts. Show people you "polished" and present something amazing, but also a picture of your kitchen after a photo shoot and the mountain of dishes and things needing to be cleaned up. This approach helps show readers what your company is all about and establishes a stronger sense of connection that other platforms may not be the best for.

Capitolo 40 Optimize Each Post

L inks After content on the Internet, relationships are the essential element! Why? Because this is how the world of the Internet is linked-through links.

This guide discusses key factors about ties and how to use them properly to achieve good rankings in search engines.

Link campaign: Every successful website has links to it. This is the core principle of rankings of search engines. A search engine connect project must, therefore, be planned and executed to gain visitors and rankings. Where links can be found, Links can be obtained in many ways. The most popular are described below.

Directories: are the best way to get your connection campaign started. There are many hundreds of directories, so it's good to start there. Others may need a backlink before you can allow inclusion, but some may require a $5-20 fee, but in exchange, you can offer 4-10 links to various pages and links on your website.

Forums and newsgroups: are another way to obtain access-everything it takes is posting to similar locations and also linking to the website with comments. If there is sufficient information, links may be included in the signature or part of the reply.

Blogs: are a great way to give its owner complete control over the process and links. Since many blogging companies offer free blogs, it makes sense to create them and use them to link and build a network of websites around the main website; however, these blogging websites must be connected to other external sites.

Articles and press releases-a compelling strategy for one-way links as well as an instant stream of additional visitors if they are republished online or offline by some media. Writing locations: DMOZ and Yahoo repositories-these two are very useful for search engines-also referred to as trustworthy pages. Links from any of these will ensure that your website is of high quality. However, free DMOZ is quite challenging to access, mainly if it is a 13-page affiliate site with links and banners around. It also applies to Yahoo and to a non-refundable $300 to $600 fee to check the inclusion on your website, which does not guarantee inclusion.

The most popular way to gain a large number of links and improve site rankings is linking exchange. Only disadvantages are worth less than one-way connections.

Connect networks-just stay away. Getting five hundred links in a day is a sure way for search engines to penalize.

Link speed Gain of links on a website is used for several search engine spam prevention filters. For a new website, more than 100 links would not be advisable in the first month. That means 2-3 connects one day as the best way for the first month.

Why? Because the site must grow slowly, as it naturally would. The number of connections can be extended at 3-5 speeds per day next month. Up to 5-10 ties, a day can be added in the third month.

For older pages with a well-known PageRank of 4 or more links and 500 + links, the pace can be higher–10 to 30 links a day.

It is important to add links to the internal sections/pages and to keep adding new content as the connection project is going.

Anchor text is essential because it is directly responsible for which keywords are placed in the search engines. However, they must be wisely selected.

If most links to your site have anchor text "Zoo," it is 100% likely that the site will not be classified as "Gardening" as it was optimized for "Zoo" This means that the owner of the website must choose correct keywords. Once a niche is selected, it is crucial to recognize that keywords are dense and smooth (low searched). For example, it would be very unproductive to choose "weight loss" as a keyword for optimization, as there are serious competitors.

One essential thing to mention is that the term weight loss is included in all these keywords. Many keywords, therefore, rank the site, and as the number of links increases, the site gradually ranks all those keywords. For some moderate searched keywords, the website could have been quite active for 3 to 6 months.

Link relevance: Today, the relevance of the situation is even more critical than ever. Engines are taking a serious look not just at PageRank and the site's reputation but also at the topic. For example, when the "Weight Loss Pills" page has links to the "Schedule," it is interpreted as a corrupt and weak quality link, which does not offer as much advantage as when the link is on the subject of the same thing or a familiar one. The more links from the topic pages in question-the better.

Link proportions: A lot of rumors are issued about the dimensions of a link to a website. How many connections should be one-way, and how many can be reciprocal? The answer is easy-the easier, the more one-way links to the website! 20, 30, 50, 90, 100%!

Why? Put, the more one way the site is valuable and the better its reputation connects.

If the reciprocal relation is heavily used, the motors may reduce their quality to a minimum. Another thing is that part of PageRank is taken away by link partners.

Exit links on a page Many webmasters make a common mistake by having many exit links to partner and affiliate websites. It sometimes leads to 10 or more exit links per page that are bad in two respects. Search engines can see this site as spam, and these multiple exit links can eliminate valuable PageRank and reduce the likelihood of proper placement in search engines.

A simple solution is to eliminate and make more efficient use of the exit connections. Twenty-five links in one write-up are not required whenever the name of the product is mentioned.

The same applies to link exchanges-there are no links to partner pages on all pages. It is quite sufficient to create and maintain a separate page for this purpose.

Exiting Links to other sites, the fact is that Google engineers say one-way links to a website and one-way exit links to other sites are usable (this means that you don't have to go back to the place that receives the connection). This makes sense, because websites are connected and can improve the visitor experience or references, but do not overdo it again. Many links are all right, but too many looks bad back and can damage your website.

Finally, add content and links: Start slowly and with the time–speed up and add content. Remember to link to the homepage, internal pages, and categories and to have one way and reciprocal links. Use many keywords in your relationships and do not exit links, particularly affiliate links per site. In no time will the website continually drive visitors and grow as you continue to promote it.

How SEO is Important for Small Enterprises

Small business search engine optimization (SEO) can mean the difference between success and failure. Today SEO should be at the top of your list with all the advertising options. Why, because you must assume that everyone would accept that a 24-hour marketing message that is always on and never off is probably the best marketing tool that any organization could ask for. But does it work for you or does it work for your competition?

Just because you're a small company, optimizing search engines could not benefit your company. When a search request is inserted into the search engine, your page will have a higher chance of achieving organic results by streamlining the platform. This is the position just under the paid list, usually at the top of the page. Statistics show that 80% of online users first look at organic results. If you are not represented, you lack a lot of potential business.

The concept behind the SEO page is to have the search engines list your website if a search is carried out for services or products that you sell. The search engines then identify your site as a service provider and then return it to the search request. It doesn't sound simple! Sounds simple! If your customer is only able to find you by entering the missing boat in your web address, he may not know your web address, and he or she will not compete.

We live today in a virtual world where small pizzerias and home-based companies are portrayed on the Internet so that they can get new customers out of their websites. It can only be a one-page website that merely sets out its business description, services, and telephone number. Your website can make a big change in your success in terms of winning new customers. Most small businesses have tight budgets. The optimization of search engines is a must, although it takes a bit of work, much of it you can throw yourself.

Don't forget this vital puzzle piece. It can bring you huge returns at a little cost. See Google Support for more information on SEO.

Small companies select SEO!

An interesting survey was carried out last year by a lead generator MerchantCircle.com that found that amongst the 2,500 small businesses in the US, most replied through search engine optimization, they preferred a marketing channel to pick just one.

The question was: "If all your marketing and budget had to be put into a single channel, what would it be?" SEO, paid search, mobile, social, and traditional media included in the list of options.

The promotion of search engines dominated all other choices; 33 percent of the respondents voted on it. 6% of businesses chose social media, 10% chose contextual ads.

Nonetheless, 20% of all respondents preferred marketing channels like printing and outdoor advertising. It is interesting that in most of these companies, there are no more than four employees (80% of the survey).

So, where to begin?

Usually, the key players have a crucial meeting to try and figure out what to do. Deciding to build an SEO strategy and budget isn't as intimidating as some experts want you to believe. You are ready to move forward once you understand a few rules. Only knowing the basics will put you a long way ahead of your competition, placing you at the forefront of your competition on the net.

At this point, assuming you agreed that you would have to do something to obtain a market position. You looked at how the search engines work when keywords or phrases are in a query that you think your website should be served, and you have found that you are not on the first page? Does further research show that you are not on the second or third page? It may not be index yet if your website has a new meaning three to six months old. It will help if it is submitted to the search engines. It could take up to 30 days, so you have to be careful.

Second, make sure your keywords and meta tags are listed correctly on your page. You may need your webmaster's help because you have to look at the source code.

You can right-click on your site and view the source code for yourself if you feel brave. The tags you are looking for are usually found in the first 50 code rows. You begin with meta name=, and the tag form follows "keywords." You can't change them without an editor or FTP. All you can do from here is look at them. It would be a good idea to print them; you don't have to write the first page more than that. Some HTML coding is very long, and only if you copy the whole script to a word document, you will get lost. Highlight the meta tags after you have printed your code and speak to your webmaster. Once you search for external support for your SEO, consider what's on your top web pages. If you understand what's there, some of the trick's advertisers use will be less likely to fall.

Indeed, in the first year following the launch of their website, the small business owners should not use paid search engine optimization services at all. You need time to learn and understand about SEO. Sign up for paid service could hurt you if it's not done right or worse if you're signing up for an extended contract, which links you to a service that doesn't. Don't invest more than one year, which will allow your blog or website to develop and gain the confidence of search engines and time to learn the basics of SEO yourself. SEO is not an overnight thing, and it can take weeks to see results. A word of caution. This may be one reason business owners are reluctant to begin their online strategy development process. In comparison to PPC payment per tap, SEO can take several weeks to several months anywhere. Bear in mind that PPC can also be very expensive, but your return on investment is instantaneous.

By now, you can subscribe to local SEO workshops or join multiple webinars to get the right approach for optimizing your website for small businesses. Even if you start reading SEO blogs for half an hour or so every morning, you can gradually learn how to distinguish the optimization of the "white hat" from the "brown" and "black" and gain practical advice on SEO, and other valuable lessons in small business marketing.

The more you learn, the less likely it is to be that you are deceived by an SEO agency, and the more chances your optimization partners must help maximize the company's on-line role and improve it.

Steps to SEO-Friendly Web Writing

What's in mind when you hear "SEO?" Most answer KEYWORDS!

For us, content originators who don't have "SEO" or "keyword" in their job headings SEO and keyword are often nerve driving.

The keyword is just one SEO jigsaw piece.

Don't be a whiz in the constantly changing Google algorithm or re-search every month for a thousand long-distance keyword to win the organic traffic game.

Fulfilling the content with keywords no longer works, as Google makes the various components in content more intelligent and evaluates to determine their relevance and ranking.

The different factors contributing to good SEO also lead to good HUMAN BEINGS content consumption.

Capitolo 41 Creating Lead Magnet Ideas

A lead magnet plays a considerable role in developing customer value optimization system. In definition, a lead magnet is anything valuable that can be exchanged for customers' contact information, especially email addresses. The sole purpose of a lead magnet is to maximize the number of targeted leads you get for every offer you make.

The Importance of Lead Magnet

The best role played by a lead magnet is making the marketing work of a blogger simpler and more manageable. In the early days of blogging, most people would market their sites and posts by asking for subscriptions for newsletters. Nowadays, things have changed.

Even though it involves no money changing hands, having the contacts of your prospects is a valuable tool in your blogging career. It converts the customers into a lead, showing that they are interested in what you have to offer, and allows you to market your services. The problem with the market nowadays is that most people are susceptible and stingy to give their emails, so there must be a catch in for them. That is where lead magnet comes in.

To grab the attention of your readers' persona, you have to give then an irresistible lead magnet, something that can deliver value to them. The moment you get the trust of your leads with free offers, you raise the chances of having them pay for the paid services and also build a positive relationship with them.

Steps to Creating a Lead Magnet

It is always easy to tell if someone puts more effort into their marketing strategy or not. And so, a lead magnet must be directed with a purpose to become active. So, the first thing to consider is the persons your lead magnet will serve.

Choose the People You Want to Target

The first market you can make as a blogger is trying to attract everyone to your site using lead magnets. To be effective, you need to be very specific to the kind of people you want your lead magnet to attract. If the people do not feel like the lead magnets meet their wants, they will never take time to download them. Most companies often have multiple buyer personas, but still, you will see every lead magnet targeting only one specific group.

You should not be worried about the people to start attracting because with the time you have lead magnets for every group of readers. What you have to do is picking the group that you feel you can add more value to and then start from there.

Identify the Value Proposition You Want to Offer

Once you have the group you want to focus on, the next step will be getting them something valuable. You must convince them with the offer for them to download your lead magnet. The value of the offer will influence the number of leads your lead magnets attract.

The best offer you can give your readers is something that they need. That would relieve you of the headache of convincing them to download it. Instead of creating something that interests you, identify the needs of the people you have chosen, and try to meet those needs. In that sense, you can offer something small, but it grabs attention than create a large eBook that means less to them.

Going for a common problem is the best way of finding out the desires of the people. You can ask what your readers like and give them just that. Solve their problems better and fast.

Give Your Lead Magnets Identities

At this point, you know your target, and at the same time, you know what to offer them. Giving those lead magnets names will not be hard. The identity should be more appealing and attractive (even more than the offer itself). The same applies to craft a catchy headline for your emails and blog posts, and you should have known why you have to do this at this point.

Choose the Type of Lead Magnets You Want to Offer

You may know what you want to offer your clients, but these things come in different options, and you have to choose the right one. And the type you go for should be able to reflect the value proposition you are making. Here are some tips to help you decide:

Make it simple: a sophisticated lead magnet defeats its purpose. The moment people fail to understand what you are offering them, they will not be convinced to appreciate it. The best way to dot it is by making it as simple as possible, concise, and valuable.

Concentrate on your strong points: what can you offer better? If you a good writer, then you can provide eBooks. If you can take popular pics, then go for that instead.

Prioritize on the in-demand areas: you have to solve immediate problems. Readers will be attracted to your blog if you are offering something that gives them quick solutions. Therefore, you must choose a format that is consumed faster and is highly demanded.

There are many lead magnets that you can choose from. Most of them fall under the following categories:

- Discounts
- Free trials
- Toolkits
- Reports
- Training clips
- Surveys
- Tests
- Sales tools

If you are not sure about the type that can attract your audience, then choose the one that you feel more comfortable about.

Create Your Lead Magnet

All the planning is now behind you, and you have to create the lead magnet. You have to consider all the aspects we have gone through as you create the lead magnets. Remember who you are targeting and what you promised to deliver. You will get things falling in place if you follow all the processes and include the details you have strategized about.

Types of Lead Magnets You Can Offer

Most people think of lead magnets as free eBooks in the form of reports or guides. Those are the most popular ones that bloggers use to get email addresses from their clients. Most customers like them, and they can be related to any niche. However, there are many other types of lead magnets that you can use to generate leads. Below are some examples that you can use to stand out from the crowd.

Reports

This form is by far the simplest and the most used type of lead magnet. That does not make it useful automatically. Most bloggers use them because they work well and can be twisted in any other direction to meet the needs of the people you are focusing on. So, in general, what makes them universal is their specificity. Once directed to focus on the persona of the buyers, they become the go-to thing. The main aim should be to deliver on the promises you made. If that is achieved, your targets will stream to your blog and offer to give you their contact information.

Handouts

Cheat sheets also work well because they can give technical aid that helps your clients to do things faster and save them the complexities. They have a different outlook compared to reports, even though they both come in the form of PDFs.

A handout can be a page or two in length, which means they must be very concise and straight to the point. You have to address the issue straight away and offer immediate solutions quickly, and in a language that is easy to interpret because you will not have the time and space to go around telling stories. In some cases, you can have some images incorporated to give it a better look.

Resource Lists

If targeted for the right people, toolkits can be a great way to offer a lead magnet. You can think of it as a reference to pieces of materials and other resources that you readers can use to solve different problems. This method is usually a way of simplifying their work. You give them what they may get somewhere else but after spending a lot of time researching and sometimes purchasing the materials. For instance, you can offer your readers a time management toolkit. By this, you will be saving them the time to download or buy such plans.

Video Training

A video is one of the catchiest and engaging formats that you can use as a lead magnet. If you dare to stand in front of a camera and teach someone a skill or two, then this should be a great way of generating leads. Take an example of a podcast. You can offer some motivational talk in areas that people want to listen about, you can demonstrate how to use some home equipment, or you can also show your readers some life hacks that can make their lives simple.

A good example is getting all the transfer rumors from the sporting fraternity if you are blogging about sports, and your audiences like to know what is happening in the transfer market. Then you can host a live webinar and talk about who is joining which club at what price and for how long.

Downloadable Software or Free Trials

Most people are glued to Netflix and have subscribed to the channel for years because of the 30-day free trial they were offered. The best way to get people to know the value of something is by letting them have a taste of it first before they can decide if they want to buy or not. And if the value is up there then you will not have to worry about the purchase, it will come. Many people like to try before they buy.

And you can also make it more effective by not including credit cards because people will not have to worry about canceling their free trials to avoid charges at the end of the trial period.

If you want to give people some software, you can have them download them and install them for free for some time to sample how it all works before they start paying for the services.

Discounts

Everyone likes getting something at a discounted price. And giving up an email address is a smaller price to pay if it means saving some few dollars in buying some essential stuff.

But this is an area that you must be cautious about. If you decide to give people a discount, then ensure that the product you are offering is high on demand. The amount of discount is also something you should consider. If you go for a meager price, you might end up hurting your financial stability. Ata the same time, people will doubt the authenticity of the product if the price is way below the normal, and that can drive them away.

Surveys and Quizzes

To some people, studies have massive value and can be beneficial lead magnets. Okay, before you get this all wrong, it does not take the form of the BuzzFeed quizzes you see on your social media networks. The questions and surveys must be ones that offer real-time solutions to emerging problems. You must touch on areas that affect people, and they feel should be addressed.

You can complete the quizzes by offering some opt-in forms for the readers to finish at the end of the question. This technique will be banking on their participation and anticipation to get some results.

Assessments

An assessment can be similar to a survey but is more specific to a person. For instance, a study can target industry, but an evaluation narrows down to target a firm within that industry. It is more effective for companies that sell their services instead of products.

S0o, in the case of an assessment, the targeted audience will not be looking to get direct answers to their problems but getting an expert opinion about their services. And views can also be used to solve problems.

Sales Tools

Some people are always looking forward to getting pieces of information that can help them make purchasing or selling decisions such as pricing.

You can give them some catalogs and other digital sales materials that are more affordable. Anything that can help them make an economical choice can be a god lead magnet that you should use.

In general, whatever you decide to offer in exchange for your readers' emails should be worth their trust. The value pack should be there for them to see and appreciate, and that is the only way that they will comfortable to give away their contact information. And when that is done, ensure that you do not misuse those email addresses by providing what is relevant only.

Capitolo 42 Why You Should Use Ads on Your Blog

I f you have ever been to a blog where you see ads scattered around, you can be certain that the blogger in question is getting paid. There are two types of ads: ones where companies pay simply to have them placed on a blogger's web page, and ones where companies only pay when people click an ad, also known as pay-per-click ads. Both of these are excellent opportunities for you to make money as a blogger.

There are two ways you can find advertisements for your blog. The first way requires that you create ad packages and directly approach companies with these packages, giving them the opportunity to buy advertising space on your blog. If you choose this route, you can create packages that vary in size and length. For example, you may offer them a single, smaller advertisement spot on a single page for a low fee, or a larger advertisement spot over several pages for a larger fee. You may also include several different spots for one company for a much larger fee. If this is the path you choose, you can choose the size of the packages you'd like to offer and offer them at your own rates. It gives you more control over the income you create off of this opportunity, but it also requires that you approach businesses and show them that your blog has the ability to draw a large amount of traffic their way. It can be more labor intensive, but it can also be more profitable.

The alternative method is to use a company like Google AdSense. With these ad program platforms, you simply register for an account with Google AdSense or whatever the platform is and follow their instructions to have their ads display on your blog.

You'll have to give them some information about you in order to be eligible for the account, and let them know that you are really serious about what you are doing and that you are a legitimate blogger who will actually help them draw traffic to their clients. Then, they will post ads on your website, and you will be paid directly by Google, or any other company you may choose to work with in this format.

Advertisements may seem to pay very little, but as your blog grows it can all add up. Many bloggers rely solely on ads as their blogs main source of income, because they're easy to implement.

Types of Ads

Text Line Ads

A text advertisement is a short advertisement that lets people know about the kind of services you provide. These advertisements work best for service-based businesses that don't have a product to sell. If you want your text advertisements to work out well, you need to make sure the text is catchy and interesting.

Banner Ads

Once you've joined some affiliate programs, if you log into your affiliate dashboard you should be able to find banners there that you can place on your blog. If you can't find any affiliate banners in the affiliate dashboard, then I recommend that you contact the respective affiliate company's support and ask them if they can provide you with some banners.

Sure, affiliate links are nice to put in your blog posts, and to put in emails, but to really set up your blog for monetization you'll need some affiliate banners.

Guest Posting

Guest posting is a win-win situation for both yourself and the blogger's blog that you post on, because your post on another blogger's blog means one less blog post that they have to write which will contribute to their SEO, and it also means you'll get traffic from their blog through the link to your blog at the bottom of your post.

You always want to make sure that your only guest posting on blogs that are bigger than yours, as blogs smaller than yours won't provide enough traffic to make it worth writing a guest post as opposed to just posting on your own blog. Also, you want to make sure that you are only making guest posts on blogs about a topic similar to your blog, because those followers would be the ones most likely to be into your blog.

Paid Reviews

A review blog is a blog that reviews products within a particular niche. For example, a review blog might review notebook computers and cover all the various kinds of notebook computers and have its own rating system for reviewing notebook computers. Each blog post will likely be a review of a new notebook computer that just came out.

How does a review blog turn a profit?

A review blog mostly makes money from the affiliate links provided on each product it reviews. A review blog might also come out with its own product related to the niche in which it reviews products in, but most of the money with a review blog tends to be earned from its affiliate links in its reviews.

There are many other types of blogs, and I'm not going to get into them all, but as we can see from this list, the way most blogs make money is by either selling their own products or promoting affiliate products, which means you need to get good at either one or the other, or both. I tend to engage in both!

Sell Ads on Your Blog

Creating a digital product may take some time, I'm aware of that, and you will need a sales strategy to get the results that you expect. However, at the beginning of this book, I warned you that you have to commit to your monetization objective and be constant and responsible.

Through your mailing list, you have a good sales percentage guaranteed. You only have to use the same principles to create products as you proceeded to start your blog. Design and create products with your audience in mind; relate to your readers by delivering high-value content products. Show them the benefits, help them become aware of what they need, and you'll be motivating them to buy what you have to sell.

Place Ads for Your Products

Social media is a perfect place to get the word out about your blog.

You want to make a Facebook Page about your blog, and each time you write a new blog post you want to post an image to your Facebook page that links to the respective blog post. Likewise, you also want to create a Twitter account for your blog and tweet a link of each new blog post you publish.

Also, you might want to consider creating a free Facebook Group for your niche, managed by your Facebook Page, and make sure you pin a post to the top of your Facebook Group that has a link going directly to your blog.

If you like making videos, YouTube is also a great place to get traffic to your blog from, by posting a video each time you make a blog post with a link in the description of each video going to the associated blog post. Now, each of these social media platforms, Facebook, Twitter, and YouTube are sciences unto themselves, but it's worth learning how to use each, since each of them can serve as a great source of traffic to your blog.

Other social media platforms you might want to consider getting into are Instagram, Pinterest, LinkedIn, and Reddit.

Since learning all of these social media platforms can be daunting. I would recommend at first just starting out with one. Focus on getting traffic from just one, and when you feel your squeezing that one out of just about all of the traffic it's going to produce for you on a regular basis, then that's when it's time to choose another one.

Using Social Media Marketing Strategies for Profit

Google AdSense

The first thing you will want to consider is the types of block formatting available to find the one that will best fit your site. According to Google, 160x600, 300x250, and 336x280 are the shapes that routinely see the best results. It is important to stick with a color scheme for the ad in question that doesn't immediately contrast with the rest of your site. The location you choose for the advertising is also important as if the potential customer sees the ad too quickly, they could easily be turned off from your site completely. As such, the far left or right of either sidebar or in the footer are generally considered the least intrusive placements.

If you are interested in giving AdSense a try, you can download a plugin to set it up easily from the plugin installation menu where you traditionally add new add-ons. Search for the Google AdSense plugin and choose the option to install. Once the plugin has been installed you simply find the plugin list and choose the option to activate AdSense. You will then need to visit the plugin settings menu and chose the option to Get Started.

You will need to start by signing into your Google Account, from there you will need to check the information it can find regarding the site in question. Assuming everything is correct you will want to click the option to Verify. Once your account has been verified you will need to go back into the plugin settings to activate it. You can set up automated ads for both the mobile and primary versions of your site. Once you have turned on AdSense you can manage the placement of your ads by using the Manage Ads option found in its settings.

The next step is to choose the template that you want to add the ads to, each template can have a different set of advertisements. You will want to Review the template in question by finding the relevant option near the Design button. This will show you a preview of the template in question with green boxes placed where the ads will ultimately go. You can place new AdSense boxes, 3 maximums, by dropping markers in specific places or delete existing AdSense boxes by selecting the X next to their locations. Save and you are ready to start profiting from impressions.

Google AdWords

Once you have found a few problems that people are looking to solve, your next step will be to determine which are the most profitable from a marketing sense. You will want to go to Adwords.Google.com and look for the keyword planner tool. This will let you filter search results to find just those you are interested in before searching for local and global results. You will want to find the monthly searches for the topics in question, the number of searches resulting from people trying to solve the problem in question, how long those terms have been returning the results in question and how readily information about that topic already is.

Additionally, you will want to do basic searches related to the niche and make sure there are plenty of advertisers already taking advantage of the customer base. If you are having a hard time finding pages with actual advertisers, you may need to ask yourself what products you are going to actually be marketing. Taking the time to stop and think about whose products you are going to advertise at this point can be a huge resource saver in the long run and is highly recommended.

Know if it is profitable: Once you have landed on several different problems that your target audience is interested in solving, you will then need to determine if they are willing to pay to solve the problem in question as otherwise, it won't be worth the time and effort involved to market content when it won't lead to a measurable number of sales. The easiest way to do this is to visit Adwords.Google.com and check out the keyword planner tool. This tool will allow you to view search results filtered by various keywords to determine how frequently they are used. You will not only be able to see how frequently the keyword is searched for but also what the breakdown is like month to month and how easily it is for people to find the information that they are looking for.

With these details in mind, you are then going to want to visit several of the sites that already exist around the topic in order to meet the current demand for information. While on these sites it is important to look for those that have an active advertising base outside of Google AdSense. Anyone can sign up for advertising via Google, but if the site has actual companies advertising on it then you know that there is definitely money to be made from the community.

Capitolo 43 : Tags, Ranking, And SEO

Who at are Tags and How to use Them in the Correct Way? Tags help you group your posts with similar details. When a visitor clicks on the tag, WordPress opens the tag page and indexes all posts with the same specific tag. Tags help to keep your content organized and have a huge impact on SEO. Tags are basically how to make your contents visible.

The Importance of Search Engine Optimization on Page (SEO on Page) How does Google work?

Google is an authority over all other search engines available. Over time, users get more value from Google search engine as it has invested in the best automated programs to ensure users get the information they need almost instantly. Delivering relevant results at any given time has been a plus.

That said, a smart blogger would want to know how Google works in order to position oneself. The primary goal here is the consumer. Google is available so that consumers get answers to all their queries and concerns. Google is out there to fetch the best results and deliver to a client. As a blogger, you are very secondary to Google. Google will prioritize you if you will in turn give the most value to Google consumers. Therefore, it is important to know that your content must be of top-notch quality and sufficiently meets consumers' needs on the web. If you are the most satisfying provider, it goes without saying; Google will rank you so highly that you will be on the first and top page of Google's search engine results page (SERP).

Google works with mathematical algorithms to filter through their database and deliver the most relevant of results to end users. They have not publicly stated what the algorithms are, and it is squarely in order so they remain anonymous since for one, they are in business and letting out why their search results are almost perfect would only be sharing company tactics and strategies with competitors. Secondly, publicizing the algorithms will not guarantee safety to users as rogue bloggers will have a chance to cheat the system. Over time, only smart and hardworking bloggers have learned how it works up the ladder. Those working right have seen their efforts bear fruit.

How Google Ranks Sites in 2019: Top Ranking Factors

The above is an all-time favorite question to any blogger who means business. It is important for one to have the understanding of Google's PageRank in mind in order to get the best out of the effort put to release quality content. Search Engine Optimization SEO is the lifeline.

Besides the fact that the top-ranking factors are anonymous to bloggers from Google, the following proven tactics have identified some factors to be true and proven to work. You cannot just fail consider them. It will be the difference between your success and failure.

Having in mind that 97% of Google users only look at the first page of the results and never bother to click on the next page, this is how to win a spot on the first page and possibly the top three organic results:

Content Quality

"Content is king" is not a cliché in blogging, rather, it is the motto. After all is said and done, the foundation of writing and having a viable presence online is quality content. Every other factor builds on this. You are already a success if you have mastered the art of juicy content. It all starts here and that is what will primarily drive people to your blog. We can't emphasize the importance of quality content enough; it is great that content quality leads to the other winning factor of quality backlinks.

Quality Backlinks

You must be an authority in your niche for another website to consider having you on their page. It means you have to have been of great value to them and they cannot do without a link to your resource.

The many links to your page by other pages is a credible voting system for Google top ranking factors. The more backlinks you have, the more credible Google finds you.

While we are at it, do not forget the word quality. Having every Tom, Dick, and Harry backlinking you is not a smart move. Therefore, seek authority websites to link back to you, as the former might be more detrimental to your blog. Be wise and carefully check out those who want to collaborate with you.

It is important to highlight at this point that your content going viral on social media and the inbound traffic to your page, is something that catches Google's eye. They are in the end always ranking your site on the quality backlinks when people choose to share your content.

Secured Sites (A shift from HTTP to HTTPS)

Google is out to protect her users from hackers and other people with ill-motives. They want to ensure that when a client is browsing through your website that all their information is kept safe from intruders. Having security in your blog will mean you mean well for your clients and it makes it a common goal for you and Google. Secure your sites if they indeed matter to you. Google will surely reward this effort.

Page speed

We live in fast times. Consumers want their results either now or now. Your page should take up utmost 2 seconds to load up. Anything other than that will see people moving fast to sites which seem to consider the value of time in this day and age. There is so much to do with so little time, so whether someone is online for work or for social reasons, you will be surprised how both do not have a second to waste.

Work on your page speed. Google in an effort to satisfy their clients, will give priority to sites with great page speed.

Webpage Content Length

After a long time of working to optimize web pages, we have learned that lengthy content wins the top ranks. We would want to assume the more you offer, the higher the chances of a client getting all they need on one stop. This is not in any way a call to have you stretching your content from East to Waste losing your focus and gist. In most scenarios, brief is sufficient. Jump in with both feet and through all lengths, short and long, in your site, watch and learn what works for you and your niche.

Mobile friendly Websites

Many websites only considered desktop user experience from the word go and as was pointed out in our WordPress section, that is a big mistake. Mobile Devices are the easiest and most accessible tool at any given time. If you even realize half your audience is on the desktop while the other half is on their phone, it is only smart to be on both service points. The fact that almost everyone has a smartphone, means that once in a while they will be doing their searches on phone. Anytime a client visits a site on mobile and it is not friendly, almost all leave for a better experience. Why would Google risk it to prioritize you?

Domain age

Whether or not the age of a domain is anything to judge its credibility on is debatable. However, the age of a site can be judged by Google or any search engine on its viability. There are too many new bloggers who do not last, so being patient and focusing on why you started in the first place is critical. Being around for a while and offering consistent and quality content from the beginning will set you up as a better authority figure.

Google Updates and How to survive them

Google updates are responsible for the most severe fears that bloggers tend to have. Why? Because you might be ranking high or appear on the first page consistently for several years and then your ranking falls due to some changes in algorithm. If and when there are Google updates, this is how to survive them.

The above points we covered on Top ranking factors still hold true, so continue to use best practices in utilizing them. In other words, be proactive and continue to update them periodically (remember trends change, so stay on the top of the wave). For example, keywords are big to garner top rankings but how and when to use them is paramount to know. Today voice search is a big deal and it is obvious that Google is big on it too. Factoring the voice search engine on your site is non-negotiable now and in the near future. It could be a top reason as to why your rank is falling after an update.

Do not be hasty. You cannot diagnose the changes with Google updates at face value. It will call for time and a great deal of auditing and reflection on your site. It is also beneficial to contract experts to do the audit for you. Once updates are out, many sources run to explain the why and the how, but few are legit. It will take seasoned digital marketers and the Google team itself to get to the truth. Be careful not to follow masses blindly and instead let all your effort count and be timely while at it.

The competition for an audience and great conversions online is great. Google updates are bound to happen to cut out the fake and manipulative participants, as well to move people from comfort zones. Remember, your top slot is sought after by many and you are only king or queen of the mountain, as long as you can hold it. Every day, you have to earn your rank.

Perfecting on good SEO skills and being in the good graces of Google (and by extension the other search engines) is a daily struggle for all content creators. Brace up for perfection and being the best always! Here are my suggestions for the most powerful SEO Strategies that you can implement from the start.

Authority

The qualitative measure that sees to it you are visible and ranking at the top is authority. You are an authority with quality content and quality links to your site. Page authority will have your site ranked higher while domain authority will also push you to the top with your popularity and age of domain.

Trust

Just like with human interactions, a site has to build an online presence that is trustworthy. Google will only rank your site if they trust you to be legit and competent with your content. Social media will go a long way in pushing for backlinks as this also makes your site trustworthy. You acquire trust when many people want to associate with your site.

Relevance

You become relevant the moment your content commands attention enough to attract backlinks. When Google ranks every backlink, it creates citation flow. They only consider backlinks from sites considered as trustworthy, thus creating a trust flow.

How to Structure your Blog for Easy and Automatic SEO

The above points will be effective if we structure our content well. The following steps show how to structure your blog for easy and automatic SEO:

Shift from using as many keywords as possible and focus on 1-2 quality long tails keywords. The rule is always clear, you are required to sound natural and not sound like you are trying to force keywords. Flow and naturally placed keywords especially with question-based long tail keywords will most likely excite your visitors and make it easy for conversions to take place.

Images are good for your blog post as they reinforce your message. However, you have to optimize images as well by putting the right caption, introducing the image with a good description, and having a short explanation of the image. Now that search engines cannot see an image as we see them, the well-intentioned texts will do the trick.

Avoid Duplicating Content and Giving Searchers What They Want

Be careful with duplicating content for the simple reason that in most cases, it is not usually a duplicated content literally, but using similar tags that can make search engines mistake them for duplicate content. Therefore, making visitors confuse your content for another person's or literally going to the wrong site.

Some ways to prevent this type of confusion is to use a URL structure guide for visitors and making sure that at every point of your site the URL matches the topic or the subtopic you positioned for the particular that link. It helps visitors have an easy time navigating your site. In most cases, they can simply change what they want to read by clicking a key work on the URL. For example, one can click the word 'contact' to 'home' and easily switch from the contact page to the home page.

The next tip is to maximize on the opportunity of using internal links. When writing about one topic in your blog page, it may require a brief intro from another relevant topic you had written on earlier and published on the same blog. You will not only sound repetitive to return visitors on your site by writing content again, but you will be limiting yourself from creating new material. Instead, create sub links that would naturally link back to all other pages you deem necessary for the current page content. This will allow your visitors to choose the topics they wish to review, instead of re-reading past information. Another suggestion is to go big on Google analytics and trends. Let me explain, many times it is easier for an entrepreneur to solve an existing problem by creating a solution. When you visit Google's console you realize that most people have interests in a particular topic, why not jump in early enough and provide the much-needed information?

A bold title with the main keyword will help the reader know whether the post is relevant to their search or not. Keywords in H1 and H2 headers also go a long way in ranking pages. Google will also rank it if it deems it important to the search question at hand. A great blog with not only good content, but with visible, clear titles and subtitles will help a reader have an easy time from point A of the communication process to point Z. Subtitles show a writer who has organized thoughts and points. It makes it easier even for a reader who is short on time or one looking for something specific on the same topic to skim through fast and successfully.

The Importance of the Sitemap

A sitemap is one of the greatest tools to employ for SEO. Submitting an XML Sitemap to Google is not a direct ticket to being indexed as Google is primarily out to crawl your content and rank it. A sitemap will require you to be consistent with your content in line with the issued side map for the following two reasons:

Usability

A visitor should have an out of this world user experience when they visit your site and click the links that you have provided. There should be good flow of information and page speeds should be as fast as possible. Also, your site should be clean and easy to view.

Responsive

A visitor wants a responsive website, whether it is you responding, an administrator, or an auto response, the visitor should be responded to as quickly as possible. When this is primarily factored in by the blogger, then one easily increases their website value.

The Importance of Link Building: Why is linking building so important? It is critical to build your page links as this makes you an authority according to Google. As well, when someone links you in their page, they are basically inviting their audience to visit your page. In most cases, they direct visitors to you as an expert and one who has something they probably would not do without.

Paying to get Link on Website with Authority

Would you be willing to buy advertising space on that blog? Or would you be willing to pay to write a guest posts on the authoritative site? The two options will see you paying to be featured there. And the visibility is guaranteed. Also, the fact that you want to associate your blog with the ones already setting pace in the market is a great effort on your part. Paying to get a link to a website with authority is considered as an unethical practice by Google. If you are caught, then the consequences will be dire on your site. Now that backlinks are a crucial part to ranking your site, Google expects a fairground for all participants.

The greatest question is, why would you prefer shortcuts? We believe the process in every product or brand ultimately makes the whole difference. A genuine blogger would take the long route at least to prove to oneself you deserve the victory that will be preceded by sweat and strategy. You may pay your way to the top and then realize you cannot sustain yourself up there, yet you already lost money paying for the site.

The only way to pay for backlinks from authoritative sites is to pay with your outstanding content. You will agree with me that it is costly to bring out a brainy and smart piece of a read, but use it as needed or as you see fit.

How to Acquire Links and What to Avoid in Link Building

When you become an expert in your niche, you will be offering unmatched content online that others would want to associate with and create leverage on. Naturally, you will attract link building networks your way or have collaboration opportunities with other large influencers in your niche.

Capitolo 44 Misconceptions about Blogging

I 've invested a great deal of energy discussing the outlook required to be a fruitful blogger. Presently I might want to examine a few misguided judgments you may have. We regularly fabricate confusions from a separation, with an absence of learning for the subject.

The main misguided judgment individuals have is that blogging is income sans work. Here's a reality: All the genuine methods for causing cash to require diligent work, however you get the chance to pick your toxic substance. At the point when you work in a field you cherish; the diligent work doesn't appear to be so difficult any longer. What's more, that is the reason energetic bloggers profit, they cherish what they do, and that makes them put forward quite a lot more exertion, which at that point receives awesome benefits.

Let's assume you are an astounding nursery worker who makes about $500 a month taking a shot at a land that spreads for a fourth of a section of land. Hearing the stories of your ability, a rich individual extends to you an employment opportunity to chip away at his one- section of land garden, while multiplying your present pay, will you accept the position? Most presumably you will, and in view of the cash as well as for the love of planting. Chipping away at just about multiple times your present region is a test, yet your enthusiasm for the field makes you need to acknowledge this demand. You realize your outstanding task at hand will increment, yet it is to a greater degree a rush for you than an errand. A similar activity may sound hard for somebody who isn't infatuated with cultivating as you seem to be.

It requires exertion to prevail in any field yet picking something that you cherish makes the work sense that play than work itself. It makes you put in substantially more exertion, which when met with consistency, gets you to greatness.

So truly, blogging will require work, tolerance, and determination, however when you pick the privilege point to blog, each procedure will get simpler. The explanation you need to blog shouldn't be on the grounds that you figure you should work less to procure all the more however about working at the perfect spot, so independent of the amount you procure, your work never feels like a task. So no, blogging isn't pain free income except if you blog about a point you cherish.

Setting up a Blog requires technical knowledge

No, you don't. Possibly 10 years prior it would have been an alternate answer however now it is truly straightforward for anybody to begin a blog and look after it, with next to zero specialized information.

Presently, we have apparatuses and administrations that deal with the specialized part while we center on the plan part. Prior, you'd need to contract a Website engineer to construct a site for your blog and afterward rely upon them to keep up it while failing to have a lot of command over it. Presently, however, you can actually set up and structure your site in under a day. These devices and administrations have a slight expectation to learn and adapt however, yet you'll get around it when you use them.

After you read the accompanying entry, you may blame me for being sermonizing, yet I will acknowledge the misleading allegations on the other hand that it causes you set up a decent establishment. Prior, I revealed to you that the best approach to pick up your group of spectators' trusts is to offer them incredible worth, yet I never revealed to you how. Well at that point, we should begin! How can one give incredible worth?

Extraordinary worth originates from a fair articulation. Truly, one more worldview to the effectively huge confound, remain with me however, this is the remainder of the ideas you have to get it. Nothing more, I guarantee.

As a blogger and substance maker, one of the most continuous inquiries individual bloggers pose to me is "Vikrant, I am an apprentice blogger/you tuber/content maker, how would I stand apart from the swarm, the online world is loaded with individuals like me, what would I be able to do to stick out and make my own personality?" My answer is a two-word presentation "Act naturally". When I offer individuals this response, I normally get a gesture yet not a persuading one, as though individuals might suspect I will give them a perplexing recipe to stand apart from the group. In the event that you solicit any from the incredible substance makers, they will give you the same answer. So how does acting naturally bring about standing apart from the group? Here's the secret:

In this universe of 7.7 billion individuals, every one of us is distinctive in light of the fact that we have experienced our remarkable arrangement of encounters that have molded us to be what our identity is. You may have had a completely unexpected childhood in comparison to me. You may have had a harder adolescence than other individuals, you may have invested more energy in the town than the city, I may love the city more than the town, and another person may appreciate the field more. We're all unique, and henceforth we've just stood apart from the group; it's only a point of fair articulation. The majority of your encounters to date have formed your feelings towards nearly everything, and when you express these, you normally stand apart from the group.

I'll give you my model: When I began composing articles, blog entries, I read a great deal about how I could make them sound impeccable to the peruse and appear to be an expert. I attempted different genius methods, began utilizing more extravagant words, increasingly formal tone, and so on. When I composed my first eBook on a cell phone guide in 2014, it resembled a textbook, all proper language, no exchanges, no mockery. Maybe I had been compelled to compose it. It had my name on it, however it wasn't me. The book had normal deals, yet some way or another I was upset about it. I realized it wasn't me.

Possibly I needed to seem like a Pro too-aesthetic to-utilize mockery sort of writer. I am a cheerful individual, and I want to joke around constantly, however none of it reflected in the book.

The theme of the book was specialized, yet at the same time, it didn't have my stamp on it! So, after around about fourteen days from the hour of the underlying discharge, I unpublished the book, took out an old notebook, my preferred dark pen and began composing. Not a consideration for the sentence structure, structure or composition. I was composing the book as though I am having a discussion with the peruse, and I needed the peruse to realize this is me. If they somehow managed to meet me on an arbitrary road by one way or another, I would sound simply as I did in the books. Following two weeks, I composed the book in my bona fide style and distributed it.

I couldn't have cared less about sales, feedback or anything. I simply needed a veritable adaptation of me in the book, regardless of if individuals got it or didn't. Truly, the book did affirm, I got a lot of positive feedback, however there was something I learned through that voyage, 'Acting naturally is a definitive street to independence and hanging out in an inventive field, regardless of whether that be moving, drawing, blogging, podcasting or anything'.

Truly, I realize my books do not have the wonderful language structure, sentence structure and substantially more of the conventional books yet you recognize what, I couldn't care less, I have acknowledged myself and my composition style. I would prefer not to be the instructor who encourages a class loaded with uninterested individuals, drawing irregular figures on the writing board. Rather, I need to be the coach who sits adjacent to you, tastes a couple runs of your espresso, and demonstrates to you what I've realized through my missteps.

So, till right up 'til today, I haven't changed my composition style, I look for discussions with the pursuer, a little giggle to a great extent and if in this procedure you discover some new information, I couldn't be more joyful!

This doesn't mean I am a complete Snob and won't engage a chance to improve myself. I can get the book composed by a Ghostwriter yet it won't be me, and I can't take that.

On the other hand, that a Million individuals read my book tomorrow and just one of them was to like it, I would love it since I give that one individual enormous incentive through my work and that as well, in my true style.

I need the equivalent for you. I need you to express your heart out without agonizing over judgment. Your blog is yours, and there is no point attempting to seem like another person. Possibilities are, the individual you are attempting to duplicate is famous in light of their fair suppositions and the bona fide style to express those conclusions. It doesn't make a difference on the other hand that you have zero or a thousand devotees, you can at present contend with the most settled of bloggers, your bit of leeway is you, and don't you ever set out remove it by difficult to be one of them.

Blogging Conclusion

Blogging is the future for most advertising and news/information sourcing.

The fact that we are seeing a global downturn in mainstream media sources and more people turning to independent media (blogging is one of these) proves that the market for advertising will continue to rise for bloggers. It is a noble call to invite people to join the profession and tell them for a fact, if they work hard and play smart that it will work out well. Their art and craft will then yield the joys of passive income for now and forever. A life spent doing what you love is the best kind of life.

I cannot end this book without commenting on the art for art's sake person. I have a great admiration for that worldview, but it can cloud real world realities. Some people only want to blog for the love of writing, but never take into account the money and income possibilities that are available to them from their art. The challenge I pose to the purists is, what is the best way to make money other than from your hobby and passion? In the real world, these kinds of people end up winning more when they learn the art of monetization, even if making money was not their end goal. They can still honor the process of writing well and passionately, but yet get rewarded for it. This will allow them to write for longer and not have to share their time with a "day job". The fact you get paid to do what you love does not discount the art or make it less fulfilling. Quite the opposite, it allows you greater freedom to practice and excel at it. The time you get because you are taking the worry of earning a living will equal greater opportunity to study and get better at your craft. There is no honor in poverty or stretching yourself too thinly, so please let go of that adage.

CPSIA information can be obtained
at www.ICGtesting.com
Printed in the USA
BVHW041512220221
600777BV00006B/242